# YANKEE
## FROM GEORGIA

Also by William Lee Miller

*Piety Along the Potomac*
*The Fifteenth Ward and the Great Society*
*Of Thee, Nevertheless, I Sing*

# YANKEE FROM GEORGIA

## The Emergence of JIMMY CARTER

William Lee Miller

Times
BOOKS

For Rebecca and Cynthia;
David and Andrew

*Second printing, January 1979*

Copyright © 1978 by William Lee Miller.

Manufactured in the United States of America. Published simultaneously in Canada by Fitzhenry & Whiteside, Ltd., Toronto.

Designed by Beth Tondreau

Library of Congress Cataloging in Publication Data

Miller, William Lee.
    Yankee from Georgia.

    1.  Carter, Jimmy, 1924-      2.   Presidents—
United States—Biography.   3.   United States—
Politics and government—1977-      4.   Southern
States—Politics and government—1951-
5.   United States—Politics and government—1974-
1977.   I.   Title.
E783.M54   1978      973.926'092'4      77-87832
ISBN 0-8129-0753-1

# ACKNOWLEDGMENTS

I have many debts for this book, and given its subject I need to underline the usual disclaimer: none of the people who helped me are to be blamed for the interpretations and judgments in it.

Betty Gail Gunter and William Gunter of Atlanta and Gainesville, Georgia, helped me in a great many ways, going far beyond what I reasonably could have expected when I first picked up the phone and asked for an interview. It was a lucky day for me. They have become my friends, and I am deeply grateful to them. The same is true of their daughter and son-in-law Gay and Randy Shingler; the Shinglers and the Gunters contributed to this book in more ways than I can list. Many other Georgians assisted me, and I thank them all. For extraordinary help at some cost, I want to name Philip Alston; Edna Langford; Eugene Patterson (in Florida now); and Mrs. Ethel Harris, of Washington, Georgia. Andrew Young talked to me about Carter before I knew this book would exist, and again in Washington when I did. Jack and Judy Carter of Calhoun, Georgia, were candid and gracious, inviting me to their house for dinner and an overnight stay. Profiting by a highly placed example, I made the bed and left a thank you note on the pillow.

Lou Cannon of *The Washington Post* talked to me many times, read a full draft of the book, and gave me the advantage both of his extensive knowledge of contemporary politics and of long letters filled with editorial wisdom. Don't blame him for the book though. Helen Dewar of *The Post* kindly granted me an interview.

June Bingham talked to me about Carter and about Carter and Niebuhr, and also generously made available to me the copy of her book showing President Carter's underlinings and markings. Morton Sosna read a full draft and assisted me with many useful criticisms.

Vernon Jordan and Frank Thomas shared with me their experiences with Carter; Mitchell Sviridoff kindly arranged the occasion for the sharing.

I have talked, of course, with a great many people—politicians, newspaper people, fellow faculty members, voters, friends—about candidate Carter and President Carter. My thanks to people who granted a specific request or made a specific contribution: Congressman John Anderson, Congressman John Brademas, Patt Darian, Jerry Doolittle, Joe Duffey, Jim Fallows, E. Brooks Holifield, Mary Hoyt, William Keel, James Laney, Waldo Lewis, William F. May, Bill D. Moyers, Jody Powell, Richard Reeves, Richard Ruland, Parks Rusk, J. Paul Sampley, William V. Shannon, Mark Siegal, Steven J. Stein, James Wall and Anne Wexler.

Robert Schmuhl drove me to a variety of Indiana events, read and marked every chapter, provided me with clippings, and helped with great generosity. Sally Sampley did research; typed, and edited so that she deserves credit for whatever merit the book may have.

Doro Fortado once again efficiently and cheerfully typed this book; Beverly Davis helped to type it, too. Linda Bernstein made many useful comments on the draft, instructed me about the South, and relieved me of many chores at the Poynter Center. I am grateful to them and to the Poynter Center at Indiana University.

Betty Horton Miller helped me again, as she always has before, and she and Cynthia, David, and Andrew Miller cheered the writer and often made useful observations about what he was writing. The dedication reflects a gratitude and pride Betty Horton Miller and I share.

Some material in this book has been printed, in different form, in *The New York Times* magazine, *The Washington Post*, and *The New Republic*.

# CONTENTS

A Personal Introduction: Singing with Brenda, Carl,
Shirley—and Jimmy    3

### PART I: SOUTH TOWARD HOME

1. The Irony of Jimmy Carter    15
2. A Georgia Yankee    26
3. The Strange Career of the Civil Rights Movement    39
4. Free at Last, Almost    51

### PART II: JIMMY CARTER THE AMERICAN

5. The Autobiographical President    69
6. The Combative Outsider    90
7. A Good Man is Hard to Find    110
8. Plan and Count; Count and Plan    130
9. The Recuperating Presidency?    150

### PART III: HOW SWEET THE SOUND

10. The Familiar Strangeness of the Bible Belt    169
11. Blessed Assurance Comes to Washington    185
12. A Man Who Read Niebuhr    201
13. Love and Justice in Politics    226

A Personal Conclusion: The Capital and Carter    241

# YANKEE
# FROM GEORGIA

# A PERSONAL INTRODUCTION:
## Singing with Brenda, Carl, Shirley—and Jimmy

In May of 1976 I drove to Indianapolis to hear Jimmy Carter. He was speaking, in an interlude between the songs, at a service thumping with gospel music. My daughter, Cindy, who went with me, was embarrassed because I sat there in church taking notes, but she liked his speech, and so did I.

It was already clear that Spring that a great plaster cast of political and personal circumstances was forming to mold Carter's "persona" into some kind of a national symbol: the diminished interest in political ideology, with Carter the most unideological of the candidates; the diminished place in his own career of that strongest tie of American politics, party allegiance ("A husk!" says his son Jack, disdainfully, of the Democratic Party); the increased importance of the instant, visual, mass communication of signs, signals, and images, at the use of which Mr. Carter was proving himself adept; the atmosphere in the nation after Watergate and Vietnam, with "trust in government" and dubiety about Washington as ubiquitous themes; and Mr. Carter's own traits as self-directed deacon and engineer (he was a post-Watergate sort of person and politician before there was a Watergate).

Cindy and I had made our way to 29th Street and Kenwood Avenue in Indianapolis, to the Second Christian Church, to hear him.

I was wondering how I could distinguish Mr. Carter's religious vibrations, to which I did not object, from Mr. Dwight Eisenhower's piety along the Potomac, to which, almost a quarter of a century earlier, I did.

I was wondering, furthermore, how much there might be in

*3*

this new figure on the American scene, this toothful Southern meteor now flashing across the political sky, of something very old: that American habit of leaping over from politics into morals. How much was there in him of that objectionable moralism and self-righteousness that afflicts certain varieties of American politicians?

I was wondering still further what it meant that Mr. Carter quoted Reinhold Niebuhr—a point perhaps of more interest to me than it might be to others. I had spent many hours, spread across two decades, inflicting the writings of Mr. Niebuhr on captive gatherings in at least five states, and Mr. Niebuhr had been important to my own life and thought.

What did it mean that Mr. Carter was sometimes called a "populist"; that his mother's father Jim Jack Gordy had been a Populist and a follower of the Georgia Populist leader Tom Watson; and that Mr. Carter had had some appeal for George Wallace voters and would certainly receive many hitherto Wallace votes in the Indiana primary?

And of course I was wondering, as was all the political world, just what firm shape this ectoplasmic new manifestation might finally assume: liberal on Mondays, Wednesdays, and Fridays, conservative on Thursdays and Saturdays, mixedly moderate on Tuesdays. (This last-named day of the week was just then particularly important. At dinner in a Washington restaurant a political woman had remarked that, whatever its merits otherwise, the proliferation of primaries certainly had enlivened Tuesdays.)

I was doing all this compounded wondering—with which this book began—while sitting on a folding chair in the balcony of that black church in Indianapolis, waiting for Mr. Carter to make his appearance.

The featured attraction of the occasion, however, was not the Presidential candidate—they come and go—but Brenda, Carl, and Shirley, the "nation's finest gospel trio." These three were dressed all in shining green and singing with skill, syncopation, and pyrotechnics songs like "We Can Make It Together If We Try" and "Come to Jesus and He Will Give You Rest." The congregation (which had paid four dollars a person to hear them) would respond to unusually elaborate effects with clapping, stomping and shouted Amens. Somebody slapped a tambourine.

The question about Carter and Ike—in particular—had come

to mind during these rousing rhythms, not only because Ike had been the most recent President successfully to link his own "character" to the nation's religious beliefs, but also because Carter seemed to share with Ike a Good-Man-Above-Politics ideological indeterminacy not necessarily characteristic of other moral crusaders and religious politicians.

Presidents are cultural symbols as well as political leaders; Ike, in particular, had filled some of the space where F.D.R. had been, and had added a frosting of "moral and spiritual values" (as the phrase went in the 1950s). Now here was Brother Jimmy talking about "trust" and "love" and the nation's moral underpinnings. A curmudgeonly critic might suggest that the difference in attitude on the part of people like me rested solely on partisanship: we were Democrats who didn't mind in 1976 in the Democrat Carter what we objected to in 1952-53 in the Republican Eisenhower.

Both men slipped quickly over policy to matters of "character" and individual goodness; the followers of both implied that exactly the requisite goodness was to be found in their man. Both called the nation back to something "higher" and "spiritual." Both men, mingling patriotic and religious language, encouraged the contrast between this higher suprapolitical spiritual something they represent and the sordid condition of national politics before their timely arrival on the scene. They did not discourage the conclusion that there is a considerable distance between themselves, on this higher spiritual-moral plane, and the rest of the pack of ordinary politicians down below.

So what was the difference?

All I had to do was look around me to see one striking difference: I could not imagine Ike being invited to, or agreeing to appear in, a black church like this one. And another difference was shortly to appear: neither Ike nor Gerald Ford nor Ronald Reagan nor any other national politician of recent memory, if he came to this church, could ever, ever, ever, ever, ever (to lapse into the rhythm of the music) have made himself at one with the congregation as Carter was to do.

That sympathetic vibration with this urban black church would symbolize a great deal. It meant that the fallout from the religious belief was likely not to be an avoidance of, but an encouragement to, social justice and sympathy with the poor.

There was another point in regard to the religion proper—just how specific and rooted was the belief? On this matter the contrast was total: Ike's spacious outlook had been the quintessence of I believe-in-whatever-Belief amorphousness; Carter, on the other hand, was a quite explicit, specific, well-read, and articulate evangelical Protestant, a point that was giving some people heartburn.

The interior of the church was painted a dramatic red. The sanctuary had a red rug. One of the stained glass windows showed a black Christ. Ushers in evening dress and three young assistant pastors (two black and one white) kept the service moving—not that that took much doing.

"I don't *like* a *polite* church!" Brenda, a large and hearty woman, called out, after a particularly rousing number. "There's not much ENERGY in it!" The congregation laughed and clapped.

Before Carter arrived the service was interrupted by a bustle of preparation. The intrusive, giant mechanical monsters of television and their human servants with their duffle bags and boxes shoved their way into the front pews, blocked the vision of half the congregation, and blinded the choir. The rumpled minions of the "writing press," festooned with credentials, typewriters, cameras, bags, purses, pencils, and notebooks, were meanwhile escorted, as befits their diminished status, to a block of seats up in the balcony where Cindy and I were sitting. They looked at each other in patronizing mirth when Brenda, Carl, and Shirley began singing once more.

It was a scene I was to see, with slight variations, repeatedly in the year that followed: First the gathering of the meek local newspersons, meekly seeking out their merely local credentials, mingling humanly with the actual human beings attending the actual local preliminary events; then the sudden imperious arrival of the traveling national troupe, with their buses and badges (Carter Press Follow Me), and tired self-importance, shoving the real scene aside to put up their giant beetles and grasshoppers and shine neon over everything and spread the machinery's intestines over the floor and distract the public from the ostensible event by their own celebrity and illusion-making arrangements.

They represented the major difference between the shaping of a President into a cultural emblem in our own day and in the day of—say—Andrew Jackson. Because Carter was already becoming the bearer of suprapolitical meaning I was reminded of John William Ward's book *Andrew Jackson: Symbol for an Age*, which shows how the folk, in their own ballads, legends, and phrases gradually made of Andy Jackson a symbol for the nation's beliefs at that time. He became a symbol of the folk's own making, at odds to some degree with the actual person General Jackson. "Of Andrew Jackson the people made a mirror for themselves." The victor in the Battle of New Orleans was seen to be "God's right-hand man," a chosen instrument, a bearer of the Providential intent, that citizens of this new country felt to be its shaping power. He was a man of iron will ("Shall General Jackson go to Heaven?" "He will if he wants to."), a pattern for Nature's Nobleman, a vindication of the merits of a people close to nature, as against those who represent cultivated civilization. Jackson was made into the symbol of Nature, Providence, and Will, these three interwoven and reinforcing each other, as the new country understood itself through the symbol it made of him. Mr. Ward sees the symbolic Andrew Jackson as the creation of his national culture in his time. One might now observe that the themes he symbolized for that age are not altogether different from those that are emerging almost a century and a half later in the public figure Jimmy Carter.

At that moment, however, he was just a Southern moderate with teeth and a smile; he was peanuts; he was the Bible class and Plains. He was of course far from being an established hero like Andrew Jackson or Dwight Eisenhower; in fact he made a virtue of his initial obscurity. But he was a figure with a life outside politics and outside Washington, a figure whose religion, region, hometown, family, and several occupations were to provide rich material for the weaving of a symbolic pattern.

In Indianapolis, the symbol waiting to be born in whom I was interested had made his entrance. Brenda, Carl and Shirley were singing "There's No Tomorrow" when Mr. Carter, for whom there evidently was a tomorrow, was escorted to the pulpit platform by the pastor, Dr. T. J. Benjamin, Jr. He was seated in a chair out from behind the pulpit and facing the alcove where the trio was singing. That meant he sat with a side view of himself

fully visible to the rest of us through twenty more minutes of
gospel music, clapping his hands, tapping his foot, and being
whispered to by Dr. Benjamin. Seen thus in the flesh, close up,
unprotected, unedited, and in profile, he was not the glamour
figure of his endlessly smiling photographs and TV appearances
but a middle-aged ex-Governor with undistinguished socks. I
liked him better for that.

I also liked the way Dr. Benjamin introduced him. I had looked
at some Carter propaganda in preparation for the evening—if you
can remember now those days before his first name became
commonplace—and although I had assumed that Mr. Carter's
first name was James I certainly couldn't find that from his leaflet.
It came not from a mere Carter Presidential campaign but from
the *Jimmy* Carter Presidential campaign; it was *Jimmy* Carter
who "has not spent years in Washington"; *Jimmy* Carter who
"doggedly fought special interests and selfish manipulators"; *Jimmy* Carter's campaign that "isn't supported by power brokers
paying back political favors"; *Jimmy* Carter on the cover; *Jimmy*
Carter on the back page; *Jimmy* Carter twelve times in two short
pages of text; *Jimmy* Carter five times in a few paragraphs under
his picture; *Jimmy* Carter every single time the text itself referred to him. Somebody somewhere surely had made a decision
about what he was to be called. So, having been Jimmied almost
into sheer Republicanism, I was glad to hear Dr. Benjamin
introduce his guest as Governor Carter.

He said he had first met the Governor as an unscheduled
speaker at a board meeting of the National Urban Coalition;
sometimes, he said, you have to put up with an *in-troo-sion* in the
agenda. At the subtly needling use of the word "intrusion" a
murmur of amused comprehension went through the black congregation. (In the "ethnic purity" incident a month earlier "intrusion" had been one of the dubious words Carter had used to try
to explain himself.) Carter's eyes abruptly turned wary and his
smile momentarily solidified. Dr. Benjamin was clearly his own
man.

The introduction nevertheless was very laudatory. Dr. Benjamin—the adroit manager of the remarkable cultural melange
created that evening in his church—said that he had whispered to
Governor Carter during the trio's last number that it would be
nice if they could all go right into the White House this way,

singing, clapping, making Billy Graham move over, and watching folks get saved. (I thought it would be a happy irony indeed if the first modern President to be an evangelical Protestant would be the one to dispense with Billy Graham.)

The pastor got the rhythm going when he brought on his guest: "Up from poverty, up from the South, freed from segregation, running with Jesus, and if it be the Lord's will the next President of the United States, Governor Carter." Carter kept the rhythm going when he ticked off, rapid fire, his autobiographical overlapping with the people of that church: "We share a common faith in Christ, speak the same language, sing the same hymns, have seen the same poverty, are bound together in spirit, in brotherhood and love."

Carter recalled his childhood: two white families and twenty-five black families; black playmates and white schoolmates, a bishop of the African Methodist Episcopal church who was his town's most prominent man; separate seats for his black friends and himself on the Jim Crow train, thirteen miles for fifteen cents, from Plains to Americus.

For 210 years, he said, his father's side of the family had all been farmers: "Nobody went to college 'til me." He forthrightly recommended himself to the black audience by claiming that *my life* is like *your life*: poverty, the South, the gospels, the same hymns.

Ike would not have described himself, as Carter did, as a "politician." Ike or an Ike-equivalent transported to 1976 would not say, as Carter did, that much of our foreign policy "makes me ashamed;" that African countries feel we don't always respect them, don't always tell the truth, "and they are right;" that though we sent our bombers over Vietnam villages and destroyed them "in order to save them," we would not have bombed such villages if they had been in France, Germany, or England. Ike would certainly not have said: "I have never seen a *rich* person in a Georgia prison," ("Amen" said the congregation); that "the criminal justice system is a disgrace"; that in the Vietnam War it was the *poor* who actually fought, and fifty thousand lives were lost, while college students mostly were exempt.

Carter made his social criticism softly and gently, and he was careful to say that the "people who write the laws," the "socially prominent," "don't do it on purpose." It is simply that the conditions of their lives are such that they do not themselves feel in their own lives the effect of the way the law works.

He contrasted the treatment his own son would receive from a Georgia judge (his son would *not* be sent to jail) to the son of a black neighbor, who would be "gone" (i.e., jailed).

When he was young he didn't know why his classmates and churchmates were white, while his playmates and friends were black, or why on that train from Plains to Americus his black friends had to sit in a different car.

Every time there had been an election, Carter said, he had had overwhelming black support, and he cited the support of Andrew Young, Maynard Jackson, Daddy King. "We have a lot in common, and they know me."

He had established rapport with the congregation and maintained it by striking other appropriate notes. "I've been in Nazareth. I've seen the Dead Sea. I went to Bethel where Jacob wrestled with the angel." He spoke of the simplicity of Jesus's life, and of the poorness of the land, and of the Jordan River. He mentioned Jesus's parables about pride, and the danger of thinking we are better than other people.

He said that the standards in government ought to be "as high as the standards you hear every Sunday from this pulpit."

His way of mentioning Watergate was not to deplore or condemn but to be wistful about what had been lost ("something precious") and to invite a sharing of the shame of the event. His way of being partisan was quietly to say that the poor people and the black people lost something the day Nixon took office.

When Carter came to the last part of his remarks, he said that through all the challenges of history and tribulations of personal life "we Christians have something that's always there, never changes" ("Amen" from the congregation). When he was young, he knew that his "daddy" was there when he needed him close by, and would pick him up if he fell. He said it with an unembarrassed simplicity and directness that not many sophisticated modern adults could bring off.

It was a more effective talk than any reproduction can cause a mere reader to understand. I was impressed, especially with the centrality and potent examples of the theme of social justice. His remarks did have a moralistic overtone, but moralistic in the direction of a particular social sympathy . . . as with the folk in this church.

"I cherish friendships with people like your pastor," Carter said. "And I'll remember this night. I'll remember Brenda, Carl, and Shirley. My life will be shaped by my knowledge of you."

When Carter finished his speech Brenda, Carl, and Shirley (at Mr. Carter's reported request) sang another number ("Sunshine, here to stay now . . . no more heartache"). He listened, smiled, and clapped some more. Then Dr. Benjamin gave roses to the musical director and an honorary membership in "Second Christian Country" to the gospel trio and to Carter. Carter kissed Brenda and Shirley and the congregation noticed that. ("It's all in the gospel," said Dr. Benjamin cheerfully when Brenda later blew a kiss to him.) Dr. Benjamin, on presenting the membership certificate, said that Mr. Carter would need a place to worship in Indianapolis, and not one of those "dry and staid and cold" places. About his own reaction to Carter he said "It takes one to know one" and "I've never *heard* a politician talk like that." Then he gave a benediction, with the members of the congregation holding hands while he held Carter's, black hand in white hand, at the front. The benediction in that setting turned out to be no perfunctory ceremony but a summary, conclusion, commentary, and rebuttal. In addition to many benedictory remarks strongly tending to favor Carter, Dr. Benjamin also prayed—into the celestial record, as it were—several amendments to Mr. Carter's remarks.

I came away thinking that a link to the members of that church should keep a leader sociologically honest, that Dr. Benjamin would make an interesting president; and that Jimmy Carter probably would, too.

# PART I

# SOUTH TOWARD HOME

# 1

## THE IRONY OF
## JIMMY CARTER

### I

It probably has not escaped the notice of an alert reader that
Jimmy Carter comes from the South. That he "comes from" the
United States in exactly the same sense has understandably not
stimulated an equivalent body of comment. But he does. President Carter, the Southerner, is certainly an American, fitting the
oldest of the national patterns.

As the purest of success stories (small town obscurity to the
White House); as an entrepreneur selling peanuts, making
money, and enlarging the firm; as a dogged competitor winning
an astonishing series of political victories; as an explicit moralist
fighting against unrighteousness from the polling places in Quit-
man County to the prisons of Brazil; as a tidying-up, reorganizing
Governor; as a planning and fixing President; as a strong-willed
follower of Admiral Rickover striving to make the world rear-
range itself in accord with higher standards, the ambitious, practical, victorious, punctual, healthy-minded, world-improving,
well-organized, speed-reading Jimmy Carter is as intrinsically
"American" as he is "Southern." Whatever one may say about his
brother, his mother, his other kinfolk and his young assistants,
President Carter himself is not a character out of Flannery
O'Connor, Erskine Caldwell, or William Faulkner. He is no man
for lost causes. He exhibits instead the clearest Yankee and
"Puritan" traits.

When in the April after his inauguration he made his "unpleasant talk" (was there a certain Puritan satisfaction in its alleged

unpleasantness?) about "the greatest challenge our country will
face in our lifetimes"—the energy crisis—he said toward the end
that "there is something especially American in the kinds of
changes we have to make." And what was it that this man from the
Deep South saw to be "especially American"? "We have been
proud of our ingenuity, our skill at answering questions." And
now: "We need efficiency and ingenuity more than ever." Was it
not the outlook—if not the accent—of a Connecticut Yankee?

To understand the irony of Jimmy Carter's arrival on the scene
let us go back to the early 1950s when Reinhold Niebuhr, one of
Mr. Carter's favorite writers, published *The Irony of American
History*. That book gave Niebuhr's own twist to familiar generalizations then being made about America, this "innocent" nation.
Our history, it was said, had been unusually fortunate. We had
had no experience of defeat in a major war, and had been able
through wealth and technology to bypass the gravest problems of
want and scarcity. We had genuine democratic virtues but "ironically" those virtues turned to vices because we held to them too
proudly, too complacently, too absolutely. ("Irony" for Niebuhr
means an incongruity that on closer examination is not merely
incongruous; there is a hidden link. Strength becomes weakness
because it prompts vanity; wisdom becomes folly because it does
not know its limits.) We Americans had generated a sentimental
picture of ourselves as a unique nation, invincible, righteous,
masters of our destiny. Our prosperity was thought to prove our
virtue and to guarantee our happiness.

C. Vann Woodward borrowed Niebuhr's theme for essays on
the contrasting irony of *Southern* history. He pointed to the
rather different—the "un-American"—experience of that region. No defeat in a war? Continual success? Prosperity? Innocence?

"Southern history, unlike American," wrote Woodward, "includes large components of frustration, failure, and defeat. It
includes not only an overwhelming military defeat but long decades of defeat in the provinces of economic, social, and political
life. Such a heritage affords the Southern people no basis for the
delusion that there is nothing whatever that is beyond their
power to accomplish."

The American people as a whole were described, in the influential book by David Potter, as a *People of Plenty*. Economic

abundance shaped the nation's character; encouraged the legends of optimism and progress; gave plausibility to the legend of individual success; shaped our unusual belief in wide open spaces for freedom of choice:

> Americans have always been especially prone to regard all things as resulting from the free choice of a free will. Probably no people have so little determinism in their philosophy, and as individuals we have regarded our economic status, our matrimonial happiness, and even our eternal salvation as things of our own making.

But the South? The South was poor. Its experience was poverty, not plenty; it was the "nation's number one economic problem." Its choices were restricted. If collective plenty shapes character, then collective poverty must do the same. The dark reality of limit and loss had a larger place in the Southern mind than in the "affluent" nation as a whole.

The most significant difference between the South and the rest of the country had to do with moral complacency. The United States as a whole, wrote Niebuhr, thought of itself as a "separated" nation, a new beginning; Americans thought they had extracted themselves from the sinful old evil world of Europe in order to make a new nation, fresh, free, and unsullied. They believed themselves to be an "innocent nation in an innocent world." The United States, said Niebuhr, was not deeply acquainted either with tragedy or with evil, and certainly not inclined to admit a significant capacity for evil-doing within itself.

But the South? "How much room," asked Woodward, "was there in the tortured conscience of the South for this national self-image of innocence and moral complacency?" For half of the nation's existence "they lived intimately with a great social evil and the other half with its aftermath. It was an evil that was even condemned and abandoned by the old world, to which America's moral superiority was supposed an article of faith. . . . The South's preoccupation was with guilt, not with innocence, with the reality of evil, not with the dream of perfection."

Americans, in a famous phrase of Tocqueville, were said to have been "born-free, and did not have to become so." But there were Americans who specifically were *not* born free, and who *did* have to become so, against the resistance of the organized will of the white South, by force of arms.

"The South's unusual experience with human bondage and its evils and later with emancipation and its shortcomings," wrote Woodward, "did not dispose the South very favorably toward such popular American ideas as the doctrine of human perfectibility, the belief that every evil has a cure, and the notion that every human problem has a solution."

Nor, might we now add, would experience with the lynch mob and Jim Crow, with masked riders in the night and the dark irrationalities of racial passion dispose the South toward Whitmanesque estimates of the innate "goodness" and "decency" of the common people—toward the belief, that is, that what we need is a government that's as good (pause) and as decent (pause) and as compassionate (pause) and as honest (pause) and as filled with love (the voice here rises gently in sentimental cadence) as the American people themselves. Such a litany, though quite "American," seems un-Niebuhrian and un-Southern.

II

Niebuhr and Woodward wrote about the contrasting ironies in the 1950s. But "history," American and Southern, did not stop in that decade, however much the nostalgia of a particular generation might wish that it had.

It might almost be said that in the more than twenty years that passed after the writing of those essays about the American and the Southerner *the two moral climates reversed themselves*.

To the South there came the Supreme Court's decision on school segregation in 1954, followed by the Civil Rights movement in all its manifestations, followed by the Civil Rights Act of 1964 and the Voting Rights Act of 1965. After passing through the fierce struggles of the 1950s and the early 1960s the South came to accommodate racial change in a way that surprised many Northerners, gratified many Southerners, and contrasted with some events in the North. Mr. Carter himself spoke for many when he not only made his flat declaration in his inaugural speech as Governor of Georgia that the day for racial discrimination was over, but also said many times that the Civil Rights acts were the "best thing that happened to the South" in his lifetime. He said, moreover, that it would be hard to judge which Southerners, black or white, benefited more. To the region that had known defeat, frustration, guilt, violent conflict, and moral torment there came—shall we say, in the phrase from the Gettysburg Address—a new birth of freedom.

Meanwhile up North, or rather in the national experience taken as a whole, the story is otherwise. No defeat in a war? However one may characterize the experience of Vietnam, it was not one designed to encourage the illusion of American omnipotence.

Prosperity as the evidence of virtue and the guarantor of happiness? The people of plenty learned that there is another America of the poor; that plenty can't last; that affluence has complicated, undesirable, un-American side-effects; and that, however rich you are, growing up in Scarsdale is terrible for the soul.

American know-how? In the late 1950's, Sputnik already raised questions.

Optimism? Masters of destiny? A young President was shot; his young brother was shot; the chief spokesman for racial justice was shot. The bright people from Harvard, clickety-click masters of world policy, took the nation waist deep into a quagmire. Racial battles moved from Little Rock, Montgomery, and Jackson up to Boston. A Georgian remarked: "Maybe we'll have to send troops up there to help them keep order. Troops dressed in gray." Northern racism and Vietnam punctured America's moral self-assurance; college youth drove the lesson home by a revolt that at its extreme condemned the whole "system."

And then as if that were not enough, this moralistic nation outdid itself by twice electing to the nation's highest office (more than an office: the central symbol of unity and of purpose in this heterogeneous, pluralistic country with no established church and no royal family) a morally tone-deaf President, the egregious and embarrassing Richard Nixon.

Troubled thinkers gathered around the big table behind the golden doors in the basement of the Ford Foundation. Crisis of confidence, they said. Loss of trust. Polls show no confidence in leaders. Vietnam and Watergate: two elites discredited. A failure

of nerve. An erosion of values. No standards. A shaking of the
moral foundations. What to do?

And then to this troubled nation there came another ironic
development. In the unlikely setting of the deepest South there
appeared, preserved as under glass, an epitome of the traits the
nation had misplaced. As from a time machine there stepped this
Georgia Ben Franklin, this Puritan in blue jeans, this Baptist in
Babylon. He predicated his presentation of himself to the nation
on such antique American suprapolitical values as to give the
deracinated modern urban political reporters intellectual hernias
from the sweaty work of trying to interpret him.

Though "American" from his nickname to his color-coded King
James Bible, he nevertheless was found to be puzzling, "enigmat-
ic," difficult to fathom. On the very day of his inauguration both
of the nation's preeminent newspapers used the word "mysterious" in their front page stories about him (Charles Mohr in *The
New York Times* and Haynes Johnson in *The Washington Post*).
Mr. Johnson, who referred to the "Carter enigma," began his
long article by writing that ". . . after tens of thousands of miles
traveled, more public appearances than anyone can recall, piti-
less scrutiny and constant criticism, he comes to power today still
regarded as somehow mysterious."

A mystery he may be, set against present-day political criteria,
but in the light of the nation's older cultural and moral values
Jimmy Carter represents the central legend of this culture—the
active will mastering the environment.

Americans—to state it now for a moment in a favorable way—
have characteristically not been morbid, cynical, defeatist, pas-
sive, fatalistic, romantic, or acquiescent, as have been many of
the other peoples of the world (including perhaps divergent
Americans in the old South). To repeat David Potter: Americans
may have as little determinism in their make-up as any people
ever had. You *can* do it; the impossible takes a little longer; there
are acres of diamonds out there in that red clay if you diligently
plant peanuts in it.

Mr. Carter as an activist and a doer fits the central American
theme of achievement in "the world" by the exertion of the
individual will. I achieve; therefore I am.

When Woodward writes of a South that "writhed in torments
of its own conscience," we do not recognize the smiling, confi-

dent face of the Baptist engineer from Plains. The American but
un-Southern legend of the solvability of problems sounds very
much like Carter's own creed. Nothing annoys him more, we
learn, than to be told there are problems that a persistent application of rationality will not solve. As to the legends of victory and
success, he said repeatedly, setting his jaw, not only as a campaigner but as a President presenting a complicated energy program: "I do not intend to lose." One of the less appealing sentences in his autobiography is an echo of Vince Lombardi and worse:
"Show me a good loser and I will show you a loser." As to human
perfectibility, Jimmy Carter has written: "Why not the best?"

That much of this resolute American Little-Engine-that-Could
action of the individual will has been put to work in the service of
career, money, success, fame—individual gain in the most tangible form—is no secret. But the underlying Puritan theme—
*purposive* action upon the external world—has expressed itself
also in more elevated ways. Mr. Carter in his celebrated interview with his fellow Baptist Bill Moyers gave this description of
his purpose: "I feel I have one life to live. I feel that God wants me
to do the best I can with it."

The best, for such a man, includes doing *good*, improving,
moralizing, making every minute count. Mr. Carter is a rather
pure combination of the American Achiever in all modes: individual worldly success; practical ingenuity; moral improvement.

It is not the self only that we are here on earth to improve: there
is the neighbor also, and the community and (not to put too small
a face on it) mankind. In the inaugural address, Carter said that
"we reject the prospect of failure or mediocrity or an inferior
quality of life for any person."

*No* mediocrity for *any* person? Well, Americans *have* believed, in a naive, comic, inadequate, valuable, and touching
way, that moral ideals may be made real, by individual action, in
the collective life of mankind.

Where great segments of the human race have been led by
circumstance and culture—by *their* history, which is not so "ironic"—to fatalism or defeatism or passivity or cynicism—Americans
have not. They have less willingness to let happen what will
happen without the intervention of their own will.

For most human beings most of the time the shaping institutions of collective life—politics and government—are not ap-

propriate objects for moral judgment or practical exertion. They
are to be understood by other criteria. They are moved by forces
too large for human agency to control, or even significantly to
affect. For many human beings on this earth the deep currents of
the historical process seem to make a mockery of the fiddling of
particular regimes and the struttings of lonely leaders on the
surface of events. Or perhaps the collective life is ruled by other
standards than moral ones—by the rules of the jungle, or by
"statecraft," which though honorable in its way is very far from
the realm of ethical conduct appropriate in the relation of person
to person. Much of the world has believed some mixture of these
things about its collective life. On the whole Americans have not.
Apparently Jimmy Carter does not.

Picture a boy in that more innocent America told by his teacher to
read *War and Peace*. What will he make of it? Where Tolstoy
primarily emphasizes what leaders *cannot* do, the young American (Jimmy Carter) will find in it rather what ordinary people *can*
do.

If there is something perilous in the return of the world-fixer,
the moralist, the innocent—the Puritan or Yankee, or evangelical, with an "interfering spirit of righteousness"—there is something promising as well. To have the mind and conscience to go
directly to the moral core of the most important matters, and to
have the unjaded will to try to set those matters straight—that
"Puritanism" is no small thing. It has been a chief source of this
country's merit. It just might happen that the world will benefit
from having a Puritan redivivus who goes straight for fundamentals, who—for just one breathtaking example—says in his inaugural that we should take steps not only to balance or even to
reduce but to abolish nuclear weapons.

On the night before the inauguration an old Georgia friend of
Carter said, "There's goin' to be a new breeze. You watch.
There's goin' to be a new breeze." After Carter had been in office
a short while an Indian academician said it rather seemed to him
that Carter was a "fresh breeze" in Washington. Prime Minister
James Callaghan, after Mr. Carter's first meetings with European
leaders in London, said that Mr. Carter was "a breath of fresh air
in the Western World."

## III

To return from the fresh breezes now to Niebuhr and Woodward: Niebuhr's view of American history was ironic, not tragic. The nation held its virtues with pride and without much depth or wisdom, but the virtues nonetheless were real. And Woodward, for his part, said that the "eccentric" position of the South need not be a handicap; in the "un-American" experience of the South there could be a consoling value that might have "enduring worth" to the nation as a whole. The heritage of the South, he wrote, "is far more closely in line with the common lot of mankind than the national legends of opulence and success and innocence." The knowledge derived from that history might serve as a complement to the more general American attitudes. This divergence from the American norm, this accord with the less happy experience of mankind, "could possibly be turned to advantage by the Southern historian."

May we add, twenty years later, by a Southern President?

There is certainly no guarantee that Southern origins give sober wisdom. Woodward published a sequel to his earlier essay, called "A Second Look at the Theme of Irony," in 1968, at the height of the folly of Vietnam. He noted that "a gentleman from Texas in the White House and a gentleman from Georgia in the State Department" offered no restraint upon the American legend of invincibility and innocence, and the people of the South supported the war as strongly as the people of any region.

But history now takes another turning, and a man at once more thoroughly Southern and more typical of older American traits than Lyndon Johnson comes now to the fore, in altered conditions.

Mr. Carter represents at once a rather pure version of the traits of the "American," Northern and Southern, in the more confident "youthful" past, and at the same time the region that may have learned from historical experience something of their inadequacy.

That older optimism and confidence, that individualism and overblown belief in voluntary action, that expectation that one can solve all problems by ingenuity and technique, that playing down of the collective and historical realities, and particularly that exemption of our innocent national self from entanglement with the world's evils, are rested upon an unusual history, quite lucky compared to the rest of the world: economic prosperity, victory in war, constitutional continuity, the expanse of a continent. They rested also upon an unusual intellectual and religious history: individualistic political liberalism, individualistic Protestantism, individualistic capitalism—all of these, bound together, reinforcing each other. They were all—capitalism, political liberalism, free church Protestantism—inclined to see the world as a field open to the free choice. Our ideas, our institutions, our historical experience has given us Americans an illusion-tinged picture of human society and of mankind's life. This nation, like others, was sure to come against "the limitation and fragmentariness of all human striving," as Niebuhr often put it. Not everything *is* soluble by free action of the human will. Human beings are not as separated from each other as our individualism implies; no one is a "self-made" man (nor will there be self-made women either). Nor is any people as "innocent" as this country has thought itself to be. Americans were certain to learn, one day, as Woodward says, that it is not true that "history is something unpleasant that happens to other people"; it "happens" to us, too.

As the national moral complacency, optimism, and self-confidence were shallowly grounded (Niebuhr's main point, in a way, in *Irony*), so the so-called "crisis of confidence," the loss of trust in leaders, the gloom and national unhappiness that followed, were also shallow. People with illusions become disillusioned; people without illusions don't.

Is there something in Mr. Carter that might deepen, chasten, broaden, and give collective and historical depth to the classic American ethic of which he is so striking an embodiment?

The recovery at the top of American self-confidence and moral energy can be something good in this new turn in the ironies of human history. It will be still better (and why not the better?) if it should be accompanied this time, as those qualities have not ordinarily been in the past, by self-criticism; by an understanding of social justice; by an awareness of the interdependence of mankind and of communal goods and ills; by a chastened, forgiving wisdom. Such added qualities might come from a President who read Reinhold Neibuhr. They also could come from a region that has lived with collective miseries, that knows what it is to have been poor, defeated, frustrated, and guilty—and nevertheless to have risen again.

# 2

# A GEORGIA
# YANKEE

Not long after I wrote an article presenting President Carter as a
Yankee and Puritan—a Yankee from Georgia—he returned to the
South to insist: "I'm proud being an American, but I'm even more
proud being a Southerner!"

He said this on his first major trip as President to the South, in
Charleston, New Orleans, Jackson, and Yazoo City. Hedrick
Smith, reporting the story for *The New York Times*, said that the
remark was greeted with "pandemonium." It is striking that
Carter and the cheering crowd should still feel the need to
formulate their Southern pride in that (as Carter himself might
put it) "aggressive" way.

That pride played a role in the administration's behavior in the
Bert Lance affair—as well as, according to Garry Wills writing in
*The New York Review of Books*, in the behavior of the President
himself: Carter defended his friend intensely and long because
he resisted the doubts of arrogant Northern outsiders about
small-town Southerners. In the week that Lance resigned, an
article in *The Wall Street Journal* drawing upon interviews with
White House associates said:

> the President is intensely loyal only to his close friends from
> Georgia and is "obsessed" with demonstrating that South-
> erners, especially his Georgians, are capable of running a
> government so long dominated by Yankees.

That "obsession" and that "pandemonium"—moral equiva-
lents of the rebel yell—indicate not only why the word "Yankee"
might still be repugnant but also the continuing emotional reality

of the Southern regional identity: that pride, those hurt feelings, the "collective egotism" and the defensive need to prove something.

There are, though, two ways to do the proving (I oversimplify). One is by way of the assertion of a superior code, a Southern ethic or way of life that is better than the busy materialistic unromantic North, a way that appealed to a long string of Southerners down to the Agrarians who wrote the book *I'll Take My Stand* and still casts up an occasional scent of magnolia today. Another way is to adopt the Yankee's code and beat them at their own game: to out-Yankee the Yankees. Mr. Carter's way is the latter.

I do not mean to cast doubt on Mr. Carter's quite evident Southern pride and knowledge of the South. In his list of roles and identities he puts *first* of all, even before American, that of being a Southerner. He has been quoted as having said that his being a Southerner explains more about him than anything else. In response to the article "The Yankee from Georgia," Jody Powell sent me a clipping describing Mr. Carter's reading of Faulkner (*all*, characteristically, of Faulkner's books) and of the other Southern writers, and quoting Carter thus:

> On many occasions I've read [Faulkner's books] aloud to my children. I think he has most accurately analyzed . . . the fallibility of human beings and the basic weakness of mankind . . . I think [the] Southern writers have analyzed very carefully the buildup in the South of a special consciousness brought about by the self-condemnation resulting from slavery, the humiliation following the War Between the States, and the hope, sometimes expressed timidly, for redemption. I think in many ways now that those former dark moods in the South of recrimination against self and others and alienation from the rest of the nation—I think they've been alleviated.

That's a valuable statement, about a significant side to the President. Meanwhile, though, the surface truth is this: if we list traits traditionally associated with the South, Mr. Carter does not fit them.

To be sure he has in addition to his regional pride and his reading of Faulkner some of the traits and associations said to be characteristic of the South: most notably, his evangelical Southern Baptist piety; and perhaps also the sidestepping of great

objective issues where one has personal loyalties, as in his dealing
with Bert Lance. The tone of his patriotism and his military
background, his love of Plains and home and family, might plaus-
ibly be added. Nevertheless the balance falls in the other direction: Mr. Carter represents the opposite of the traits that have
traditionally been associated with a distinctive Southern approach to life. A Washington newsman said that Carter is Southern in the way Edward Brooke is black.

To be sure the notion of distinctive Southern traits is in part
myth. There are many different parts and aspects of that enormous region, from hill country to delta, black belt, tidewater,
piedmont, many layers of geography and life, black and white,
rich and poor, each state a story to itself (as V. O. Key indicated in
*Southern Politics*). Moreover it keeps changing, New South following upon New South. Still there is a powerful legend, and one
side in the scholarly debate on the subject—represented by the
historian Carl Degler's *Place Over Time* and by the sociologist
John Shelton Reed's *The Enduring South*—finds the legend
grounded in fact. The South is distinctive, and the distinction
persists.

The Southerner, whose life was said to be gracious and not
ruled by the clock or the dollar, was said to be sociable, gregarious, good company. But Carter consistently has been described
like this: "Fellow governors who served with him in the South say
he was never 'one of the boys' . . . Once during a Southern
Governors' Conference, while most other governors were playing tennis or golf, Carter had a helicopter pick him up and take
him to study a county health-care center."

When David Broder of *The Washington Post* told me (in the
spring before the election) that Carter had been disliked by his
fellow governors, I asked the then Congressman Andrew Young
about it. Rather than deny the charge he turned it to Carter's
credit. Carter, said Young, doesn't do the governors' conference
stuff—banter, chatting, sitting around telling jokes. "He wants to
talk serious talk," Young said. "He would rather go somewhere
and read a book than engage in small talk."

President Carter does not like to be called a "loner," but the
description persists. Elizabeth Drew wrote in *The New Yorker*:
"Governing does require collective action. It remains to be seen
how good Carter—a loner—is at that." White House staff mem-

bers I talked to accepted the word as accurate. When Carter
himself was asked about the word *loner* his answer was revealing.

> It's not true. I have a lot of close friends that I've had from my
> infancy all the way up through college and my naval career
> and, of course, now . . . because of the tightknit friendships
> that I've had, large groups of Georgia people who knew me
> well, who have been very close to me, went at their own
> expense to campaign for me.
>
> So far as I know, no other candidate in the history of the
> country has had that kind of home base support.

His response in fact shows an interesting inversion. He notes that
people follow, and reach out for *him*. Commitment of friends to
him, yes; support for him, yes. The not quite answered question
goes the other way around.

"He likes to work off paper," says a member of the administration. Among the words used about him by his staff are "cool" and
"aloof." Curtis Wilkie, the Mississippian writing perceptively
about his fellow Southerner for *The Boston Globe*—sometimes
to Carter's annoyance—wrote in the third month of his Presidency:

> By nature, Carter is more like a commanding officer than a
> congressman.
>
> He prefers to make unilateral decisions that are not subject
> to compromise.
>
> He dislikes small talk and believes the ritualistic flattery
> which members of Congress heap on one another is a waste of
> time.
>
> "Some of these qualities that you find in legislators," said
> one Carter associate, "are the very things that Jimmy can't
> stand."

The long analysis of Carter the Man in *The Wall Street Journal*
for September 26, 1977, written by James Perry and based on
interviews with the Carter staff explicitly contrasted him to the
Southern politicians:

> Some of the officials profess surprise that Mr. Carter is so
> unlike the stereotype of the Southern politician that he is
> supposed to be. "Unlike most Southern politicians," says one

official who himself is from the South, "Carter despises the
use of political 'grease.' He doesn't like bull-sessions. He
doesn't like making your standard deals."

As to Southern hospitality and manners, there are continual
reports that his staff gets no thank-yous. After Carter's witty
remarks at the White House correspondents' dinner at the end of
April, 1977, a high official said, "Too bad he isn't that congenial in
private." When Carter simplified the ceremonial dinners for
visits by heads of state he remarked: "I don't want to waste my
time or theirs. I want to make maximum use of my time and
theirs."

As is evident in his best forum, the press conference, Carter
may be the most intelligent man to run for President in modern
times, but it is a "Yankee" intelligence—particular, didactic,
concise, inductive, exact. (I use "Yankee" and "Puritan" often
just to stand for the older core of the generalized American; if the
words are used, as here, more strictly they suggest the essence
that goes back to New England.) One of Carter's staff told me "he
is intelligent but not speculative. Most of his political values come
from inductive reasoning, not a priori." Carter can master, remember, and manage a complex body of materials, and he can
make close distinctions. This shy man moreover has used his
intelligence and his will to make himself articulate. (In 1966,
when he had the opportunity at a gathering at the Piedmont
Driving Club to impress Atlanta's elite, he wasn't articulate, and
he didn't.)

The defect of this high intelligence is important—perhaps the
most important reservation one may have about the rather clear-
cut old-fashioned disciplined character, admirable in so many
ways, that I have here in the teeth of Southern resentment called
Yankee. One does not look to Poor Richard for "vision," for
imagination, for conceptual, speculative power. If one described
the mythic mind of the South its primary quality would be
imagination—imagination, "creativity," the seeing of visions, the
dreaming of dreams, the investing of drab reality with the fire of
memory, and a passionate re-formulation. Mr. Carter's man
Faulkner is a prime example, alongside clusters of Southern
novelists, newspapermen, and a whole school of social theorists
before the Civil War. But that is not Carter's mind—"high intelligence but not speculative."

I found in *Parade* magazine, while sitting in the Morris Inn at Notre Dame waiting for the commencement service that President Carter was to address, a cover story on Ruth Carter Stapleton, with many quotations. What she said about her brother was of course thoroughly laudatory but I noted one phrase: "He is a very logical, methodical, punctual, well programmed man with a mind like a steel trap. *I would not say that he's particularly creative or innovative . . .*" That sentence sprang at me; the emphasis is mine.

I was to be struck also by the sweeping conclusion in the James Perry article in *The Wall Street Journal*:

> "To the extent there is a vision in this administration," one adviser says, "Carter is the visionary. Nobody else really has one. Domestically, though, his only vision, if it can be called one, is to make programs work better."
> That idea—that Mr. Carter wants to make things work better—was repeated endlessly.

Making things work better and making speeches are not the same thing; the legendary South has excelled at the latter. College debaters who cross the Mason-Dixon line from the North have long shared the experience of sound transformed: Logic, argument, one-two-three facts are replaced by rhythm, style, flowing words, platform oratory. One might not be able to locate the verbs or even identify the subject, but one knows one has heard something. The archetypal Southerner, like the Irishman, loves words, knows how to talk and sometimes to write, to use the imagination and to tell tales. Whatever the value of these traits, Carter doesn't have them.

He is no Southern talker, orator, or writer. He writes and speaks without embellishment. Jim Fallows, his speech writer, told me that he *does* care about words, and works on speeches, but strives for a simple style without ornament (so did the Puritans, by the way). In his interview with Harvey Shapiro of *The New York Times Book Review* Carter was appealingly self-deprecatory about his writing and speaking: "I've only written one book, in a very amateurish way," he said, and, later, about the talented writer's giving expression to a vision in words: "I don't have talent in that respect." He said this as an aside while asserting the importance of the talent he lacks. Though verbally agile, he uses words as instruments only, to convey facts, points, arguments. He found no apparent difficulty with the boring iterations of the campaign platform. His formal speeches ("and another point . . . and another point"—10 of them, no less, in the energy speech) are not particularly well-written. His spontaneous talk is not eloquent. In a particularly un-Southern way, his speeches have no rhythm. Big words pop out in unexpected places. Complex formulations intrude when he is trying to be simple. Parallels don't parallel. Though he can give effective terse answers, I heard him speak, in a press conference, about "some attenuation in the rapidity with which we will implement programs." The newsman sitting next to me told me that at the last outing Carter had said we have "tapped the reservoir of bi-lingual excellence."

Here is a sentence from his inaugural address, presumably a sentence upon which he expended care:

> Our commitment to human rights must be absolute, our laws fair, our natural beauty preserved; the powerful must not persecute the weak, and human dignity must be enhanced.

With those flat final verbs, it sounds like a translation from the German; "preserved" at the end of the first series lets our spacious skies down with a bump.

Another example:

> We will be ever vigilant and never vulnerable, and we will fight our wars against poverty, ignorance and injustice, for those are the enemies against which our forces can be honorably marshaled.

Again it seems to have been translated from German, and the sentence is a bit of a roller coaster. "Ever vigilant and never vulnerable," not a happy alliteration, is the work of the man who could keep saying that our tax system is a "disgrace to the human race" without grinding his teeth at the jarring little rhyme.

Nevertheless, the inaugural address had its own pawky personal attractiveness; Carter's language has its own unassuming appeal; what he says is often more effective when one hears it than when one reads it. My point is simply that it is a long way from either the verbosity or the eloquence of the "Southern" use of language.

Each of these traits can be presented either as a virtue or a vice; there certainly is an undesirable side to "Southern" talkativeness. That other side—and a merit in the characteristics ascribed here to Carter—may be exhibited by making a contrast with another morally earnest President, Woodrow Wilson.

There are a number of parallels between these two Presidents. Wilson might well have written to his father, a Southern Presbyterian minister and leader of that denomination, the statement Carter made to Moyers about God putting us on this earth to do our best. Wilson, whose family moved to Augusta, Georgia, when he was one year old, grew up in the South, and was enough identified with it still to leave the room in anger during an argument over the Civil War when he was a student in Princeton. As with Carter there was in Wilson an explicit replacement of ministry with politics, in the interest of a larger service. Perhaps it can almost be said of Carter, as Edmund Wilson wrote of Woodrow Wilson:

> All that language of . . . idealism—truth, righteousness, service, faith—which the ordinary public speaker makes use of without believing in it and, as it were, without expecting to be believed—all these phrases were in some sense a gospel with Wilson, and it was the realization of this that arrested the attention of the public.

But the link between the two morally earnest Southern Protestants breaks abruptly when we turn to their roles on the platform and in the office. "Making speeches was the thing he did best," wrote Edmund Wilson of Woodrow Wilson; such a sentence would not be written of Carter. On the other hand, there will be no criticism of Carter comparable to that of Wilson. Niebuhr wrote in his notebook at the time of Versailles that Wilson "is too much a child of the manse. He believes too much in words." Wilson himself once referred to his intoxication with his own verbosity. John Maynard Keynes wrote a memorable description of the post War disappointment of his European admirers:

> The President's programme for the world, as set forth in his speeches and his Notes, had displayed a spirit and a purpose so admirable that the last desire of his sympathizers was to criticize details—the details, they felt, were quite rightly not

filled in at present, but would be in due course. . . . But in fact
the President had thought out nothing; when it came to practice, his ideas were nebulous and incomplete. He had no plan,
no scheme, no constructive ideas whatever for clothing with
the flesh of life the commandments he had thundered from
the White House. He could have preached a sermon on any of
them, or have addressed a stately prayer to the Almighty for
their fulfillment, but he could not frame their concrete application to the actual state of Europe.

Now with President Carter, for all his twenty-five prayers a
day, the traits that Keynes found in Wilson are almost reversed.
Carter does not deliver an eloquent Wilsonian address, a mighty
sermon, or a stately prayer, of the sort that lifts the hearers out of
their seats, vibrating with hope and warmth and idealism. One of
his love/hate maybe-admirers in the press corps said in despair
after Carter's remarks at Warm Springs commencing his campaign (which were a rather jerky exercise in ideological coun-
terpoint): "Won't he *ever* rise to the occasion? Won't he *ever*
make an inspirational speech?"

But on the other hand when the time comes to apply the words
to "the actual state of Europe" he *would* know the details. By all
reports he is Wilson's opposite on that score: he has a "prodigious
memory"; he soaks up details; he *listens*; he *loves* being briefed;
he presents himself as a good student, and is one; he reads stacks
of paper until his eyes are red. Speechwriter Fallows says that
Carter does not want "the rhetoric to outrun the reality," a phrase
that might almost be taken to describe Wilson's career. Carter is,
in a nice phrase from another aide, "very big on being tutored."
His daughter-in-law Judy, that most interesting observer in the
family, says of her father-in-law: "He *loves* it, listening to people
explain a foreign policy problem—two hours with Brzezinski, or
five hours in that conference on energy policy."

Before the end of Carter's first year in the White House he was
being criticized and praised for traits and behavior almost the
opposite of Wilson's. He spends too much time on detail, it was
said, and on detail a President shouldn't spend time on; he is not
as good with concepts, with general ideas, with the overall issues;
he rarely makes formal speeches, and when he does lifts nobody's
heart. He does however, as Charles Schultze of the Council of
Economic Advisors said, have "a mind for numbers."

Woodrow Wilson's traits fit more closely the mythic Southerner; up North the prosaic Yankee, like Carter, knew the details,
read the dull papers, had a mind for numbers.

Southerners were reported to have a penchant for nostalgia,
for Faulkneresque memory, for drenching the present in a
romanticized past. The Southerner, in W. J. Cash's *The Mind of
the South*, was "a romantic and a hedonist." He remembered, he
dreamed, he escaped, with the encouragement of the clinging
vine, Sir Walter Scott, bourbon, and the Southern climate, into
unreality. In all of this, one is describing someone that is the
opposite of the Georgian who was elected President the night we
were told, at the World Congress Center in Atlanta, that the
victory celebration going on around us was the greatest event in
the city's history since the premiere of "Gone With the Wind."
Carter is not a romantic but a realist. Anybody who thinks he is a
hedonist hasn't looked up what the word means.

As to living with the burdens, resentments, and glories of the
past: on the central memory-choked issues of race and regional
guilts and hypocrisies, Jimmy Carter has shown a deft touch of
the necessary forgetfulness. After the trauma of Bert Lance's
departure one of his associates said, "He doesn't look back or
second guess himself. He will push on." Mrs. Edna Langford of
Calhoun, Georgia, friend and campaign comrade of Rosalynn
Carter, mother of Jack Carter's wife, Judy, and grandmother of
little Jason, is an impressive woman who manages to be at once
brisk and attractive. Telling, one day in Atlanta, in swift, well-
organized detail the story of their early campaigning in Florida,
she mentioned an injunction that Rosalynn (that first, best student of Jimmy's) had "absorbed from Jimmy" and often repeated:
"Don't look back." A listener, another friend of the Carters,
broke in and said, "That's it! That's Jimmy! *Don't look back*." So
much for romance, nostalgia, memory and the great Southern
entanglement with the past.

The most important of all the distinctions between the South—
mythic or real—and the rest of the country, especially New
England, had to do with *time*—with time, work, and "the Puritan
ethic." Woodward quotes Tocqueville: "As we advance toward
the South the prejudice which sanctions idleness increases in
power." How much is real and how much myth, how much or
little still true need not concern us here, nor should I make a

layman's stab at explanation (climate, slavery, poverty, hook-
worm and other candidates). It is enough that the myth was there.
The North was associated with the word "bustle," as a noun, a
verb, and, suitably suffixed, an adjective. The South, except
when "new," unbustled. It unbustled particularly in rural places
like Sumter County. Woodward examined the Janus-faced
Southern trait of leisure (the attractive face) and laziness (otherwise). One face of the mythical South was plantations, magnolias,
mint juleps; a slow, pleasant, mannerly, unhurried, sociable,
hospitable, leisurely life. The other face was redneck, lazy, good-
for-nothing trash sittin' on the porch, and broken-down auto-
mobiles without tires rusting in the front yard in the middle of the
chickens.

Does President Carter represent either aspect of this trait? The
testimony in the negative is overwhelming. He is the furthest
thing from lazy. He gets up early, works a very long day, wastes
no time, records everything, counts everything—especially the
minutes. If leisure-laziness be the measure of the mythical
Southerner, Jimmy Carter is from Vermont.

Here is a journalist's description of the start of the President's
day: "Good morning, Mr. President . . . It's five-thirty . . . Jimmy Carter slipped quietly from bed, leaving his wife asleep in the
darkness to begin another day in the White House. The day
would last until nearly midnight, a grueling eighteen
hours . . . Each segment is duly noted on the neatly typed
schedule that awaits him on his desk every morning, even when
he goes to work at 6 a.m." Descriptions of the intense, long,
meticulously planned Carter workday abound. As candidate his
campaign was the only punctual campaign known to political
man; often he would arrive at his appointments early. An aide in
the White House says he "would never play tennis with him";
tells how Mr. Carter would be "pissed off" at players on his side
who made errors in the softball games in Plains; how he never
wants to do anything "half-assed"; how "hostile" he is to "lazy and
fats."

Spanish lessons; speed-reading exercises by the whole family—Amy, too—gathered on Tuesday evenings around the
Cabinet table; attendance at the King Tut exhibition, the ballet,
symphonies; visits backstage; rereading *Anna Christie* before
attending the play; Vivaldi, Schumann, and Bach echoing

through his study as he works; exercise every day (back from bowling with Chip: "I really worked up a good sweat"). Time is to be used, filled with what is good and right and improving.

Spokesmen for a classic Southern ethic spoke of the "inestimable boon of leisure," of the "gentleness and dignity and leisure of the old Southern life," of avoiding "the fault of being intemperately addicted to work," of the attractive "dualities of fellowship and leisure."

For the Yankee world, on the other hand, the most characteristic voice was Ben Franklin's, whose phrases might be mottos of the Carter White House: *Dost thou love life, then do not squander time, for time is the stuff that life is made of . . . There will be sleeping enough in the grave . . . Sloth makes all things difficult, but industry all easy . . . Leisure is the time for doing something useful*. Every American knows, although he may not know where the saying is to be found, what early to bed and early to rise will make a man. (It may also make him President and/or a millionaire—two conditions more combinable than they used to be.) Every American knows also what a penny saved is. Yankees balance budgets, watch the account books, "scrimp and save" (Mrs. Carter's constant phrase on the hustings), often are "tight as a tick" (Mr. Powell's description of his boss). *Newsweek* reported that Carter charges Cabinet members $1.25 for the orange juice, roll, and coffee at their "breakfast" with the President of The United States.

Count the pennies, count the minutes.

Life should be predictable, managed, planned. Connecticut was known, when it was a Yankee state, as the state of "steady habits." Rosalynn Carter, campaigning, stood at Gate 11 in the Indianapolis air terminal and indignantly condemned the waste and incompetence, the unsteady habits of the Washington her planner husband, her businessman husband, would straighten out.

Straighten things out; be competent; save money, save time: time is money. Save time, use it wisely, because for a Puritan to do so is Godly and for a Yankee to do so is remunerative.

How did this apparent anomaly come about—that these older, Puritan-Yankee traits should be incarnated in a modern Southerner? One answer has to do with Carter himself. Annapolis, a national institution, was his college. As a naval officer he lived much of his life outside the South—San Diego, Honolulu, New York, three times in New England. He is (as he kept reminding audiences) an engineer and a business man, and the traits I have been calling Yankee are as much those of early industrialism as of Old New England.

The Old South was seen to lack the Yankee-industrial virtues, but Southerners were still Americans too. Therefore the lonely earnest achievers in that region—the upwardly mobile first children, the straight A students—may adopt the allegedly missing virtues in a particularly unqualified, insistent way: to show the Yankees, for example, that Georgians can run as "competent" an administration as any Northerner.

The very distinctness of the Southern experience—defeat, poverty, racism, tortured conscience and Northern disapproval—that insulated the South from the rest of the nation, and that hobbled that sequence of modern industrial New Souths, provided also a crust under which the Puritan substratum of American culture was preserved. It was preserved in parts of the South even as it was eaten away elsewhere by the acids of modernity. It was preserved especially in parts of the South that were not included in "Society": in the Sunday School of the Plains Baptist Church more than in the Piedmont Driving Club. The religious historian E. Brooks Holifield wrote that "the Southern Baptist convention is among the last great repositories of the Puritan tradition in America."

When the Civil Rights revolution ended the long moral isolation of the South and burst open the regional crust, Brother Jimmy, the Puritan-Yankee deacon and warehouse owner, was ready to step forth into the world bearing the marks of an older, almost forgotten America.

# 3

## THE STRANGE CAREER
## OF THE CIVIL
## RIGHTS MOVEMENT

In the early morning after election day, while we waited to hear
the results, Coretta King spoke to the immense crowd in the
World Congress Center in Atlanta. We certainly did represent,
as we wondered whether we would overcome or not, black and
white together—crowded close together. Mrs. King took note of
the racial composition of the crowd. She referred to the "remarkable story" of Carter's rise. She cheerfully said—the results were
coming in slowly—"let me stall." Respectful voices called out
"no" to reject that utilitarian interpretation of her role. "Jimmy
Cah-tah," she concluded, "will bring the kind of America Martin
Luther King, Jr., talked of at the Lincoln Memorial in 1963. He is
a product of the Movement."

As a white man from Sumter County Georgia he was certainly
an unlikely product of the Movement. The band of low country
counties stretching across the deepest South, called the black
belt, had more intransigent racism and more reactionary politics,
more violence and more lynching than other parts of the South.
Sumter County in Georgia is one of those counties.

People in Atlanta asked disdainfully: "Can any good come from
Sumter County?"

The Bible reading citizens of Plains no doubt heard the echo in
that question: Can any good come from Nazareth? On January 2,
1977, in the Men's Bible Class at the Baptist Church in Plains the
teacher Clarence Dodson, dealing with a lesson from the New
Testament in which Nazareth was mentioned, noted the obscurity, and perhaps the dubious reputation, of that little town. Looking up over his glasses at the President-elect of the United States,

who was seated erect and listening in the second row, he said:
    "Brother Jimmy, you'll have to bear with me.

    "What people said about Nazareth was like the people who now
say: Who would have thought the next President of the United
States would ever come from Plains, Georgia?"

Sumter County was by reputation "the nastiest county in the
state," partly because the interracial Christian commune called
Koinonia Farms, fourteen miles from Plains, had been bombed,
presumably by local whites, and boycotted for supporting (ex-
hibiting) racial integration. "There is no record," wrote one critic,
"of Jimmy Carter, a prominent businessman in the county, step-
ping forward (as some local ministers did) to remind his neighbors
that firing shotguns at people's houses and burning down their
barns constituted un-Christian behavior."

In Atlanta in 1976 I learned how conservative some of Carter's
chief supporters were. Many who had backed Carter for Governor in 1970 voted for George Wallace for the Presidential nomination in Miami in 1972. Many hated and refused to support
McGovern. One Carter campaign worker had been heard to say
that he "don't much like niggers." A man in Calhoun said to one of
Carter's supporters, "If he turns out to be a blankety-blank liberal
I'm going to get you." A close Carter friend said to me that she
didn't like it when Carter took back his "ethnic purity" remark:
"That's the way we believe."

Carter courted and willingly accepted the support of George
Wallace, and he praised segregationist senators. In the election
he received the votes of hundreds of thousands of sometime
Wallace voters, Goldwater supporters, white segregationists,
and conservative whites. He carried every one of the Confederate states except Virginia. That Southern base was essential to his
nomination and especially to his narrow victory. And conservative white voters helped him not only in the South but in other
areas that he needed in order to win—particularly the counties
south of Route 40 in Ohio.

Despite everything that might have been held against Mr.
Carter, key leaders of the Civil Rights Movement not only gave
him their support, but gave an *active* support, gave it *early*, did
so at moments in the primary campaign when it really counted,
and did so again throughout the general election in a way that was

decisive to his victory. They held no grudges. They applied no test of perfection.

The vote of blacks on election day was only one part of the service done for this unlikely product of the Movement. He would not have been there on the ticket to receive those votes had he not had that active support of the widow, the father, and the most effective associate of the Civil Rights Movement's most noted leader.

At the end of his first year in office, with all of the intervening distractions and inevitable changes in his perspective, Mr. Carter still, in his interview with James Reston, explicitly remembered the support of Andrew Young and the Kings as part of the good fortune that made him President.

Back in April of 1975 Andrew Young, sitting at breakfast in the Indiana University Memorial Union, surprised his questioner by saying he was supporting his state's ex-Governor Jimmy Carter at least until the Florida primary in order to defeat George Wallace. A year and month later in the House Dining Room the then Congressman Young explained that as he had come to know Carter better (he had known his mother longer) he had moved to an unqualified support. And that decision by Andrew Young was a key to the "remarkable story" of Jimmy Carter's arrival—more than peanut brigades, more than the magic of his smile, more than his adroit fuzziness or the brilliant planning of Hamilton Jordan's memos, more than the endless shaking of hands. By Young's decision (and the Kings') Carter was made legitimate to millions of blacks; by the support both of Young and the Kings and of black voters he was made legitimate to white liberals. Already attractive to Southern whites and some conservatives by his regional identity, he now represented a formidable combination, and, showing himself intelligent and competent, began to get the benefits of looking like a winner, like power. A friend of mine said he could feel the Ford Foundation building begin to lean toward Carter.

Young also gave practical advice to Carter. In April of the primary season, when the phrase "ethnic purity" appeared in the sixteenth paragraph on page 134 of a story in *The New York Daily News*, it was picked up by a CBS executive and used to prod from Carter some further dubious language—"intrusion" and "alien groups." It was Young who persuaded Carter to recant and then Martin Luther King, Sr.—"Daddy" King—who gave him the imprimatur of a soul handclasp. The picture of that handclasp, circulated nationwide, stamped out the fire.

At an Indianapolis park during the fall campaign, Nikki Giovanni, young, black, beautiful, not long ago militant, spoke a couple of her poems into the cold air and the unresponsive white crowd of millwrights, lathers, roofers, cement masons, and retail clerks, in support of this unyoung, unblack, unbeautiful, and certainly unmilitant cautious white Georgia rural male.

At an airport rally, Coretta King, svelte in a red jacket and grey slacks, a gold peanut in her lapel, almost upstaged the candidate. A black newsman interviewed her; Senator Vance Hartke gave her a very tentative kiss; Mayor Richard Hatcher of Gary gave her a more assertive one.

At Madison Square Garden after Carter had been nominated, there was Daddy King again, like a William Blake drawing for the book of Job, giving what must be the most extraordinary benediction in the history of American party conventions, praying up a veritable storm of religious, moral, American, and partisan passions for this Georgia white man.

On the day before the election itself when we had heard that Jimmy the Greek was giving six to five odds that Ford would win, there was Andy Young yet once again, his voice growing hoarse yet once again, calling out to the crowd in Atlanta's central city park that the pollsters always undercounted blacks and that Jimmy would win. There was Daddy King again, in the brown hat that he wore everyplace, just in from speakin' across America for Jimmy, attacking this late-minute "trick" (the much-publicized last-minute effort by the old black minister to integrate the church) "they" pulled to smear Jimmy down at Plains.

"Why not six months ago?

"Don't you *buy* that *lie*; don't you *buy* that *trick*.

"They got the money; they always got the money; they cater to the rich folks. Don't *buy* that *lie*."

He also answered, in his unique pastoral style, the worries over the *Playboy* interview. His answer did not follow the line of other clerical defenders of Carter, that was testimony to the scriptural soundness of the point that Deacon Carter had been making in his comments about lust. Daddy King took a different line: "They can't kill you for lookin'."

"Old as I am, they STILL look good.

"When Ah see a good lookin' woman, I look, and I wipe my mouth . . . and I wished I could . . . but I'm a preachah!"

However it might have served in other circles, this defense of Mr. Carter's interview was unmistakably effective at the peanut roast at Atlanta's central city park on November 1, 1976.

A day and a half later, in the early morning of November 3, there was Daddy King again, still in the brown hat. He made a joyful noise as he got onto the elevator in the Omni Hotel: "It's a new day! It's a new day!"

Carter received, according to *Congressional Quarterly*, 94 percent of the black vote. The black vote was larger than his margin of victory in at least seven states. His margin in the electoral college was small; though his margin of the popular vote was not as thin as that of John F. Kennedy in 1960 or Richard Nixon in 1968, the way the vote was distributed meant that his electoral college margin was thinner. Although a close election gives every group of voters the opportunity to claim a decisive role—if several thousands just here and just there had switched—it takes no such neat placement to know the overwhelming importance of black voters to Mr. Carter's election.

He could never have been elected had it not been for the Voting Rights Act of 1965, which made it possible for the multitudes of black citizens in the Deep South to vote. One may also say therefore that he could not have been elected had it not been for the marches, culminating in the Selma march that led directly to the Voting Rights Act—marches by "outside agitators." The memory of those outsiders still more than a decade later makes the eyes of the widow of "Brother Bob" Harris—the longtime pastor of the Plains Baptist Church—flash with anger. It is unlikely that Carter would have risen to a position to be the beneficiary of those marches if he himself had been a participant in them.

It is remarkable enough that so soon after the slogans of Black Power echoed through the land—taught us, indeed, to say "black" instead of "Negro," and filled the air with epithets against honkies and white liberals and white devils—that so soon after all that militant antiwhite outlook the enormous preponderance of American blacks should cast their votes for a white man from the Deep South with the connections I have described. It is all the more remarkable when one puts alongside those black votes the Southern white support, the conservative and hitherto segregationist white support, that Carter received.

Carter won both the nomination of his once deeply divided Southern/Northern party and the election to the office Lincoln once held with the decisive support of black voters and, simultaneously, the solid return to the Democratic ranks of every Confederate state except Virginia. He won his victory with a combination like that of the crowd lining up in cheerful interracial disorder to acquire their paper cups of beer in the World Congress Center in Atlanta on election night—a mixture of ordinary black Americans not long before disdained by white fellow Georgians and of ordinary white voters who were in turn themselves disdained, sometimes with reason, as "racists."

The state that clinched Mr. Carter's victory—flashed onto the huge television screens in the Atlanta center—was, appropriately, Mississippi, the state that was once called a "closed society" by a professor at its university—where Carter was supported by Aaron Henry of the NAACP and by Senator James Eastland; by Medger Evers, Hodding Carter III, and the son of Ross Barnett; by Fannie Lou Hamer and by Senator John Stennis. The Civil Rights Movement may appear to have had a strange career indeed to cast up now as a leader of the free world this self-confessed white nonhero from Southwest Georgia, where in 1962 the movement suffered some of its worst setbacks.

The Civil Rights Movement, capable of much "overcoming," has a meaning for American politics going beyond its own immediate and tangible accomplishments.

I mean by this something different from Andrew Young's claim that the Civil Rights Movement started progressive juices flowing. These juices, he said, fed into the Women's Movement, the environmental movement, the consumers' movement, and the progressive politics of the congresses of which he was a part, and on to Jimmy Carter. Mr. Young tells about women in the Civil Rights Movement in the South being unhappy that, while they were actually doing the work, the men rode around in cars with two-way radios and gave press conferences and got their names in the papers. Out of the perception by the women in the Civil Rights Movement of a certain unfairness in that arrangement, says Young, the modern women's movement was born.

The Civil Rights Movement had a still deeper effect on the shape of American politics: it furnished an example of politics addressed to fundamental matters of justice; it had moral underpinnings; it had ideas; it had a carefully thought out strategy (direct nonviolent action) founded in and compatible with its ideas. The movement had a long history of thought as well as action, and a complex doctrine and strategy. It placed its claim about equal justice explicitly in the framework of the nation's founding truths, constitutional guarantee, and principal religious heritage.

The civil rights leaders were, to be sure, "activists," as the newspapers always called them, but their activity was founded to an unusual degree on *ideas*—stated moral ideas—which guided, gave form to, and restrained their "activism." Their "action" was purposeful, disciplined, nonviolent, and collaborative, with clearly defined objectives. And that movement, even though it had to resist the phony change-resisting appeals (like that of President Eisenhower) to "a slow process of education," did, in fact, a great deal of educating.

There was, indeed, a "slow process of education"—a real one—in the development from the scattered antislavery Quakers and others in the colonies through the antislavery movement in the South before 1830 to the larger movement in the North that came out of the revivals of the 1830's down through a long moral education since the Civil War.

The twentieth-century Civil Rights Movement was not another one among what Mr. Carter calls "special interests," like the Southern Florida Orange Growers or the Union of Pastry Cooks or Mr. Carter's own Certified Seed Growers. It was a movement grounded in a justice—in "human rights"—that transcends the interests of a particular group.

The black power movement that followed the Civil Rights Movement in the late 1960's made, no doubt, its own contributions in the recovered awareness of distinctive values in black culture and black history and black community and in completing the break with white paternalism. Where collective self-esteem has been so systematically expunged, a movement to counteract that by underlining racial pride and identity filled a cultural need. As a larger program, however, the black power movement, unlike the Civil Rights Movement, had this defect: it made its claim specifically for "power"; it spoke for a particular group in behalf of its interests. Where the Civil Rights Movement sought justice, a transcendent claim, both required of and benefiting black and white together, the black power movement seemed to be saying: "What's in it for us?" It seemed to be saying, in other words, what much of modern American politics allows one to say, under prevalent theories of politics and economics ("What does labor want?" Samuel Gompers: "More."). The Civil Rights Movement, by contrast, went back to a deeper foundation: What was claimed was a justice which transcended the interest of any individual or group, and could one day serve another person or group apart from those it serves today. The Civil Rights Movement represented the active recovery of transcendent moral truths in the operating work of American politics.

The movement directed toward overturning this nation's "One Huge Wrong" reflected, in the manner and success of its doing so, an underlying rightness—a "rightness" present, although quite imperfectly, in the laws and the "self-evident truths" held by the people of this country.

They are "truths," as truths must be, of universal validity; that "we hold to" them suggests in the pronoun and verb the limitation of, the relativity, the grasp a particular community has upon them (still it is fortunate that Jefferson used the strong word "truths," however much it may set on edge the teeth of modern philosophers, rather than the weak word "ideals"). Reinhold Niebuhr used to preach a sermon called "Having and Not Having the Truth," a title describing the simultaneous possession and nonpossession, absoluteness and relativity, moral confidence and self-criticism, that may be adapted from the religious truths of which he spoke to the political and ethical truths that Jefferson referred to. Americans, for all our violation of them on the one side and our excessive confidence in our absolute and even sole possession of them on the other, have been sufficiently in touch with the moral truth of human equality for the Civil Rights Movement to be efficacious in our recent politics.

Already before the American Revolution there was in the Bible that the colonists read, even though they rarely found it there, the possibility of a universal affirmation about all persons that contradicted racism and the slavery system. It followed then in the Declaration of Independence, even though Thomas Jefferson himself may not quite have realized the full implications of the enormous generalities that he wrote, there was the claim of a universal human equality. The nation tussled with the moral substance of equality and the actuality of slavery, and then of Jim Crow, through nearly two hundred years of its life, including the "terrible scourge of war."

The years since that war have seen moral doctrine revised, reexamined, guiding action and much persuasion based on the doctrine.

Lillian Gordy, for one important example, sat at her father's table and heard the interracial doctrines of the early populist movement ("I guess it just rubbed off on me") and was ready then to persuade her son of racial views different from those of her husband.

I was explaining to Patt Darian, the white Mississippian who is the State Department's Human Rights Co-ordinator, where I thought Carter's emphasis on human rights might have arisen in the recent history of thinking about international politics.

"That may be," she said. "But I think it began in Plains when Earl and Lillian Carter talked about how they felt about black people and their son Jimmy decided his mother was right."

Andrew Young, a most significant example of the effect of the Civil Rights Movement, was, in his college days, a handsome young dentist's son interested mostly in girls and in sports and not even a member of the NAACP. He was jarred out of that by a talk he heard given by a young divinity school student; he went into the ministry and in his first pastorates became caught up in the movement led by his wife's friend's husband, Martin Luther King, Jr.

The developing clarity about racial justice—that segregation must go, that separate but equal is never in fact equal, that prejudice alone is not the problem, that a *structure* in society reinforces prejudice in a vicious circle—all this is a story not only of politics in the half-truth sense that Americans have come to understand it, that is, of *power* and *pressure*, but also of reason, justice, and human understanding. This is one part of what is to be learned from the Civil Rights Movement for other aspects of

American politics: that wise and good politics takes thinking, educating, shaping mind and attitudes. It takes the abolition movement and the early Populists and the NAACP and W. E. B. DuBois debating Booker T. Washington and the long history of Southern white liberals and the Urban League and lots of Methodists hearing the Social Gospel and the 1941 threat of a march on Washington and A. Phillip Randolph and Bayard Rustin and a book by a Gunner Myrdal and an immense action by the U.S. Supreme Court and the Montgomery bus boycott and Martin Luther King's letter from a Birmingham jail and thousands of popular pamphlets and sermons and speeches giving the ideas that guide and discipline and clarify action—it takes all that and more one day to persuade and convert people to take different kinds of action than they would otherwise have taken, or at least to acquiesce in changes in society they might otherwise have opposed.

Then after (or during—it never ends) the fight for what is just there is another stage: healing; forgiving; binding up the wounds. In order to do that it is necessary to overcome guilt; to set aside expectations of gratitude; and to avoid the vindictive looking back toward the settling of old moral scores out of the past.

Daddy King had made an appearance again, in his brown hat again, at the Lincoln Memorial on the cold morning of the day Jimmy Carter became President of the United States. By that time the tune had subtly shifted from the effort to elect Jimmy Carter, because of the good things he would do, to the effort now that he was elected to be sure he would do them.

At the morning service on January 20, 1977, Mrs. Stapleton read the scripture from I: Kings; Leontyne Price, wearing a stocking cap, sang "He Has the Whole World in His Hands," and then Daddy King talked about "these hallowed grounds"; "Fo-teen years ago my son stood here and gave his gret GRET speech on I have a dream . . .

"Ah didn't know ah would be here . . ."

Daddy King's theme, texts, and refrain were "feed my sheep" (John 21:18) and, from the parable about "and ye did it unto me" . . . "the *least* of these."

"The *sheep* must be *fed*.

"Loveth thou me more than these? *Feed* my *sheep*.

"The *least* of these are never to be forgotten.

"That's what Martin Luther King, Jun-i-ah, was all about.

"That's why Jimmy Carter is President-elect; that's what he is all about.

"The sheep are bein' *fleeced*.

"Instead they need to be *fed*.

"I was in prison and you didn't visit me. Sick and you didn't come to see me. Stranger and you didn't let me in.

"Do these things for the *least* of these."

In conclusion Daddy King prayed that the new President would "REMEMBAH ALWAYS THE *LEAST* OF THESE . . ."

At the end of the service Coretta King and Andrew Young both made it a point to tell television reporters that Daddy King had said the right thing about President-elect Carter. One suspected from a certain insistent emphasis that they were already striking this note in the hope that it *would* be so, in an effort to *make* it be so, more than in the sure confidence that it would be. It was a moment of transition from the Carter campaign, in which Carter's position on the older issues of civil rights was known to be sound, to the Carter Presidency, in which his position on issues of economic welfare was not . . . his position on the plight of the cities, of the sheep bein' fleeced—of the *least* of these—really was not.

The Kings and Young already on that morning, and Vernon Jordan of the Urban League criticizing President Carter's performance for blacks and the poor six months later, were carrying on the endless work of politics at a new stage. Jimmy Carter was elected: that's good. Next comes the effort to bring the Carter administration to do as much as can be on the more complicated problems of the cities, of the poor, of economic justice . . . of the "least of these."

When Mr. Carter had been President about three months Fannie Lou Hamer died. Mrs. Hamer, a black woman from the little town of Ruleville in Mississippi, was one of the most respected and best loved of civil rights leaders. The white Georgian in the White House sent a plane with a delegation to Mrs. Hamer's funeral: Andrew Young; Vernon Jordan; Patt Darian; Hodding Carter III, another white Mississippian, bearer of a famous name in liberal journalism in the South, now the State Department's spokesman. When the plane landed at Indianola, Vernon Jordan reported "there were all the SNCC kids who not long ago wouldn't have gone near an Air Force plane." The moving funeral in the crowded little Ruleville church went on for three and one-half hours. Among those who spoke was Ambassador to the United Nations Andrew Young. Young said the seeds of a human rights movement that led directly to the election of President Carter were "sown here in the sweat and blood of you and Mrs. Hamer." (Sown, in other words, by the sweat and blood of Mrs. Hamer, Mr. Young, and others who fought against institutions like the Sumter County school board.) Civil rights veterans like Young filled the chapel in Ruleville where fifteen years before they had been threatened and denounced as "outside agitators." "Ruleville, Mississippi, got known even before Plains," said Young. "In fact, if it hadn't been for Ruleville you might never even have heard of Plains."

# 4

# FREE AT LAST, ALMOST

Since Martin Luther King, Jr., delivered "his gret GRET speech on I have a dream" on August 23, 1963, one of the "dreams" has acquired a particular geographical poignancy: "that one day out in the red hills of Georgia the sons of former slaves and the sons of former slave-owners will be able to sit down together at the table of brotherhood."

In memory King's resonant voice rolls out that sentence to the enormous throng (250,000 people, they said) that came to Washington that day in—as Hubert Humphrey put it—"an immense town meeting." It was "dissent with dignity, protest with decency, citizens peacefully petitioning their government." Mr. Humphrey's eyes grew misty once as he described it as "one of the most beautiful occasions in American life."

The specific objectives of that beautiful occasion have in part been accomplished and some of the dream made real. But as with most dreams made real, the reality has some rough spots not featured in the dream. What would be the past of the white Georgian—"the son of the former slaveholder"—who would sit down with his black brother in that red hills reunion scene? Almost certainly he must bring a history that will need some explaining and some forgiving: "You have to remember what the conditions were . . ." He may have been (to choose an example not exactly at random) a member and later the chairman of a school board that operated racially segregated schools for seven years, 1955 to 1962, after the Supreme Court had declared such schools unconstitutional; a deacon in a segregated church; a man capable of discreet silence during Martin King's marches and

jailing in a nearby city and of racial ugliness in his own county; a
politician capable as late as 1970 of subtle campaign appeals for
white bigots' votes: that is, a Jimmy Carter. Or he may have been
an upwardly mobile service station owner's son whose career as a
Governor's advisor in the segregation days is susceptible to more
than one interpretation, a man morally obtuse enough to join and
to defend joining the Piedmont Driving Club (Wherever those
two sons sit down together at the table of brotherhood it will not,
alas, be there): that is, Mr. Carter's appointee as the nation's chief
law enforcement officer, Griffin Bell.

In other words the white person in the fulfillment of King's
dream will almost certainly come to the table of brotherhood with
dirty hands. He will bring a history that requires some overlook-
ing and forgetting and understanding.

At its best the movement for which King spoke had the capacity
to do that forgiving and to rise to the generosity that allows life to
go on. The story of the liberation of the South—the breaking
open of isolating crust, so that a Jimmy Carter could move to the
top and center of the nation's life—is largely the story of that Civil
Rights Movement, and of the moral profundity in its best expression. There is also the subordinate story, not quite so widely told,
of the Southern white accommodation. There is some "overcoming" in that direction, too. Jimmy Carter's arrival on the world
stage is of course thoroughly entangled with these two interwoven stories of militancy foregone, of vengeance and anger overcome.

The greatest American expression of such overcoming is also
the greatest speech by any of Mr. Carter's predecessors:
Abraham Lincoln's Second Inaugural Address. The entry into the
central seat of the Union of a man from the secessionist South,
with his friends from Atlanta proudly staying in the Lincoln
bedroom, and Daddy King preaching on Inauguration Day at the
Lincoln Memorial, sets off new reverberations in the "mystic
chords of memory" linking black and white, North and South, the
President during the Civil War and the new President from the
South. It recalls that Address. The election of a white Georgian
by the votes of the sons of slaves and the sons of slaveholders
represents something of that binding up of the nation's wounds,
so long postponed, for which Lincoln's Address was a moving
appeal.

Mr. Carter's own Inaugural Address, though well this side of Lincoln's in eloquence and style, had nevertheless an echo of that greater speech: his quotation of the familiar passage from Micah (to do justly, to love mercy, and to walk humbly with thy God) introduced the theme of humility—political, collective humility—which is a chief theme also of Lincoln's address. Mr. Carter, as the President whose adherence to the Christian religion has the most visible connection to his political life calls to mind the Address by the other American President most profoundly rooted in Christian themes.

The rereading, in the year of Mr. Carter's election, of the nation's most celebrated documents (to the accompaniment of bicentennial music) left out, ordinarily, this most remarkable of those documents. But howevermuch it may warm our patriotic heart to read again Mr. Jefferson's Declaration, or the Preamble to the Constitution, or the First Amendment, or the most famous of the Federalist papers, number ten, there is not to be found in these passages of the national scripture, nor even in the Gettysburg Address, the distinguishing notes of the Second Inaugural: malice toward none and charity for all; the Almighty has his own purposes; both sides pray to the same God; bind up the nation's wounds. These themes have as a premise, of course, "firmness in the right"—resolute action in a just cause, as we see it. It is the genius of that speech that it combines the endorsement of such resolute action with an eloquent appeal for reconciliation with those who oppose it.

The sectional, ideological, and racial themes caught up in Jimmy Carter's emergence call for that profounder Lincolnian combination: the fervor of action in a just cause that does not obliterate charity to opponents, or the awareness of a judgment larger than one's own, or an eventual healing, forgiving, and reuniting.

When Carter was inaugurated the black choir from the collection of Colleges in Atlanta that includes Morehouse College gave a rendition of the best known and most stirring of all American songs, "The Battle Hymn of the Republic," the song of the Union side in what they did *not* call (as Carter did still after he was President, and in a New England town meeting in Clinton, Massachusetts) the "War between the States." That singing of the Battle Hymn must have made Americans (Northern or Southern)

to their toes. "Truth" was "marching on" indeed, though,
ɔrrow from another familiar quotation, in crooked lines, or, to
,row from yet another, in mysterious ways.

But if in a cooler moment one listened to the words of that
Battle Hymn one would hear rather a ferocious point-of-view:
God's hero, says the song, will "crush the serpent with his heel."
God is enlisted unequivocally on the Northern side. He has
"loosed the fateful lightning of His terrible swift sword," by
means, exclusively, of the Union armies. His Truth is marching
on, strictly on that side of the war.

It is a curious historical footnote that President Carter, the son
of the South, sent his daughter Amy to a heavily nonwhite public
school in Washington named in honor of Thaddeus Stevens, the
post-Civil War radical Republican and fiercest critic of the South.
Thaddeus Stevens considered the defeated Confederate states
"conquered provinces."

The modern parallels to the outlook of the Battle Hymn or
Thaddeus Stevens are easier to find than parallels to Lincoln's
outlook. They are always easier to find.

And one heard something of the condemnatory point-of-view
when Mr. Carter appointed Mr. Bell as his Attorney General—a
partner in the Atlanta law firm of King and Spalding and a
member of the Piedmont Driving Club, neither of them institutions noted for its devotion to racial justice. There followed upon
this appointment an exhuming of a section of Georgia history
about which judgments differed: although Georgia blacks defended Griffin Bell's role in the days of segregation, many national black leaders and liberal leaders attacked him. Mrs. King
herself said Bell was "a bad appointment"; Julian Bond said Bell
was "a turkey"; the ACLU and the Congressional Black caucus
opposed him. The national NAACP, in the person of Clarence
Mitchell, testified against him. Perhaps the most effective statement, however, by those who are inclined to look unfavorably on
Bell and on Carter, was an article by Calvin Trillin entitled,
"Remembrance of Moderates Past" in *The New Yorker* magazine
for March 21, 1977. Mr. Trillin quoted the wry remark of a black
lawyer made back at the height of civil rights activism, about the
white people who say they've been "working behind the scenes."
"Yes, sir," he said, "it must be getting mighty crowded back
there, behind the scenes." Mr. Trillin made full comic use of this

picture of the great crowd of white people (like Bell and Carter) working of course not out on the stage but "behind the scenes." He described them as "moderates," a word he managed to give a heavy satirical load: "A moderate . . . was someone who had never been caught throwing a rock at a Negro"; the moderate was "a white man without side arms." "Carter was, after all," wrote Trillin, "a member of the Sumter County Board of Education when . . . a liberal was someone who didn't object to putting a coat of paint on the colored school."

Such reconstructionist righteousness was not confined to condemnation of Southerners. It was very common also in the struggles over racial integration in the cities of the North. The liberal in a two-acre lot in the suburbs with his child in a private school, or in a school district outside the city limits (I indulge here in a stereotype myself), bravely summons the working class white in the city to solve the moral crisis of our time—and calls him a "racist" in the bargain. Italian and Irish working-class people in the city are described in stereotypes that would be totally impermissible if applied to Blacks.

A white working man in New Haven, Connecticut, responding to such righteousness from the suburbs, said he was reminded of what the pig said to the chicken about a ham and egg breakfast: "For you it's a contribution; for me, it is total commitment."

If you live in the middle of one of those struggles you perceive that the moral sensitivity of the white has its own sharp boundaries. The Yale person did not notice or care about the Italian immigrant coming into New Haven nor deplore the fact that there were streets in New Haven on which an Italian-American still alive was told as a boy he was not allowed to play.

The plaintive overwhelmingly familiar comment in that setting—"they didn't have any Civil Rights Act when my grandfather came over to this country"; or "nobody helped us"—has its partial justice.

And a whole body of stereotypical and categorical attitudes about the Southern white man is not hard to find, as Carter's candidacy showed. Where there is so clear a social evil as the Jim Crow system and its aftermath outsiders can indulge in an orgy of moral superiority. They have what Robert Penn Warren called "a treasury of virtue," stored up from their apparent dissociation from the evil they have opposed from a distance. The Southern

white man, whether or not he is a racial bigot, has known through
the centuries that there was something wrong in the point of view
of the Northerner for whom the moralities of the thing were so
clear as never to include himself and never to separate carefully
among others.

There was a revealing moment for me during Inauguration
week. A white Southern friend of Carter who has a thick Georgia
accent remarked at dinner on the evening of January 19 that that
week in Washington was the first time in his life that the black
people of the nation's capital city had not responded negatively
when they heard the way he talked. He was pleased by that
experience: that his white face and his unmistakable rural Georgia mode of speech did not provoke a wary and negative attitude
on the part of the black people of Washington.

Lincoln's Address is a particularly appropriate text for these
reflections for the reasons I have given—historical, sectional,
racial, religious—a text both for Jimmy Carter and for the Civil
Rights Movement of which his Presidency is such a curious
product or by-product.

In his Cooper Union speech Lincoln explicitly rejected, in the
way with which we are familiar in a hundred such "moral issues"
in American politics, any "groping for some middle ground between right and the wrong"; he might almost have written about
"moderates" "behind the scenes." Elsewhere he rejected being
silent or undecided on any issue about which *no one can be silent*
or undecided; for a moment he has the accent of the STAND UP
people, the SPEAK OUT theme, of America's moral crusaders.
In his rise to national significance there is in Lincoln a more
clearly articulated moral conviction about a specific issue than can
be found in the rise of Jimmy Carter.

Despite compound reasons for righteous indignation Lincoln
was not unforgiving, self-righteous, or absolute. Quite the contrary.

About slavery, there appears in the middle of the Second
Inaugural, almost as an aside, this sentence:

> It may seem strange that any men should dare to ask a just
> God's assistance in wringing their bread from the sweat of
> other men's faces; but let us judge not, that we be not judged.

Reinhold Niebuhr wrote that this passage "puts the relation of our moral commitments to our religious reservations about the partiality of our moral judgments more precisely than any statesman or theologian has put them." First the moral judgment: "It may seem strange that any men should dare to ask a just God's assistance in wringing their bread from the sweat of other men's faces." Then the religious reservation: "but let us judge not that we be not judged." (As President Carter surely would tell the Men's Bible Class, that is a paraphrase of a sentence from the Sermon on the Mount, Matthew 7:1.) The adding of these relativizing reservations is characteristic of Lincoln. In the familiar ending of this address, when he invokes "firmness in the right," he adds the qualifying apposition "as God gives us to see the right." Even in his earlier phase, when his role was more to heighten the moral tension than, as in 1865, to diminish it, he did something of the same. He ended his Cooper Union speech (in 1859), to great applause (it is reported) from the gathering of New York leaders, thus: "Let us have faith that right makes might, and in that faith, let us, to the end, dare to do our duty as we understand it." Perhaps it crippled his peroration a little to end with the qualifying phrase "as we understand it," but it is to Lincoln's moral if not his rhetorical credit that he did so. It is characteristic and desirable that even in the very moment of a ringing affirmation of "right" and "duty" he adds the grace note that implies that his and his audience's understanding of what is right and dutiful may not be quite the whole story.

The chief parties to the Jimmy Carter phenomenon are capable of this "religious reservation," at least by their familiarity with the Biblical thoughtworld: the Civil Rights Movement; the best of the white South; Jimmy Carter himself.

With a self-restraint remarkable in an embattled leader, Mr. Lincoln blamed neither the war nor slavery on the South. About the "impending civil war" he wrote "all dreaded it—all sought to avert it. . . . Both parties deprecated war." His description of the coming of the terrible war—still not finished as he spoke—has a generous passivity: "And the war came."

Neither party expected for the war the magnitude or the duration which it has already attained. Neither anticipated that the cause of the conflict might cease with, or even before,

the conflict itself should cease. Each looked for an easier
triumph, and a result less fundamental and astounding.

He did not blame the South for the war, or for its size or
destructiveness: neither party expected (or, by implication,
wanted) this "terrible" destruction; neither party expected it,
wanted it, is to blame for it. His own side did not know what it was
getting in for. He does not reach back and claim retroactively a
sweeping moral objective to vindicate the outcome now known, a
"result" so "fundamental and astounding."

He said, with generous imprecision, that all knew that slavery
was "somehow" the cause of the war. The "somehow" reminds
me of the "almost" in his phrase about this country, the "almost
chosen people." I like the Lincoln of the "somehow" and the
"almost."

Lincoln set aside judgment about who is right and wrong in the
first place, and explicitly refers to larger forces than those of the
contending parties. He puts those points in religious terms:

> Both read the same Bible, and pray to the same God; and each
> invokes His aid against the other.

Lincoln's sentences represent one of those thoughtful moments when there is no drumbeat of a battle hymn, no serpents to
be crushed by anyone's heel, no conquered provinces, no catalogue of "racists" or score-keeping about the inadequacies of
"moderates." In such a moment, the observer of the complex life
of humankind, and the role of religious belief in it, notices the
irony of the two sets of believers killing each other, each praying
to the same God for victory over the other. In this remarkable
case the reflective observer is himself a central participant.

This is by no means to undercut the seriousness of one's moral
understanding. The spirit of Lincoln's address is *not* relativistic
or shoulder-shrugging or "conservative." Its attitude is not "live
and let live," or "there is no accounting for tastes," or "deliberate
social action does more harm than good." He certainly did not
say, with a modern reductionist, that some people "prefer" slavery, some people don't "prefer" it: who is to choose? He certainly
did not say that being for or against the Union was a matter of
"preference" merely, determined by geography or taste, with no
rational or objective foundation. In his Cooper Union speech he

had explicitly repudiated a "policy of 'don't care' on a question about which all true men *do* care." He did not say: "Leave things alone and they will work out better in the long run." Instead he had solemn convictions about these matters, upon which he acted. Only when a person has such convictions, and takes such action, does one appropriately add with Lincoln the qualifying, chastening, deepening themes of this address.

Why add those themes? Because the absolutism even of men whose cause is just can itself be the cause of a new injustice. The commendable abhorrence of human slavery gathers up a great many less commendable motives as it flows on into Reconstruction after Lincoln's death. The just repugnance at racial discrimination spills over into an epithetical contempt for "racist" rednecks and ethnics and Wallacites that ironically is not unlike the stereotypical prepossession it started out repudiating. The legitimate claim of women to an equal treatment becomes then an instrument for personal advancement and revenge. Self-righteousness is an invitation to cruelty, malice, and blindness, even in men (or women) who are indeed generally "right" about the issue at stake. Fanaticism is a menace even on the part of those whose cause is just. Why is this so? Because the egotism and irrationality to which we are all tempted are by no means obliterated when we fight for a righteous purpose. Because the field of "battle" is never as simple as in our crusading right/wrong pictures of it (in the metaphors of "battle," fight, crusade). There are other issues, too, beside the ones that occupy us; the people we oppose are human and complex, not simple instruments of the evil we oppose. And there are other human beings affected by our outlook and action whom self-righteous blindness may prevent us from seeing. And the cause today is not the same as it was yesterday. Tomorrow's injustice is created or fed by the vindictive spirit in which today's injustice is combated. The historical drama is never so simple that actors in it need pay attention only to one cause, one issue, one purpose without regard to the mystery and freedom of the historical drama in which they play only a single part.

The Lincoln who delivered this speech was no poet or essayist "composing for anthologies" (as the late Justice Robert Jackson once wrote, in an opinion from the bench) nor even your ordinary President, but rather the nation's leader in a war which would "rend the Union." Nevertheless, despite all the accumulated reasons for Lincoln to be righteous, angry, argumentative, and partisan, his speech resounds with a quiet acceptance of purpose beyond his own, and an absence of vindictiveness, that would be remarkable even if written by that solitary essayist in his chambers.

The address, as given by that man in that circumstance, combined active moral "engagement" (to use a word that would come to prominence in a later war) with an explicit awareness of the larger drama within which that engagement played its role. That awareness, then, led to the rare humility and evenhandedness about the conflict, and the magnanimous attitude toward opponents, for which the address is remembered. It is the combination, in such a setting, that makes the speech remarkable. To turn the combination around, the generosity for which the address is renowned did not cloud the speaker's moral perception or diminish the executive force with which he pursued his purposes. The address, therefore, is a model, not simply of charity and largeness of spirit; it is a model of these qualities held by an engaged, "committed," political being. It is an example—better perhaps than bullfighters—of "grace under pressure."

And so now back to the present, or this century at least. I did not, in my youth in the 1940's, fully understand two commonplace claims of the interracial movement: that segregation and discrimination were damaging to whites as well as to blacks, and that enlightened white Southerners could be sounder on race than most of us Northern liberals. The first of these was a phrase I repeated in speeches to unlikely and unreceptive audiences in places like Fremont, Nebraska, but with a sense that it was propaganda. Of course there was the obvious meaning—that the whole country lost a great deal because black talent was suppressed or distorted—but anything beyond that I did not feel in my bones. A Southerner like Carter, on the other hand, knows (or can come to know) that his own life was also stunted by a false, foolish, and cruel social convention. He can see and feel that in a way most Northern white liberals, living daily at a distance from it, are not likely to. Mr. Carter, on the issue of race, has a sureness of touch that comes from moral soundness underneath, derived from experience and reflection on that experience from the way he appropriated his hours in the pew and the Bible class, from reading, from his mother. It is reflected in his autobiography in the calm unapologetic way he recounts the stupidities of segregated life he grew up with, fully aware that they were stupid and cruel but without condemning anybody, without self-flagellation, without proclamatory fervor. When he says—as he regularly has—that it is not clear who has benefited the most by the Civil Rights Act, whites or blacks, it is clear that as a white beneficiary he means that.

Which brings me to the second familiar statement of the older Civil Rights Movement, which though I repeated it and could see the surface meaning of it I did not understand inwardly: that many liberated white Southerners were sounder on the issue of race than most of us Northern liberals, and that when the day of liberation came the South could be better than the North. I repeated those phrases, and could make out dimly the outlines of their truth, but it is not clear that I understood why they were true, or even that in my Northern heart I fully believed them.

Now that history has vindicated their truth we can look back and see why they were true. In the North it was hard for a white liberal to avoid some sense and flavor of "doing something for" someone else—the victim of injustice, the black man, who stood before him in need of his, the white man's, generous and humane social and moral action. The one who is "doing something for" someone else has difficulty avoiding the expectation that the one who has something done for him should be grateful; he has some temptation to regard himself favorably, as a bit of a moral hero. Certainly he can let himself go in rich condemnation of those who stand on the other side of a sharply defined moral issue: he can condemn "racists" with an unqualified fervor.

The morally sound Southern white man has a knowledge of individual human beings who are black, in sufficient numbers and variety and familiarity, to base his relation to them not on abstract social moral categories, but on the real and the human. He also knows "segregationists" in sufficient numbers and closeness and complexity to realize that that phrase does not describe one type either. Therefore, a Jimmy Carter wants to stand on a platform in Biloxi, Mississippi, with Senator Eastland on one side and Mississippi's leading black politician on the other; and he is willing in that setting to praise Eastland and Stennis and accept their support. When he is asked about it he can speak of them as "two great Southern statesmen," even though that surely will bring down upon him the wrath of *The New York Times* editorial page—as it certainly did. At the same time, in their presence, without condemning them by name, he can speak favorably about "the new relationship between black and white citizens, with equality of opportunity and with an integrated society that we now enjoy . . ." He can say that it "has liberated the South and the rest of the nation from the long preoccupation with the race issue." When asked about serving on a local Georgia school board that perpetuated racial segregation during the 1950's and 1960's, he can respond, "It obviously would have been better for our country had I refused to participate, but I did it." He volunteered this experience when reporters questioned him about how he could campaign as a racial progressive alongside Eastland and Stennis. "I'm part of the South and I was part of the county school board that carried on and operated a segregated school system here, right here where we're standing," Carter said. "I can't undo my action twenty years ago or the votes of the U.S. Senators twenty years ago."

There are three dimensions to the point here discussed, the point underlying, in a different context, Lincoln's Second Inaugural: first toward oneself, letting go of guilt; second, toward victims, avoiding patronage and the expectation of gratitude; third, toward the people who are "in the wrong," one's opponents, avoiding vindictiveness and stereotyped condemnation.

The overarching point is healing: binding up the nation's wounds, or the world's wounds for that matter . . . whatever the torn community may be. In order to do that it is necessary to have malice toward none and charity for all.

It is evident enough not only in the South but also in the North that the history of American racism requires these qualities. The vindictive looking back toward the settling of old moral scores out of the past—remembering the day when "a liberal was somebody who would put a coat of paint on the colored school"—keeps open the wounds, and in its own stereotyping someday creates a new unfairness.

In June of 1976 I asked Andrew Young about the wariness

concerning candidate Carter. Is he, I asked, one of those proud moralizing men whose religion reinforces his ego, his stubbornness, his sharp division of the world into the righteous and the unrighteous?

Congressman Young's answer—he was then still a Congressman, sitting natty and handsome at a table in the House Dining Room—was not precisely to the point. I believe it told more about Young than it told about Carter.

Young told the story about the first time he met Jimmy Carter. He referred to Sumter County and to the associations he had from the hard days, the civil rights battles, of 1962: Sumter County was the nastiest place in the South. Young mentioned Laurie Pritchett, the police chief of Albany who put Martin Luther King, Jr., in jail. Carter, hearing all this from Andrew Young, need not have responded at all—certainly need not have defended Chief Pritchett, a notorious figure in the lore of the Civil Rights Movement. "All he had to do," said Young, "was to leave that alone." But Mr. Carter didn't do that. "He's not that bad," Young quoted Carter as having said. "He probably was more afraid of you than you were of him."

Carter (as Young tells it) did not do either the political thing or the Northern antiracist moralizer's thing. It was not politic for a Deep South Sumter County white Georgian to defend Chief Pritchett to Andrew Young on first meeting. Young's interpretation of this response was that it represented "sympathetic understanding of a sinner."

Young took for granted, with considerable generosity, Carter's full identification with him and his side—so that therefore Pritchett was a "sinner," to be forgiven.

Young's interpretation of Mr. Carter on race is that he is quite different from the "converted redneck" or the paternalistic Northern white liberal, those who need continually to overcome guilt, prove their superiority, show their righteousness. Jimmy Carter, said Andrew Young, knew from his youth, before his teens that his mother was right on the issue of race and he knew it not only intellectually but also in his experience with the playmates to whom he often referred in his talks. He never had to rebel, to be converted on this subject—and therefore did not have a need either to demonstrate his rightness on the racial issue; or to condemn "racism" in others, to banish "racists," to sharpen the lines of division. Andrew Young looked at Jimmy Carter and perceived moral soundness there in that white Southerner and committed himself, and hence added an ingredient to the politics of his nation in the history of the world—he saw that Mr. Carter was sound at bottom on the issue of race and unembarrassed and unguilty about it.

When Mr. Carter had been in office for about half a year two events, one happier than the other, showed the blend of his relation to this history and its future. Vernon Jordan, an old friend and supporter from Georgia and now the head of the Urban League, made a major speech criticizing the Carter administration's failure to do all it should for the unemployed, the poor, the cities' blacks. Carter, stung, implied that Jordan was "demagogic" and said his remarks hurt the cause of the poor and black. It was a thin-skinned response.

A short while later Carter made his first extended Presidential trip to the South. Before an integrated audience in Yazoo City, Mississippi, he made a moving statement. "I think it took a great deal of courage for the South to . . . change," he said, appealing thus to Southern pride, as applause grew in the hall. "I wouldn't be here as President had it not been for the Civil Rights Acts and those leaders—and I don't claim to be one of them—who changed the bad things to good things in the South." It was skillful and touching that he could now appeal to that fierce Southern pride, exactly in behalf of the condition and the persons that pride had long resisted. It was affecting, further, that he praised the civil rights leaders and admitted that he would never have been President had it not been for that leadership of which he himself did not claim to be a part. It was his better moment.

A friend of Martin Luther King, Jr., says that King's youthful aspiration did not reach to a Nobel prize or world fame, but only to a college president's office, and specifically to the presidency of Morehouse in his hometown. Life's mysterious ways worked otherwise. Jimmy Carter, meanwhile, a slightly older man attending all-white schools farther south in a town smaller than King's, came to be Governor of the state in which both of them had been born; as Governor Carter had King's picture hung in the state capitol. Once, after he had announced that he would run for the Presidency, candidate Carter was asked a hostile question, with a plain racial meaning, by a member of a white audience. "Didn't you get an honorary degree from Morehouse College?" "Yes," Carter shot back. "I'm going to be the first Morehouse boy in the White House." As indeed he is.

# PART II

# JIMMY CARTER
# THE AMERICAN

# 5

# THE AUTOBIOGRAPHICAL
# PRESIDENT

## I

I am a writer and an American, a former alderman, a husband and father, a basketball fan, a teacher of ethics, a student of politics, a sometime speech drafter, a university person, a Presbyterian, and a reader of both Reinhold Niebuhr and Robert Benchley. I have been born, at most once. I live in Bloomington, Indiana, which has a population of 48,672.

When I heard Jimmy Carter in Indianapolis he had already told the people of Iowa, New Hampshire, Massachusetts, Florida, and, by news reports, the United States and the World (I leave out a few stops) the list of roles and identities by which he chose to define his life, not omitting his love for Bob Dylan's songs and Dylan Thomas' poetry, and the characteristics and population of his hometown (Plains, Georgia, in case you didn't know; population 683). He displayed a persistent tendency to tell about his own life. I noticed that his subject in the church was mostly his own life. I thought it quite an autobiographical speech; I knew he had written an autobiography; I thought he was conducting an autobiographical campaign; I have since felt his to be rather an autobiographical Presidency: "Last night I spoke to the people of Clinton, Massachusetts; tonight I address the delegates to the United Nations." "I come from a part of the United States which is largely agrarian . . . so I can sympathize with the leaders of the developing nations." "I feel at ease. I feel good. I pace myself very carefully. I enjoy the job." "Bert Lance is my friend."

One of the more tactless examples of this habit was reported by that scrupulous observer of Presidents, John Osborne of *The New Republic*. (If ever a journalist deserved Carter's word "fair," Osborne does.) Reporting on a "poverty forum" in Detroit at which the President appeared on a Western trip in October, 1977, Osborne told about the comments of a 56-year-old black steel worker from Gary, Indiana, named Hall, struggling to meet his family obligations while unemployed. Osborne commented: "Carter's replies to this and several similar statements at the forum were generally sympathetic and understanding. But he made my flesh crawl when he said in part of his reply to Hall, 'I also have a ten-year-old daughter . . . so I feel a kinship with you'; and in his answer to a former migrant worker who had told of picking tomatoes 20 years ago for 14 cents a basket, 'I picked tomatoes by the hamper myself, and I picked cotton.' Jimmy Carter picked tomatoes and cotton on one of the several farms of his Daddy, who in Jimmy's boyhood was becoming one of the richest landowners in Sumter County, Georgia."

Early in my explorations of the Jimmy Carter phenomenon I bought his autobiographical book, which deals in large part with those days in Georgia, and I composed my own contribution, such as it may be, to the collection of jokes about its title. Carter tells about the mistake he made when he was twelve and Miss Julia Coleman (the school superintendent he quoted just before the prophet Micah in his Inaugural Address) suggested that he read *War and Peace*. He thought from the title it would be a book about cowboys and Indians. Well, wrote I, the uninformed today might think *Why Not the Best?* the title of a sales catalogue for one of those snobbish, distinctly unpopulist stores dealing in "exclusive" menswear (Benchley once referred to "the place where I am allowed to buy my shirts").

Titles aside, I thought autobiography a particularly appropriate genre for the American achiever, whether or not for a Presidential candidate. One question about this man, I realized, was the degree to which he was the latter merely as a version of the former: whether for him and for his most characteristic followers there was any difference between individual careerism, "competence" rewarded by success, on the one side; and political leadership and statecraft, on the other.

In any case it was significant, I thought, that this Georgia Ben Franklin, like the original, had told his own life story as a way of offering moral guidance to his readers. Such autobiographies, in their American way, focus not upon timeless ideas but upon *facts*, and not upon facts about great masses of people but upon one particular human being in one particular time and place: He is to be taken as significant. The individual person matters; the detail of concrete life matters; the sequence of external events— human "history"—matters, and is not an endless repetitive cycle or a shadow world to be fled. The telling of the story of one's *own* life, separated from others (*I* matter) accentuates the separate self in a way that dwellers in Teutonic cloudlands or Eastern mystics swallowed up in the All would not be inclined to do. The American religious equivalent, in churches, gospel tents, street corners, has been *testimony*—I am, or was, a "wretch" but "amazing grace" saved me: "I once was lost, but now I am found; I was blind, but now I see." Autobiography and testimony—I tell the story of my own life, and how it got from *there* over to *here*, in order that my telling may be instructive to *you*.

Autobiography and testimony flourish in this country—in contrast not only to impersonal, abstract metaphysics, political philosophy, or theology but also to *confessions*, as in Augustine and Rousseau. *Confessions* imply that the *inner* life is of primary significance; unkind critics might say that the American achiever does not have enough of *that* to make a book.

The American autobiography deals with *external* events. The true thread of course is the hero's progress. Here is a characteristic paragraph from the model, *The Autobiography of Benjamin Franklin*:

> My original habits of frugality continuing and my father having among his instructions to me when a boy frequently repeated a proverb of Solomon, "Seeist thou a man diligent in his calling, he shall stand before kings, he shall not stand before mean men," I from thence considered industry as a means of obtaining wealth and distinction, which encouraged me, though I did not think that I should ever literally stand before kings, which, however, has since happened; for I have stood before five, and have even had the honor of sitting down with one, the King of Denmark, to dinner.

When he wanted to illustrate the "spirit of capitalism" in its connection with the Protestant ethic, Max Weber went to Ameri-

ca and specifically to Benjamin Franklin (five-kings-Franklin) for
the essential idea: "Time is money." I learned that Mr. Carter had
read Franklin's *Autobiography* several times.

These American autobiographies *get somewhere*; they tell the
tale, told again at another level in fiction by Horatio Alger books,
the story deeply implanted in this culture, of a rising career, of a
young man starting out in humble origins and by his industry,
diligence, and ability, getting, as the saying goes, ahead. The
young man rises from humble beginnings to sit at dinner with the
King of Denmark, and from Plains, Georgia, to travel as Governor to many foreign countries as a member of an international
commission which provided (I quote from Mr. Carter's book) "a
splendid learning opportunity."

Mr. Carter's splendid learning opportunities markedly increased after January 20, 1977. Returning from the economic
summit in London in April of 1977, his first trip abroad as
President, he said "I learned from each conversation. I was a good
student. There was a ready acceptance of me and an eagerness on
[other leaders'] parts to teach. . . . I have had a chance to learn a
lot."

I was amused to note that that other American learner, Benjamin Franklin, not only enumerated the moral virtues one-two-
three, but tried to acquire them, one by one, in an orderly way.
He wanted to attain temperance first, and once that was—to
quote what Carter's good friend Charles Kirbo said in the very
early morning of November 3, 1976, in another connection, "in
the burlap"—then *silence* would be easier to achieve, and so on to
order, resolution, frugality, and industry—eleven virtues
achieved seriatim. He made of course a little book in which he
allotted a page for each of the virtues and kept careful track of
how he was doing, exactly as we may picture Jimmy Carter doing.

Such I-tell-my-story writings, though much more likely to be
produced in this culture than metaphysical speculation or epic
poetry, are nevertheless not ordinarily written by candidates for
office. "Memoirs" can come later, at the end of a career. If the
*candidate's* life story is to be told in a campaign document, then it
were better done by some other person, who can celebrate the
realization to the full of all of Ben Franklin's list of virtues without
impairing the candidate's claim to the last one, humility. A campaign biography is written, for example, by Nathaniel Hawthorne

about Franklin Pierce, not by Pierce himself, and by hundreds of lesser writers about better candidates. If a book is to be produced under the candidate's own name, then that programmatic or hortatory book, with words like "vision" and "challenge" and "greatest" in the title, will deal with "America," with the "future" or "progress" or "conscience," or "courage" and will glorify the candidate only by indirection.

But Mr. Carter, a declared candidate, in an extraordinary act of ingenuous gall, presented his own life as a chief argument for elevating him to the nation's highest office.

Sometimes it seemed to me that this proud, able, and un-ideological American treated the office he has come to hold as though it were a personal prize, to be won individually, to be *earned* by hard work, a *success* to be checked in one's book of accomplishments (five kings, eleven virtues, one Presidency) like first place in the spelling bee in Miss Julia Coleman's classroom.

## II

When I started to read Mr. Carter's book I did not like it. The first and last chapters have one sentence paragraphs and rhetorical questions ("two great questions face America") that are the routine political sort of thing that any of us speechwriters might produce for any politician. The last chapter thumps out we *must* this and we *must* that in a series of unpersuasive peremptory exhortations. Looking at the beginning and the ending, I was tempted to turn the title of the book back against itself.

But then when I read the second chapter and the chapters that followed, I changed my opinion. When the book deals with the life of the author it becomes much better. Mr. Carter tells with detail and authority about plumbing, crops, farm, town, father, mother, Annapolis, submarining, campaigning, governing, evangelizing. He conveys with precision and economy what his early life was like: how peanuts grow; how to boil them; what it was like plowing with mules against the continually invading grass; why cleaning the "after head" on a submarine was nobody's favorite job; how unpleasant it is to do the job called "mopping cotton." Like most books of this sort it is more interesting when it deals with his youth than later. I liked his story of the radio

broadcast of the Joe Louis-Max Schmeling fight. He tells how the
blacks in Plains gathered under Mr. Earl's mulberry tree and
listened to the radio in the window while the Carters sat inside
the house. When the racially significant fight was over, the blacks
politely thanked Mr. Earl, silently withdrew to a black home one
hundred yards away and then celebrated with a joyous pandemonium. His recounting of the story about his fight as Governor with the Army Corps of Engineers to resist their building a
big dam on the Flint River had a kind of passion about a public
issue that the rest of his book does not contain. His description of
the Chattahoochee River, complete with a poem from Sidney
Lanier, has an impressive quiet passion of another kind.

Whenever Mr. Carter is telling particular details out of his
experience, about how something is done, how something works,
how something looked and felt, he writes a good book. Although
he was criticized as a person without a sense of humor—wrongly
it seemed to me already, given the apparent quality of his mind—
there are repeated little touches of wryness or of very slight
mockery, even including a faint (very faint) self-mockery, that
would have refuted even then, before Mr. Carter was President,
the mistaken notion that he was lacking in humor. It turned out to
be an unusually good book for an active politician to have written—better than *Conscience of a Conservative* or *Profiles in
Courage*. Nevertheless, given his situation and his purpose, it
was a work of revealing audacity.

The book includes of course Mr. Carter's list of his roles and
identities.

> I am a Southerner and an American. I am a farmer, an engi-
> neer, a father and a husband, a Christian, a politician and
> former governor, a planner, a businessman, a nuclear physi-
> cist, a naval officer, a canoeist, and, among other things a lover
> of Bob Dylan's songs and Dylan Thomas' poetry.

Almost every campaign speech he gave had some variant of
that listing, and when members of his family gave speeches in the
campaign they regularly used it, too. They would select items to
recommend him to the audience. I went twice to hear Rosalynn in
Indianapolis and found her to be an excellent campaigner,
poised, pretty, straightforward, and adept. And very sober. What

she talked about was partly her own current and past life, but mostly "Jimmy's" life. Mrs. Carter, apparently thinking "Indiana," did her "Jimmy's a *farmer*" sentences; perhaps thinking "conservative state," did "Jimmy's a *businessman*." Then came "Jimmy's a *planner*." When he got to the Governor's office, he found Georgia government a mess and fixed it; Washington is a mess and needs a planner to fix it.

Chip Carter came to Bloomington and forthrightly made a point to the students in the Indiana Memorial Union that it might have been a little indelicate for his father to have made explicitly, although it was clear enough that he believed it: "Dad is smarter than Gerry Ford (laughter)."

In the list of roles in the senior Carter's book I notice *canoeist*. I hear in my imagination some Carter, in northern Maine perhaps, saying "Jimmy's a canoeist," with some reference perhaps to the yachts, sailboats, and battleships of other candidates and to Jimmy's unique, personal mode of water travel featuring the verb "to paddle."

Mr. Carter's autobiography centers (perhaps more than his life) around his perfectly chosen hometown. On Labor Day, 1976, after watching the opening of the Carter campaign in Warm Springs, I was driven to Plains, where, in the almost deserted hometown of the Democratic nominee three of us spent a pleasant day. Although the full tourist invasion had not arrived, there was already a bus tour. When we got back to Atlanta and told a Georgian about that, his eyes grew wide with astonishment. "Two dollars and fifty cents? For a tour of *Plains*?"

The tour showed the window of the room in the hospital where Jimmy was born; the house Jimmy lived in when he grew up; the house in which he had lunch when he went to school; the public housing project he and Rosalynn lived in when they came back to Plains after Mr. Earl's death; Miss Lillian's old house; Miss Lillian's present house; the house of Mrs. Smith (Rosalynn's mother); the elementary school Amy then attended; the tree in which Jimmy had his tree house; the lawn where Mr. Earl beat Jimmy in tennis; Billy Carter's service station; the house where Jimmy and Rosalynn and Amy lived.

It was all, in its way, perfect. . . . that pleasant small town, perfectly named, with its sleepy main street, one block long; its white-frame Baptist Church, with its stained glass windows, its

pulpit in the center, and its Men's Bible Class in the basement;
the mother, the registered nurse, a humanitarian indeed, be-
loved to all, and comical besides ("President of *what*?"); the
brother, a good ole boy, a drinker of beer and a teller of tales to
the other good ole boys in his Amoco gas station, outspoken,
perhaps slightly wayward, but underneath, good, and comical too
(President and Mrs. Carter are a pair so serious that the family
stage set required not one but two characters for comic relief, not
counting Amy); the sister, a modish and attractive blond called in
the press (with its limited vocabulary) a "faith-healer," who
blends popular religion and popular psychology in an "inner"
healing, a person with a following across the country, independent of her brother's; the uncle, the owner of a *worm farm* and an
antique store, complaining about the prices they charged for
hotels up there in New York when he went there for his nephew's
nomination ("*fifty-seven* dollars a *night* at the Americana").
There is the farm, the green fields of peanuts, the red soil; there
is the warehouse, the small family business, growing steadily into
a larger family business through the earnest application of the
steady work of the hands of the hero himself and of his wife. And
there is the wife, beautiful, intelligent, rising from that same
lowly beginning, a full partner, devoted to her husband yet not
subservient . . . but I need not go on. I could imagine some
moment when some alert public relations agent of the Eastern
establishment, looking for a likely growth stock in the political
industry, looked up and down the main street of Plains, Georgia,
cast his eye over this unbelievable list of surrounding characters
and symbolic circumstances, and rubbed his hands with a dis-
coverer's lascivious glee. "It's a gold mine!"

It was a political gold mine, of course, not because it is representative but because it isn't. Small townness, farming, self-made
business men, deacons in Baptist churches, district officers of the
Lions Club; these were once coins of value in the democratic
politics of the American nation because they were the reality of
much of the nation's life. Now they have value because they are
not. They now have the value of nostalgia, of return, of romanticized memory turned into a norm.

Obviously any candidate's life and origins are instructive to
some degree, and the public loves that kind of thing. Obviously,
too, Mr. Carter's (overstated) Southern rusticity and varied roles

were more interesting and useful symbolically than other backgrounds. Suppose Rosalynn had won the argument, they had not returned to Plains in 1953, and he had presented himself to the public as naval engineer James Earl Carter, Jr., of Schenectady, N.Y.?

But at some high point in the stratosphere of statesmanship, as of literary art, those biographical particulars should be left behind, and it becomes appropriate to say what Ernest Hemingway (of Oak Park, Illinois, population 62,511) grumbled once when he heard some fellow writers going on about their origins: "It doesn't matter where you came from."

## III

The resolutely autobiographical American Jimmy Carter managed to fulfill the American injunctions to achieve, to work, to rise in not one but three different careers:

—In the navy, where his success apparently was sufficient to make plausible his calm expectation, in which David Broder found an amusing example of the Carter hubris, that he would one day be Chief of Naval Operations;

—In his peanut agribusiness, which he built sufficiently to cause meticulous undervaluing in the 1976 campaign in order not to make him a millionaire (as in the Soviet Union there are proletarian millionaires so in the U.S. there are populist millionaires). A symbol of his multiple successes occurred the day he was driven back to Plains exulting alternately in two recent acquisitions: a big million-dollar peanut sheller and "the Big Z" (Brzezinski).

—Most spectacularly in politics, where his career appears to have been written by Benjamin Franklin and Horatio Alger for inclusion in *McGuffy's Reader*.

Four efforts to be elected, very similar in their shape, exhibit a tenacious ambition: 1962, when he was first elected to the Georgia State Senate; 1966, when he ran unsuccessfully for Governor; 1970, when he was elected Governor; and 1976, when he was elected President.

In each case the odds and the logic were against him, sometimes very heavily against him. In each case observers outside the

Carter camp did not see why he particularly needed to run, since there were alternatives already in the field. Homer Moore had already won the original Democratic Party primary for the State Senate seat in 1962, and had been pitched into a second primary only by the accident of a court decision reapportioning the district; his claim on the nomination would seem solid enough to most traditional politicians. In 1966 Ellis Arnall, the "moderate" Governor out of the middle 1940's, was already the candidate of the North Georgia moderates and the Atlanta press. Again in 1970 former Governor Carl Sanders, another "moderate" with that Atlanta support, was already in the field. In 1976 the harder line position already had its candidate in Scoop Jackson, whom Carter himself had nominated at the 1972 Miami convention, or possibly in the hardy perennial Hubert Humphrey waiting in the wings. There was a plentiful supply of more liberal candidates like Morris Udall, Birch Bayh, Fred Harris, and Sargent Shriver. It was not apparent to outsiders that Jimmy Carter fulfilled some ideological necessity by entering the race.

In each case there were overtones of his moral superiority to other candidates.

In every case, the tenacity and persistence and hard work of Mr. Carter and his family go beyond the ordinary bounds. His battle against the vote fraud in one of the counties of his state senatorial district in 1962 is a complex story of multiple repeated persistence against multiple rebuffs: vote fraud in the primary election; the unwillingness of the Democratic leaders of the state to hear the story about that vote fraud; Carter's bringing in an investigative reporter to light fires that brought the fraud into court; the arduous rounding up of affidavits to appeal to the County Democratic Committee; the rejection of that appeal by the county boss responsible for evils they were protesting; the appeal to the State Democratic Committee, and again to the courts in the nick of time before the general election. It is an astonishing story of repeated rebuffs and repeated persistent attack. William Greider of *The Washington Post* quotes one of the heroes of the Carter effort: "I saw the real burning desire to win that I had not really seen before. It really meant everything to him. I guess it was partly a desire to win and partly a desire to clean up that situation."

In 1966, after two terms in the State Senate, he had a safe shot at the seat from his congressional district in the United States House of Representatives. When he received word, though, that the failing health of one of the gubernatorial candidates opened the possibility for election to that office, he decided not to run for Congress but to run for the Governor's chair—a much more problematical effort, in which of course he failed.

He "never worked so hard in his life" as during the next full four years of campaigning for Governor, again in a complicated race in which there was another nonsegregationist candidate, Carl Sanders, and with tactics which do not suggest perfect accord with the title of this autobiography. Elected Governor, Carter had not been in office very long before the possibility of running for still higher office began to be seriously discussed.

The drama of Mr. Carter's rise to the White House, told many times now, is effectively suggested by a paragraph in *Running for President* by Martin Schram. Schram is recounting the day, November 21, 1974, when Walter F. (Fritz) Mondale withdrew from the campaign for the Presidential nomination. Mondale said then that he did not have the overwhelming desire to be President the campaign required; later he said that after campaigning hard he had not made much progress and hovered around three or four percent in the polls. "But," remarks Schram, "it is worth noting that this is higher than Jimmy Carter was—in fact, Carter was not even ranked at the time, he was so unknown."

*The Washington Post* published a long page one story on Mondale's withdrawal, in the next-to-last paragraph of which there was an announcement that the executive director of the National Democratic Committee was resigning to head the Jackson campaign. And in the very last paragraph there appeared the apparently quite insignificant news that Governor Jimmy Carter of Georgia planned to announce officially on December 12 that he would be running for President.

Mr. Carter himself dramatized the point in another way in a conversation with James Reston at the end of his first year in office. "I remember," President Carter said, "in 1975 meeting with *The New York Times* editorial board. Gallup had a poll on the 1976 election. I think there were thirty-eight people on it, including Julian Bond and Ralph Nader and so forth—and they didn't have my name on the list."

Surveying Mr. Carter's two-year effort to become President,

or the whole of the fourteen-year rise from private citizen to the
White House, one might say, in the manner of America's inspirational literature of success: he did not know that what he was
proposing was impossible, so he did it anyway.


# IV


During 1976 I was regularly reminded of the events of 1956, and
not only from the round numbers. Twenty years before Mr.
Carter's remarkable victory I had helped to achieve Mr. Stevenson's remarkable defeat. The little gold-colored peanuts the Carter staff wore reminded me of the little silver-colored shoes, with
the hole in them, the Stevenson staff wore. The happy, worried,
busy, orderly, chaotic people stir-crazy in the paper-strewn war-
rens in Colony Square, Atlanta, reminded me of the same condition in our building on Connecticut Avenue in 1956—three quarters hard work, three quarters "sterile excitation," as Max Weber
once called it (too large an enterprise to be limited by the ordinary
logic of fractions), a great part of the day spent asking each other
how things are going, and reassuring each other that things are
going well, and reporting to each other pieces of news, and
struggling with each other over political strategy, and taking
phone calls from excessively helpful supporters around the country, every one calling in his urging that the candidate do this and
the candidate do that—Oh! their flood of ideas!—and still a lot of
work getting done somehow anyway. At a fund-raising party
featuring Rosalynn Carter, early in the general election campaign, I found myself, while talking to Mrs. Carter's assistant
Mary Hoyt, verging on making—an observation, maybe even a
*suggestion*—but I was stopped by Ms. Hoyt's wry remark about
suggestions from Democrats all over the country. What you don't
need, living twenty-four hours in the constant flow of it and not in
command anyway, are more *suggestions*.

Our candidate in the 1950s, Adlai Stevenson of Libertyville,
Illinois (pop. 11,684), made two extraordinary speeches to the
Democratic convention that he first addressed as a potential
nominee. In one of those speeches he said, "*Who* leads us is less
important than *what* leads us—what convictions, what courage,
what faith—win or lose." I could not imagine the Democratic

nominee in 1976 saying that. When later he returned, a victor (barely) in the election, to his little hometown, his first remark had a very different character: "I told you I wasn't going to lose!"

When I went to Georgia I found that to the Georgians I met, as to Carter, it certainly *did* matter *who* leads us far more than "what convictions" lead us, if one could figure out what those were to be. There was among his admirers a kind of Jimmyism that seemed the counterpart of his own autobiographical bent, a focus upon his unique and personal distinction, without much reference to policy or philosophy. "Jimmy" transcended ideology, transcended the Democratic Party, and of course transcended all organized (equals "special") interests. This Jimmyism would put me sometimes at cross purposes with these Georgia friends of his. I was told about the enormous ideological spread among the people who would come to the Sunday evening quasi-revival meetings at the Dinkler Plaza Hotel in Atlanta to report what they were doing in their counties for Jimmy's election as Governor. They ranged in their political opinions from people who were segregationists and tempted to vote for George Wallace at the 1972 National Democratic Convention through conservatives and moderates to a few liberals. When I asked, I was told that the Carter support did not have any ideological consistency. It included a wide range united only in their belief in Jimmy. Whereas I was supposed to find this impressive, a positive recommendation, I found instead that it made me uneasy. I spent my youth arguing against people who would say, in the American individualist fashion, and proudly, as though giving themselves medals for moral superiority, that they vote for the *man* and not for the *party*.

On the Sunday before the election I remarked that I was pleased to see Mr. Carter had said he was indebted to Andy Young. "And nobody else!" the Carter friend shot back instantly, proudly. But I had meant something quite different from that; I was pleased to see that Carter, who seemed to me lacking in acknowledgment of the collaborative aspect of politics, at least admitted owing something to *somebody* outside his own family and "the people" (projections of himself). Moreover I was pleased that the somebody was Andrew Young. My Carter friends thought the point, rather, was to be free of ties.

These friends had seen the whole arduous undertaking; had

had the Carters stay in their apartment (the secret service, now, checking it); had still as the centerpiece on the dining room table a giant peanut with comic adornments made for the last visit of Rosalynn; knew how many hands had been shaken and how many planes had been flown in and how many speeches had been given and how much work, work, work it had all been. They were not pleased by any suggestion—especially when made by an interloping Northerner—that others might have a remotely comparable claim on the office. But the unrepentant Northerner had to demur. Earned it? There is no *earning* if that office is rightly understood. Earned it? If it were to be earned, had Jimmy Carter earned it more than—say—the battered, vulnerable, inadequate but gallant Hubert Humphrey (battered, incidentally, by among many others Jimmy Carter)? President Carter himself, safely in the White House, sent Senator Humphrey a picture of himself in the oval office, inscribed "You deserve to be sitting here." But individual "deserving" and "earning" does not apply to the Presidency.

One consequence of the politics of autobiography and Jimmyism may be a derogation not only of the legislative body, as was much discussed while President Carter was getting his Washington sea legs, but also of the political party.

The pre-Washington Carter may be seen to have been a lonely achiever more comfortable with the clarity of command than with the messiness of collaboration. Those personal characteristics may combine with the accident of his coming from a one-party state to downgrade the political party (already in bad shape as an institution for reasons independent of Carter). Congress, another ailing institution, has at least the leverage gradually to bring this President to understand—as it was regularly put in 1977—that it is not the Georgia legislature, and gradually to bring him from a certain Rickoverian peremptoriness in his first dealings with it to a near collaboration with Speaker O'Neill and more respectful coping with Senator Byrd and their colleagues.

But the Democratic Party has no such leverage.

Mr. Carter's entourage was Jimmyist before it was Democratic. Though one close supporter insisted upon his party loyalty to the point of voting for Lester Maddox, others deserted McGovern for Wallace. One key supporter voted in the 1950s for

Eisenhower. All were proud of the ideological and partisan tossed salad that Jimmy attracted.

Though Carter himself has been a loyal Democrat, that loyalty apparently has not been the outward and visible sign of a particularly strong inward and spiritual belief. It is mixed with Southern pride. Mr. Carter was a lonely supporter of Harry Truman at the New London submarine base in 1948. He proudly tells how Georgia gave John Kennedy a greater percentage support than his home state of Massachusetts (for that matter, Georgia even went—against strong cultural currents—for Al Smith in 1928). But the old solid South commitment to the one party need not include the belief in the organization that marks the Democratic Party in a Northern city, or in the party as the bearer of an ideological heritage that marks liberal Democrats since F.D.R. For those who believe in the importance of the two-party system and in the "responsible" political party as an important American institution, Jimmy Carter is a person of whom to be wary.

The important political battles of Mr. Carter's past were against Democrats, not Republicans: against Homer Moore, Ellis Arnall, Lester Maddox, Carl Sanders, and the string of contenders for the Democratic Presidential nomination in 1976. Some commentators explained the comparative failure of his general election campaign as against the deft footwork of his in-fighting within the Democratic Party in the primaries by this history: He was running against a Republican opponent.

One of his non-Georgia staff members told me Carter feels he got the nomination in spite of the Democrats and is not a part of that central old Democratic group, toward whom he feels—this was after Carter had been in the White House for three months— a "lingering hostility."

Moreover, said this aide, the Democratic Party as a continuing organization does not evoke his loyalty or understanding. Why would anyone be, year after year, a precinct captain? It must be self-interest. All he hears from the organization is their desire for jobs for party workers, and he has contempt for an organization with that characteristic.

Mr. Carter's organization in 1966 and in 1970 and in the peanut brigades and Carter organization of 1976 were composed of people who did not necessarily have a great loyalty to the national

Democratic Party or to its ideological heritage. When Carter campaigned in the general election as the nominee of the Democratic Party, he was not careful to lend his support to the party and its slate. I saw David Broder in the Atkinson Hotel in Indianapolis after a Carter rally and mentioned Carter's perfunctory endorsements of local Democrats. Broder's response was quick and critical: "He doesn't do that well. And all it takes is a three-by-five card!"

It had seemed to me on hearing both Jimmy Carter and Rosalynn that their endorsements of local candidates, if indeed they made them at all, were of the most transparently routine sort. Rosalynn Carter obviously was speaking for "Jimm-eh" and not for the Democratic congressman in whatever district it was.

Carter's speech at Warm Springs, with all the Franklin Roosevelt paraphernalia around him, including an introduction by James Roosevelt and "Happy Days Are Here Again" played on the accordion by Graham Jackson who is the black accordionist crying in the famous picture taken after Franklin Roosevelt's death, did speak some words (alternately with praise for the balanced budget and fiscal responsibility) for Franklin Roosevelt and the tradition of the Democratic Party. There were paragraphs in his speech that might well have been written by Theodore Sorensen. But very shortly thereafter in the first week of the campaign Rosalynn Carter and others persuaded Jimmy to stop sounding like a person in the heritage of liberal Democrats, and he did stop.

A month after he was President the old New Dealers got together at a party at the Statler Hilton; Benjamin Cohen and Tommy the Cork and Grace Tully and Rex Tugwell. President Carter did not attend that party; the White House, occupied by a Democrat, sent no representative.

At a press conference in his ninth month in office he comfortably admitted that on some matters the Republicans in Congress were more helpful to him than the Democrats.

All Presidents present themselves as leaders of all the people and borrow as much support as they can from independents and from the opposition party. That certainly includes Franklin Roosevelt himself, and Mr. Carter's immediate predecessor as a Democratic President, Lyndon Johnson. Other Presidents have tended to derogate the party organization in favor of an organization built around their personal leadership. But in the past there has still been a continuing link to the party organization and to an ideology which that organization very loosely serves. Though we do not have ideological parties in this country, we do have traditions built around those party organizations; they have grown by small increments of experience to have discernably different lines of policy.

In Mr. Carter the line of policy growing out of the heritage of the Democratic Party and its absorption of the immigration to the American city and the problems of the economy in the Great Depression is not very strong. He and his followers either sink below it or rise above it; they believe either in that individual hi-neighbor campaign of the Carter's multitudinous handshakes and of the cheerfully naive visits from the peanut brigade (an Ohio politician said that the peanut brigade coming with their cheerful Southern accents into a Slovak suburb of Cleveland caused it to be the one Cleveland district Carter lost) or to rise above the party organization into the good-man-above-politics, making his appeal to all the people and morality itself by means of television.

V

Let me return now to the early morning after election day when Mr. Carter learned that he had won—finally it was in the burlap, like one of the doves that he used to shoot, also in the early morning, with his father.

Carter returned home from Atlanta to Plains, and the whole world saw a touching moment. He came down the main street of Plains and spoke to the five hundred or so citizens of that town still waiting up to see him. He hugged his mother and his sister-in-law, and he began speaking. Then the emotion of the moment took over. He said "I came all the way through—through twenty-two months and I didn't get choked up until I . . ." There were tears in his eyes, and he turned to embrace his wife, who had tears in her eyes, and a whole nation watched the couple embracing tearfully in the moment of the fullest realization of an extraordinary accomplishment. The echo of that moment included not only the twenty-two months of active campaigning for the Presidential office to which Mr. Carter alluded, but, really, the fourteen years of collaborative effort, often against very heavy odds, which brought him from that very small town in southern Georgia—by then we certainly did know the town's population—to the leadership of the most powerful nation in the world. Jimmy had done it.

We were watching the moment when he and his wife realized that. The tears in the eyes of both as they embraced could not help but have an effect on everybody who saw it. I saw two anchorpersons (perhaps a record) with tears in their eyes—Barbara Walters on ABC, and John Chancellor on NBC. I watched it myself in the Atlanta apartment of Georgians who had themselves been a part not only of the twenty-two-month quest for the Presidency but of eleven years devoted to the career of Jimmy Carter . . . now thus incredibly fulfilled. There were tears all around the room; a visitor, somewhat tearful himself, could not help but be affected not only by the scene of the Carters on television but also by the emotion of the Georgians watching it.

It was a moving triumph. In that instant one's critical powers were suspended, in admiration and in a human fellow feeling for what had been done.

It is to take nothing away from that moment to say that later one's critical faculties returned to whisper this observation: In a sense it was not a *public* moment but a *private* moment, not *our* moment but *their* moment. To a degree we television watchers were intruders, as I was a bit of an intruder in my Georgia friends' condominium. Excepting some moving scenes from the terrible days after John F. Kennedy was shot—and in them historical meaning and private emotion were inextricably woven together—the other moving occasions of our recent televised public life have not been like that . . . have not partaken of the intrusion into private emotion of television entertainment, "Queen for a Day," "This Is Your Life," the camera zooming in on tears and laughter. Adlai Stevenson's concession speech in 1952 was moving because of the grace of it, because of the links he had built with a community of followers. When Lyndon Johnson—the other first Southern President—used the phrase "we shall overcome" in his remarkable speech after the Selma march, the emotion evoked was unmistakably linked to public policy. But in the case of Rosalynn and Jimmy on the platform in Plains, looking at each other and embracing in tears, the rest of us were in the sense

onlookers at a moment of remarkable, private accomplishment—
as when a young person overcomes all handicaps to achieve his
diploma, or as when a victor in a difficult sporting event wins
against all odds, or a deserving but hitherto unknown actress wins
the critics' award.

All this took place in Plains, and Mr. Carter, as he said, was first
moved to tears when he rounded the corner and saw his fellow
townsmen waiting for him; at least he felt their collaboration.

More important, there was Rosalynn. Benjamin Franklin certainly does not tell how Mrs. Franklin helped him achieve virtue,
eminence, and a meeting with five kings, nor are the tattered
Toms of Horatio Alger accompanied by a meaningful partner.
The embrace in Plains did not say: *You* did it, Jimmy, you won
the prize, and I congratulate you (as at graduation day or the
Olympic gold medals); instead it said: *We* did it, you and I, and I
couldn't have done it without you. *That* collaboration, at least,
was real, and a principal reason the moment was so moving.

We are moved, of course, vicariously. *They* have won, and we
observe their victory. It seemed an accomplishment of the
strenuous exertion of the individual will, which might equally
well have happened in fields of business, or education, or art. We
watched; we were moved; but we were watching a moment that
seemed to belong more to them than to us.

Finally—Carter did admit he hadn't done well in the general
election. In a rare public display of self-criticism he said he had
had "the best family support, the best friends, the best campaign
organization . . ." and so on, so that "the only reason we were
close last night was because the candidate wasn't quite good
enough as a campaigner. But I'll make up for that when I'm
President." It was a rare glimpse of a self-critical Jimmy, autobiographical still.

During the transition when his nominees for the Cabinet were
together for the first time on St. Simon's Island, Carter said they
would carry out his campaign promises because "my honor is at
stake." That seemed to me rather more self-referential than was
appropriate for so immense a collaborative undertaking: *their*
honor? the Democratic Party's platform? the long heritage of the
more progressive party? In the nation as a whole Mr. Carter ran
well behind the Democratic Party ticket so that it can certainly be
argued at least that the Democratic party's "honor," having

helped pull Mr. Carter into office, was also at stake. And there were the obligations to groups that supported Mr. Carter: These obligations are not uniformly nefarious, as Mr. Carter's individualist theme, the People-and-I against the "special interests," implies.

The symbolic acts of the early cardigan sweater months of his administration had a high component of the personal ("Hi, Jimmy"; "Hi, Michelle"); his speeches and press conference replies did too. When Mrs. Carter traveled to South America, one item in her reporting was "they love you in South America, Jimmy." When Vernon Jordan of the Urban League made the first major speech critical of President Carter, in July of 1977, Carter (using his wife's comment for a billiard shot in self-defense) said that Rosalynn had told him, "Vernon doesn't think you are doing as well as I think you are doing, Jimmy."

"He wants to give the Cabinet more responsibility," said a newspaper report after his first month, "but clearly intends to set every policy and keep a finger in every pie." A Carter lieutenant said, "There is going to be only one star in this administration, and his initials are J. C."

Presidents in general and candidates for President, by the selective process by which they become such, have sizable egos. Lyndon Johnson's was gargantuan. In some ways (the surprisingly solid role given to the Vice-President) Mr. Carter has shown a remarkable restraint, compared to most others in that select company. A man who worked for both men compared him to Eugene McCarthy. "Gene has a big ego but not a strong one; Jimmy has a strong ego but not a big one."

If one has (as I think one should have) high expectations for Mr. Carter as a teacher, as a source for a moral advance in this country, then one should hope for a correction of the balance in this sheer individual achievement thing, this careerism, this mere success ethic. Throughout the much maligned Washington (maligned by—among others—candidate Carter) there are able and honorable people whose values have a different balance than the classic American combinations symbolized by Poor Richard and Horatio Alger—a combination including more disinterested service to the common good.

The old creed says: I have worked hard, therefore I have achieved—therefore I deserve to have achieved. What I ha ⌐

achieved is *my own doing*. I have *competed* against others—and *won*. It is *my* accomplishment, the result of *my* hard work. The autobiographer goes on to say: now I will tell you my story, so that you may learn from it.

But I thought (and think) the Presidency of the United States should be more than that. It doesn't matter where you come from (not so much anyway); *who* leads us *is* important—more than Adlai Stevenson believed—but still it is less important than *what* leads us, or what shapes him.

Another ambitious provincial, from towns that also had small populations, in Kentucky, Indiana, and Illinois, said once during the Civil War, "What we are dealing with is too large for malice." It is larger now, too large for malice, too large for egotism, too large to be treated as a merely personal accomplishment.

# 6

# THE COMBATIVE
# OUTSIDER

## I

The classic American autobiography maker—the man on the rise—may find other men *also* on the rise, and in his way, *competitors*. He compares himself to them, puts himself in competition with them, beats them out. Indeed, it is exactly in the beating out of others that he *proves* his quality.

Mr. Carter himself tells about his decision to run for Governor in 1966—a most interesting decision; a most interesting paragraph in his book. The Republican candidate for Governor was to be Howard (Bo) Callaway, who had also been the Congressman from Carter's home district. Friends who were urging Carter to run for Governor told him, he says, that he was the only candidate who could beat Callaway. He writes: "Although it is not especially admirable, one of the major reasons [for deciding to run] was a natural competitiveness with 'Bo' Callaway." Carter spells out the parallel elements of their lives that made the competitiveness, in his view, "natural": they were the same age; Callaway had gone to West Point, Carter to Annapolis; Carter had wanted to have a college built in southwest Georgia, and Callaway tried to block it; Callaway was the leader of the Young Republicans, Carter, in some ways, of the Young Democrats.

This paragraph in Carter's autobiography calls to mind the more familiar one, repeated often in his speeches, in which he explained how he began to think he might run for the top office: "During 1971 and 1972, I met Richard Nixon, Spiro Agnew, George McGovern, Henry Jackson, Hubert Humphrey, Ed-

mund Muskie, George Wallace, Ronald Reagan, Nelson Rock-
efeller, and other Presidential hopefuls, and I lost my feeling of
awe about Presidents." His own self-confident competitive
measuring of himself against these others is the clear point: they
aren't so much. If they can do it, so can I. In fact, I can do it
*better*.

During the general election campaign I twice heard him say: "I
doubt if one percent of this audience ever heard my name a year
ago." He took pride in his triumph over obscurity. The opening
line of his acceptance speech—"I'm Jimmy Carter, and I'm running for President"—was amusing and effective; it also may
contain a trace of "I told you so." It seemed to imply: "I showed all
of you people—unknown, as I was, opposed by most of you, as I
was: I used that line all the way from nowhere to this victory."
Later in the speech Carter noted that he had never met a Democratic President. It was a note he was to strike again, even after he
was one. Why? It was another way of underlining his accomplishment—his arrival from nowhere, from outside, knowing none of
these people, then—on his own—beating those others, joining
those Democratic Presidents he'd never met. Carter is not one to
neglect the romance of his own attainment.

One detects something more intense, emotional, and communal than the mere desire for individual success inculcated into
any American boy. There is also the combative attitude of the
outsider who has been slighted and disdained. He's *proving*
something, and not just for himself: for his region, his county, his
people.

I heard echoes of this when I talked at dinner with Jack and
Judy Carter at their house in Calhoun, Georgia, in May not long
after Jack's father had spent his first Easter as President there.
(When Jack had given me directions to his office he used as a
landmark the Calhoun National Bank, later to become famous for
its policy on overdrafts.) At one point Jack asked, a little belligerently, "Do these people think my father is naive?"

I did not altogether deny it. "These people" by implication
included me.

Jack Carter was getting something out of the refrigerator when
he asked his question, so the vigorous shutting of the refrigerator
door punctuated his comment on my non-denial.

"*He's* President. All those guys who say he is naive are *not*."
Bang.

In that defiant sentence and slammed door there was an angry
assertion that went beyond pride in one individual's achievement: there was implied a riposte by a whole people. One often
heard something like that in conversations with Southerners who
supported Carter.

And one heard in conversations with non-Southerners some of
the reason for it. It's a big country, and more of our life is directed
by mutually held stereotypes and reciprocated antagonisms than
we would like to admit.

*He's* President—the others are *not*. Jimmy Carter is in many
ways the epitome of the American legend of success; the pristine,
able, ambitious American achiever—but with a difference. As he
himself has said, the first clue to understanding him is that he is a
Southerner. That fact, and the related fact of his "outsideness,"
give an extra turn of passion to his quintessential Americanism.
He is in important ways the American, even the Puritan and
Yankee—but also very much from *Georgia*. From Sumter
County.

One feels that Carter's ambition goes beyond that of a mere
Northern Horatio Alger hero, achieving only for himself. It is
tinged with regional defiance, with pride of place, with the need
to demonstrate something—perhaps even to retaliate.

Everyone mentions his "self-confidence." But is his self-confidence what McGeorge Bundy's is, or Robert Hutchins's was? It is
not a self-confidence supported by a social class, a prestigious
college, a nationally prominent family, an easy, automatic, taken-
for-granted connection with the great—a *birthright* self-confidence on the national scene. It is self-confidence achieved instead, once he left the support of home, in the teeth of many
prejudices: can any good come from Sumter County?

During the rise and election of John Kennedy, one of Hutchins's associates explained to me what was bothering "Bob" about
the newcomer from Massachusetts: he didn't know him. Hutchins was accustomed to knowing all Presidents and all candidates
for President. If this reading of Mr. Hutchins was right then
surely he would have been still more indignant about this Carter
person from southwest Georgia.

With the Carter person himself the foundation of pride was

quite different. He took pride exactly in his identity with his remote locale, and in *not* knowing any of those other, allegedly superior people—in becoming a Democratic President without ever having met one, without owing anything to Northerners and big shots. Elizabeth Drew quoted a Carter aide as having said, "We don't owe anybody anything"; a distinguished American political scientist then quoted that remark with his angry gloss: "And nobody owes *them* anything, either!" That exchange tells in capsule the underside of the Carter story.

During the transition, economic experts from prestigious places (Bundy—Hutchins people, in a sense) were summoned to Plains by the President-elect, loaded on a bus for the hot trip from Atlanta to Plains, given a box lunch including fried chicken, and then crowded into the pond house where there was one bathroom with a door that sometimes stuck. One may infer that something was being said, beyond the comments on public policy. A reporter who saw it all reports a swagger and a possessive attitude on the part of the host: these Harvard professors came to *him* in *Plains*, on a bus.

If there is an attitude expressed in this deed, and these words, it is not only that of Jimmy Carter, but that of many who are, as the lawyers say, "similarly situated." It was a response in part to real and fancied antecedent prejudices, especially against small-town Southerners, against "crackers" and "rednecks."

The Southern President previous to Carter, the accidental President Lyndon Johnson, gave this response in a virulent form, writing sadly in his memoirs, *The Vantage Point*:

> I did not believe, anymore than I ever had, that the nation would unite indefinitely behind any Southerner. One reason the country could not rally behind a Southern president, I was convinced, was that the metropolitan press of the Eastern Seaboard would never permit it. My experience in office had confirmed this reaction. I was not thinking just of the derisive articles about my style, my clothes, my manner, my accent, and my family—although I admit I received enough of that kind of treatment in my first few months as President to last a lifetime. I was also thinking of a more deep-seated and far-reaching attitude—a disdain for the South that seems to be woven into the fabric of Northern experience. This is a subject that deserves a more profound exploration than I can give it

here—a subject that has never been sufficiently examined. Perhaps it all stems from the deep-rooted bitterness engendered by civil strife over a hundred years ago, for emotional clichés outlast all others and the Southern cliché is perhaps the most emotional of all. Perhaps some day new understanding will cause this bias to disappear from our national life. I hope so, but it is with us still.

It was with us in 1976-1977, at least in the perception of Carter people. "The Northern liberal press didn't want Jimmy Carter," said his son Jack, angry even after his father was four months safely in the White House. "They concluded a priori that he was a conservative. They wouldn't look at his statements, which were reasonable; they never read what he said. They looked instead at where he was comin' from and drew their conclusion from that."

Judy Carter, an unusually bright and able person, burst out once when she remembered unpleasant encounters from the campaign: "In California and the West they *really* hate Southerners. The minute they heard my accent they wouldn't even *listen* to me." The phenomenon I am describing is not one-sided. And it is not only regional, although the South vs. North thing is its strongest manifestation.

There undoubtedly is a prejudice against the South, and there are stereotypes of Southerners. At the same time, the prejudice is overestimated by a thin-skinned Southerner like Lyndon Johnson.

There are also in the cosmopolitan and upper-crust worlds dismissive and disdainful attitudes toward the provinces and toward small towns; toward Fernwood and Winesburg, Ohio, as well as those little towns in Georgia whose names are pronounced in a funny way by the natives. But defensive people with unglamorous addresses discover the disdain even where it doesn't exist.

And the same pair of assertions holds true for educational background. Nobody cared nearly as much as Lyndon Johnson did that his college was San Marcos State Teachers College rather than Harvard.

In Carter's case there is yet another complex of prejudices: those having to do with Born Again Baptists, Evangelical Protestants, Fundamentalists. In this bias the precipitating initial disdain is much more explicit (perhaps stronger) than in the

others. All through his rise to power, and even after he was
President, his religion received from the Northern liberati sar-
castic treatment in the Mencken tradition. He had been President a year, for just one of many examples, when Lewis Lapham
wrote a sneering article in *Harper's*, recording the developing
view in his circle "that Mr. Carter didn't know what he was doing
and that perhaps he should resign his office in order to give more
time to his Sunday school teaching and his Bible studies." The
article ventures interpretations in this vein:

> To those members of the congregation fortunate enough to
> have been "born again," Jesus appears as the savior who
> guarantees admission into a state of grace. If Mr. Carter
> believes himself rescued by Jesus (a figure somewhat compa-
> rable to a Southern banker who lends unlimited amounts of
> money without charging interest), then I can well imagine why
> he would find it difficult to take much of an interest in a world
> elsewhere.

And this:

> Mr. Carter considers it his business to bring visions from the
> desert. If the lost tribe chooses not to act on the news that Mr.
> Carter brings them . . . then the lost tribe has nobody to blame
> but itself.

The religious prejudice is to be found not only among folk who
were born up North and outside the Southern Protestant culture
but also, perhaps with special intensity, in some native Southern
Protestants. Persons raised in the South who left the region and
its religious culture behind—James Wooten of *The New York
Times* and John Osborne of *The New Republic* for two important
examples—must then be tempted either to impute to Carter all
the beliefs they themselves have escaped (the sweet nothings of
Sunday school, the ferocious rigidities of fundamentalist preaching) or to believe he is faking for political purpose. James Wooten
is quoted by Richard Reeves in Reeves's book *Convention* as
having said, "I know he doesn't believe that religious stuff. I
know it! I know it!" John Osborne went out of his way to make a
circle of interviews in Plains that imputed to Carter a literal belief
in heaven and hell that we have not heard from Carter's own lips,

and Osborne has applied the word "fundamentalist" to him. But Carter is not like the fundamentalists of Osborne's youth; indeed, he is not a fundamentalist at all.

I talked with Helen Dewar, whose coverage of Carter for *The Washington Post* I thought to be particularly perceptive, about his religion. She wasn't disdainful but she *was* baffled. She admitted that the problem was her own lack of experience with that world, but still—she couldn't believe it. How could he engage in that sophisticated discussion about public issues on Monday after that simple Bible class on Sunday?

Finally, Carter was an outsider in Washington. Many men have come from smalltown Southern backgrounds, and from Evangelical churches like Carter's, and have gone on to long careers and powerful positions, perhaps punctuated by Prayer breakfasts, in the nation's capital; Washington used to be called, not without reason, a Southern city. For all of Lyndon Johnson's hurt feelings it was an enormous help to him when he came to the Senate in 1948 as a Southerner, with immediate access to Sam Rayburn, Richard Russell, and the Southern powers on the hill. But Carter is no Lyndon Johnson, Richard Russell, Walter George, or Carl Albert. Most of his career had been outside politics, and his short political career had been outside Washington.

So Carter, by his residence, his region, his religion, his cast of mind and his experience and occupation, was not a part of the world that does most of the interpreting of national affairs. Much that he represents is unfamiliar to the centers of national communication. To understand the Jimmy Carter phenomenon one has a dual problem: not only interpreting him, but also interpreting his interpreters.

Carter is indeed an outsider, and an outsider from a region marked by a considerable defensiveness; he comes from a small town and he holds to religious views not held by the community of sophisticated conversation in the city. He is not the gregarious sort of person who would seek to break down those barriers. Therefore there is a reciprocity of misinterpretation back and forth between him and the world into which he has moved. The latter may be at least as much off the mark as he.

Already as a Southerner he may have had the feeling of being unfairly regarded that throbs through Lyndon Johnson's paragraph and rang out in Judy Carter's voice. The other items I have listed would then add to that feeling.

These two sets of attitudes mutually reinforce each other. Working on a magazine in New York or teaching at Yale one is struck by the quick flash of defensiveness some innocent remark can provoke in an Italian-American, Nebraskan or, even more, a Mississippian. But at lunch or in the faculty club one can hear remarks that prove that the slights are not all just fancied.

The Southern white, as observers have said, is comparable to an ethnic group. Billy Carter, drinking beer for a fee at a Terre Haute auto race, cast himself as a real-life equivalent of a Southern Archie Bunker. The "popularity," if that is the word—the celebrity—of the President's brother is itself a curious study in the complicated relationship I am trying to describe.

Though the Carters were eminent and secure in their own small world, it was a very small world; and outside that world their little town, their county, and their region were not highly regarded. So Billy's abler older brother Jimmy encountered a whiplash. He was accustomed to being the most capable person in the surroundings in which he moved, from Plains elementary school where he made his A's, and the Baptist Sunday school, where he was the ablest interpreter of the Bible, to being the ablest business man, and an able State Senator and Governor. His father and his family had security and eminence in his home county; he was himself the smartest person around and a leader in the smaller worlds he knew; but then he found himself categorically disregarded in the larger worlds outside. In Atlanta they looked down on South Georgia and particularly on Sumter County. In New York City they were *very* nervous about a Georgia cracker, a red-neck, a Born Again Baptist. (After his first year in office a New Jersey Democrat said, "That's the last time I vote for a Born Again candidate.")

And so there is combativeness, defensiveness, resentment, defiance, the hurt that comes from repeated slights. And there are also condescension, stereotyping, the slighting and dismissive attitudes that give those attitudes some basis in fact.

## II

Of course Carter's identities *helped* him, on balance, in the 1976 elections; he would not have won without them. There was political mileage in his outsideness not only among Southerners, Evangelicals, smalltown folk, and people who don't like Washington but also even among some of the elite whose attitude was supposed to be negative. There was a mystique of the South, and a good deal of romanticizing of Plains and of solid old-fashioned religion on the part of people remote from all these worlds. Carter and his political advisors knew perfectly well that there is and was in American democracy a social psychological equivalent of "affirmative action" long before that phrase existed, making it sometimes advantageous to be "disadvantaged," if your disadvantages are the right ones and timed right. (There is of course a converse: going to Harvard hurts you with the broad populace, unless you compensate in some way, like being an Irish Catholic.)

But victories with the public aside, the reciprocating antagonisms continued into Carter's Presidency and colored his relations with a circle of institutions: with Congress, the Democratic Party, the bureaucracy, Washington society, the press. In each case there were lingering hostilities.

The press is particularly important, and is a kind of reflection of the rest. The post-Nixon, post-Vietnam press is puffed with its importance, especially in relation to Presidents and potential Presidents. To the outsiders this national press is the visible surface of the whole patronizing insider's world. It is in this regard both the front line of the partly fictional national elite, especially the Washington/New York/Cambridge political elite, to which all the resented prejudices are imputed, and also the bearer in stereotyped images of the prejudices. It doesn't matter that all those "media" people came originally from St. Joseph, Missouri; the entity of which they are a part is felt to be the "Eastern liberal establishment press." It is no accident that, in the quotations I gave above, both Lyndon Johnson and Jack Carter focused on the press resentments that really have a wider target.

When I drove to Atlanta on the Thursday before the election, I found among some Carter people there—old friends of his, new friends of mine—a sizzling antagonism to the press. I sensed an angry thesis taking form in Atlanta's Colony Square: if their man lost, it would be "the media" that (in Eliza Doolittle's phrase) done him in.

A column deploring the whole campaign as "Dreary, Dreary, Dreary," written by Al Otten in *The Wall Street Journal*, for just one example, had indignant underlinings and marginal outcries scratched all over it: You media people who *did* it, are now blaming him for what *you* did! I even heard the argument that the polls and the Carter critics in the press *needed* to make the election *seem* close in order to sell papers and magazines. The irrepressible Billy Carter gave voice to antimedia views on national television, to the consternation of anchorman John Chancellor, who rather unnecessarily then and there, with millions watching, argued *back*.

And what of the candidate himself, undergoing just then the immense historical metamorphosis from candidate to President-elect? It had not gone unnoticed in "the media" that the candidate in the *Playboy* interview had disdainfully remarked upon the lack of interest in "issues" on the part of the national press. Then the President-elect—in a press conference from which the camera people were excluded—said he had had "some real concern about news coverage," especially on the nightly news. I think an Agnew cloud was gathering in Georgia, and moved on to the White House. Carter as President has been careful to say in public that the media has been in general—with individual exceptions— "fair," but there is a pause and apparently a bit of a struggle before he says it—for example in the press conference on Lance's resignation (signs back in Calhoun said: MEDIA: WHO'S NEXT?). In interviews the President says gently that his larger purposes can get lost in the media's "transient" analyses. At another press conference he quite evidently restrained himself from the comment he was tempted to make about Sam Donaldson's reports.

Meanwhile an anti-Carter cloud had gathered over Peanut One, which also was to move on to Washington.

When after the election I drove back to the state university where I work, I entertained in quick succession, for several days each, two well-placed journalists recuperating in academe from the political year. I heard them in enough classes, TV interviews, public meetings and other forums to be able to repeat their standard speech, even as they could repeat that of the candidates with whom they had rocketed and bumped around the country. These standard lines included, along with some surprising *mea culpas* for the press, much anti-Carter material. One of these journalists (a "highly placed source" for me, I suppose) gave voice to this material in his own right; the other, not altogether sharing its bias, nevertheless confirmed its existence among his colleagues.

The standard lines go like this (although when I combine and compress them here, they sound even more anti-Carter than they actually were): Carter does not like to be crossed; does not bear frustration well; does not suffer fools gladly; does not reach out to others—equals—and collaborate with them; holds grudges, gets even; is stubborn and rigid; thanked *no one* in his acceptance speech; has an excessively "managerial" approach to politics and government; needs to be in charge and to have things go well— isn't good when he isn't and they don't. He does not like or understand the press; takes criticism personally; perceives analytical articles to be hostile; and once cited as an example of good journalism a puff piece about his triumphs as Governor. While I was hearing these anti-Carter lines, *The New Yorker* arrived, with an ill-tempered post-election attack on Carter's "wretchedly run campaign." Then came *The New Republic*, with TRB reporting press attitudes toward Carter on Peanut One—"cynicism, distrust, even hatred"—and the way Carter himself seemed: "aloof, cold-eyed, distant."

Well now, what is one to make of that? As a citizen with the advantage of never having been on Peanut One, or in the White House press room, I propose that the case against Carter in the press was not much nearer the whole and rounded truth than the case against the media in Colony Square and the other parts of the White House. They are each fractional truths at best, spiked with personal interest and momentary irritation, grounded in the contrasting characteristics of different roles and institutions, and—above all—distorted by recent history (the events that staggered the Presidency inflated the press).

There are personal ingredients as well. Jimmy Carter is in some ways uncongenial to newspaper people. Richard Reeves, that sharp, early analyst of Carter, wrote that whereas Jody Powell is good company, Jimmy Carter is not (as he doesn't butter

Congressmen or butter George Meany so he doesn't butter newsmen—in fact, takes pride in nonbuttering). Reeves wrote in another place that a man who gets to be President is "not your basic nice guy." And he said in private that Carter is a "grind." The knights of the clattering typewriter like wit, flash, sensation, the interesting and new: for anything long, complicated, old, and dull they use the phrase MEGO (mine eyes glaze over). Jimmy Carter is a man whose eyes do not glaze over.

But behind these personal reasons for hostility, and those grounded in the recent history of the press and the Presidency, there are the social divisions, in which the "Northern (Eastern) liberal (establishment) press" is simply the most visible and available epitome and conduit of the reciprocating social antagonisms and stereotypes I have tried to describe.

## III

Southerner, outsider Carter is "tough." He says so. He used the word "tough" seven times in his election eve television program. "Aggressive" is another of his words.

And an interesting variant is Carter's recurrent repudiation of timidity: "I will not be timid"—as President, as proponent of this or that policy. In a wire service interview after he had been President nine months, Mr. Carter was asked how he would like to be remembered as President. He mentioned peace, national pride, and the alleviation of suffering. Then he said in conclusion: "I would like to be looked on as someone who administered the affairs of government well, who was not timid." I find the repeated use of the word "timid" intriguing—"timid" as something neither he nor his policies are ever going to be.

Without falling into psychohistory one may still say it is a curious sort of self-confident toughness that even raises the issue of "timidity," and that repeatedly underscores its aggressive, tough, active, self-confidence. Another sort, not under siege, secure from the start, would not feel the need to make the explicit assertions.

Helen Dewar told me how on the plane after his victory Carter came back to the press seats exulting, chortling, rubbing it in: you were *wrong*. I *won*. His need to score that point, and nail it repeatedly, emotionally, caused her then to be stunned when in Plains the exultant victor suddenly admitted that he had made mistakes—that the closeness of the election was the *candidate's* fault. It was a very different Jimmy from the one who had shortly before been taunting the press.

Vernon Jordan is one of the many who were reminded by Jimmy Carter that they had told him he shouldn't run, couldn't win. Jordan, telling the story himself, remembers saying to Carter in the Governor's mansion in 1974: nobody knows you; you're from the South; you are a damn fool to run. Carter, says Jordan, replied, "I'm going to run. I'm going to win."

Three weeks after the election Jordan got a call from the President-elect: "You remember that conversation we had in the Governor's mansion? Guess what. You were wrong as hell."

Carter, says Jordan, does not forget; he remembers everyone who discouraged him, everyone who got in his way. That's part of his political problem. Carter, the efficient Yankee, does not look back; Carter, the combative Southerner, remembers. A Northern urban politician, for whom politics is collaboration and basic loyalty combined with a continual pragmatic shifting of strange bedfellows, might say that Carter seems to forget what he ought to remember and remember what he ought to forget.

I had seen Philip Alston in his Atlanta law office on Monday, the day before the election, when he was not very happy; on Inauguration Day, at his party in Washington, when he was happy; and on the day in March after he had learned that he would be appointed Ambassador to Australia, when he was ecstatic.

Alston is wealthy, gracious, gentlemanly, and the chief figure in an Atlanta law firm that represents Northern businesses. He was Carter's most important early supporter from the Atlanta establishment, one of the few from north Georgia, an essential figure in the providing for Carter of financial support and of legitimacy in the world of the Piedmont Driving Club. He came to be, as he said, "hooked on Jimmy Carter" and helped raise money for him at crucial points in the gubernatorial race of 1970 and the Presidential campaign of 1976.

Mr. Alston had learned the good news about Australia at a dinner at the White House with Prime Minister Callaghan of Great Britain as the guest. He had arrived late in Atlanta, his flight delayed, and I had expected him to cancel our appointment. Instead he asked me to stay after hours in his deserted law office to talk about Jimmy, the White House dinner, and how impressed and happy he was.

Two themes ran through his conversation: the naturalness of the Carters in the White House, and the toughness of Jimmy Carter.

I had encountered both of these themes in other conversations: Georgia associates of Carter trying to prove to me, as a Northern writer, that Jimmy had qualities that I was never inclined to doubt that he had. I expected him to be informal and I expected him to be "tough" and I expected him to be intelligent. I never doubted that he could behave gracefully at a dinner for the Prime Minister of England.

As part of the discourse on toughness Mr. Alston repeated an exchange at the dinner. A series of parallels were drawn between the Prime Minister and the President: the President is a Baptist; the Prime Minister is a Baptist: the President has a sister who is in religion; the Prime Minister has a sister who is in religion: the President proposed to his wife in a churchyard; the Prime Minister proposed to his wife in a churchyard. This presentation went through a series of such parallels, and ended. Here Philip Alston leaned over his desk at me and gave the punch line with intensity: "And each of them has the strength to cut your goddam guts out if you do wrong."

He repeated this story proudly. That strength to do the necessary guts-cutting on the part of his man—paralleling this other world leader—was to him a point of pride. He went on to say that we need "never fear his abilities to sit down with Brezhnev."

Again the Southerner preserves an older characteristic of the nation as a whole—especially the mainstream of the nation as it moved West and South in the nineteenth century. Many observers have said what Robert Osgood wrote in his book *Limited War*: "The nation's moral and emotional aversion to violence is joined by a strong streak of pugnacity. There broods in the American mind a fighting spirit that recalls the days when the United States was a bumptious young nation trying to prove itself to the world, as well as the more recent days when the populace boasted that the country had never lost a war."

It is indisputable that the South still has all those qualities,

doubled. It has a greater inclination to support belligerent action
by the nation, including the Vietnam War ("The South was not
touched by the protest against the Vietnam War the way the rest
of the country was," said one Carter supporter to me). And the
greater willingness to resort to violence individually and in private life is a staple of the interpretation of the characteristics of
the South. John Shelton Reed's *The Enduring South*, for example, makes it one of the three characteristics by which he can
distinguish Southerners from other Americans on the basis of
empirical data. In the Southern Yankee toughness, personal ambition and competitiveness are interwoven. The old American
competitiveness—getting ahead personally by one's own efforts,
ahead of somebody else—is given a defensive edge: that of need-
ing to prove something to those people who have looked down
upon you, people in the North.

Eugene Patterson, editor of *The Atlanta Constitution* during
important years in Carter's rise, left Atlanta in 1968 and now is
editor of *The St. Petersburg Times* in Florida. He recounted his
relationship to Carter, in swift and pungent detail, on the day that
he was editing the issue of his paper that dealt with the incident of
the Hanifi Muslims holding hostages in Washington—telling me
part of the story, being interrupted to make a decision about the
breaking story, returning to the tale of his relationship to Carter
where he had left off.

Patterson's story was rather intricately revealing, because he
and Carter are much alike. They are the same age and have the
same background in rural Georgia. It is a background, says Patterson, by which both are "forever marked." "He knows where
he comes from." "His populism is genuine because mine is." "He
thinks the same way I do." He "went into the military to break
away from the parochial background, as I did; came back from
military service to see that racial discrimination was wrong, as I
did."

But Patterson also represented the other side of the mutually
provocative worlds I have been describing. Though he comes
from Carter's rural Southern background he had been a prominent member of the national press at *The Washington Post*, and
before that had been editor of *The Atlanta Constitution*: the
establishment papers in the big cities. Moreover he committed
the cardinal sin of endorsing Carter's opponents. My talk with

him gave an interesting echo effect: being much like Carter he gave the sound of Carter's own feelings, even when the two were in disagreement.

The Atlanta editor had been struck by the "total animosity" that Carter felt to Bo Callaway. "Typical of the South," he said, "to reduce politics to personality." When Patterson wrote a mildly nice paragraph about Bo Callaway as a bright young man showing fresh blood in the Republican Party, this then unknown figure from Sumter County, Jimmy Carter, wrote him, as the editor of the state's preeminent newspaper, a fierce, negative letter, a letter which Patterson says "blistered me." "Here I was posing as the editor of a liberal newspaper, supporting a Republican who inherited his wealth and who set up Callaway Gardens as a rich boy's paradise in an area where other people sweated out their living." Carter said Callaway was the beneficiary of the Goldwater movement in Georgia, and represented the country club Republicans who were suddenly "in" with Barry. Carter's letter was a "mean attack" calling Callaway a "real bastard" in "fierce populist terms." (I am quoting Patterson.) "The letter really chewed me out" for saying anything favorable about Callaway. Now—here comes the interesting part, for the Northern listener. "His letter," said the Southern editor "won my immediate respect. I liked his letter chewing me out."

As Carter has said, one of his motives for running for Governor was his rivalry with Callaway, who was to be the Republican candidate for that office. When Patterson tells the story it has a pungency it lacks in Carter's book. Carter, said Patterson, "trailed Callaway like a bird dog after a quail." The feeling "goes deep." That Callaway should be representing the people of Georgia seemed to Carter "a damned outrage"; Carter "went right after Callaway; he felt it deeply."

In this bird-dog-after-a-quail pursuit of Callaway, Carter came to *The Atlanta Constitution* and visited not the mere editor (Patterson) but the President of the corporation that publishes the paper. The President, in turn, called Patterson to say "there is a fellow here who wants to see you." (Anne Cox Chambers, the heir to *The Constitution*, was to be appointed our American Ambassador to Belgium in 1977, after much water under the bridge, by President Jimmy Carter.)

The fellow came into Patterson's office: "little ole Jimmy Car-

Little ole Jimmy Carter sat in a big over-stuffed chair with
sharp blue eyes and said he was goin' to run for Governor and
u.._t he had a better chance than Arnall. Patterson did not give
him any encouragement because he had already decided that the
paper would support Ellis Arnall.

Here was this little guy from south Georgia, said Patterson,
telling me "you got nowhere else to go." He did *not* smile when
he said it, either. He left. We—*The Constitution*—endorsed
Arnall. The primary was "a shocker": a shocker to Patterson and
*The Constitution*, as well as to Carter and his followers. Carter
narrowly missed the run-off. The eventual winner of the Governor's race was a figure entertaining to the rest of the country but
not to Georgians, the ax-handle segregationist restaurateur
whose talents include riding a bicycle backward—Lester
Maddox.

(Another citizen of Georgia, a supporter of Carter then and
since, said that there were wounds going back to that primary that
still are not quite healed. The Arnall people felt Carter's entry
was an unnecessary division of the moderate vote. The Carter
people felt Arnall, "a Claghorn on television," could not win.)

Patterson, like others in Atlanta, was startled by how well
Carter did, with no press support and little support from the
establishment (Alston almost alone). "Damned if he didn't almost
make it in the primary." "The kids at the University of Georgia
discovered him." In that campaign, in contrast to the campaign in
1970, he put blacks and whites together, and the kids with their
elders, and almost brought off an upset. But he narrowly missed,
and that led to the period—was there one or was there not?—of
Carter's unhappiness, of his walk in the woods with Ruth, and his
starting over again to run again for Governor in 1970.

Patterson wished *The Constitution* had supported Jimmy Carter. "I had underestimated him."

Carter, said Patterson, regarded Bo Callaway as a major threat,
more of a threat than Lester Maddox. Moreover after the events
of 1966 the word was brought to Patterson in his editorial office in
Atlanta that Carter was brooding, "really beating up on you down
there; bad-mouthing you down there; he never forgets." (I myself
discovered that even yet early supporters of Carter do not have a
great enthusiasm for Gene Patterson.)

Patterson left Georgia in 1968 and went to *The Washington*

*Post*, but he kept connections. In the 1970 gubernatorial race against Carl Sanders he did not expect Carter to win. He heard from his friends in Atlanta that Sanders had the press, had the organization, had the major Democrats, had the money, had everything.

All Carter had was the people. And a "tough" campaign.

Carter—Patterson heard in Washington—was "segging it up" down in Georgia. He had positioned himself to *win*, a little bit to the right of Carl Sanders. And he did win.

The moralist may here observe that the politics of toughness, of combative competitiveness, doing whatever is necessary, may have its costs.

An oft-quoted Carter statement in that 1970 gubernatorial race in Georgia—in which his tactics were not such as to make his supporters proud—was made to Vernon Jordan, then a Georgia black leader, now the head of the Urban League. The statement was this: "You *won't* like my campaign, but you *will* like my administration." Both parts of that statement proved to be true.

But in the Spring of 1977, with Jimmy Carter now in the White House, Vernon Jordan (who says to himself in unbelief every so often: God damn! Jimmy Carter is President!) was sitting at dinner in New York remembering that incident. A short time later he was to give a speech criticizing Carter's neglect of the poor, of cities, of blacks. Jordan remarked ruminatively about the fiscally conservative budget-balancing business-confidence-seeking President, his old friend, Jimmy Carter: "I suppose Jimmy may have said last Fall to *business* leaders what he said to *me* back in 1970."

But whatever the tactics, in 1970, as in 1976, Carter did win. The head of the advertising agency for Sanders in 1970 was astonished that his man "got his plow cleaned." Patterson said: "It was the second time I underestimated that little guy."

(Patterson, a big husky man, referred often to Carter's size. It is not only in Indiana that that fact is noted, although in rural Georgia I believe it may be for different reasons than in Indiana. Once after Carter had spoken in one of our basketball palaces, while the orchestra wafted the strains of "Georgia on My Mind" up over the smell of tired fried chicken and old tennis shoes, I looked down from the balcony to watch Mr. Carter shaking hands with voters near the free-throw line below. I heard a Hoosier fan behind me calmly assessing him by a prime local criterion. "He's kind of a short fellow, ain't he?")

When Patterson, now in St. Petersburg, heard that little ole Jimmy Carter had been announced for the Democratic nomination for the Presidency he thought: "I knew I had underestimated that little guy twice before—but *President!* JESUS! That was too much."

In February 1975 Carter called Patterson and arranged to come to *The St. Petersburg Times* for a conference with the editors. He sat in a chair in the center of the group, a small figure who handled all the hard questions from the "hard-nosed newsmen" in a way that "mesmerized" that group. He dropped names in a way that showed them he had been around and he handled questions about nuclear energy in a way that showed that he had done his homework. Patterson, still a little embarrassed that he brought "this nobody" to the editorial conference, asked where he was getting the money for his Presidential campaign.

"Raisin' it in Georgia."

"Why in Georgia?" "Why should they give?"

Didn't he have a flimsy financial base?

Carter grinned. They are "scared to underestimate me again." (Carter knew he was getting to Patterson.)

Jerry Rafshoon, who came with Carter to this meeting in Florida, said afterward that they had wasted their time. "No," Carter replied. "Now Gene understands."

Patterson wrote a column in February of 1975: "Don't underestimate this guy."

In May, 1975, some editors of the nation's major newspapers touring China stopped in Tokyo. These editors discovered in the Okura Hotel the ex-Governor of Patterson's ex-state, a candidate for President not being taken very seriously. Carter was there for a meeting of the Trilateral Commission. Patterson said he thought he'd give him—Carter—a thrill by leading all these notable editors over to talk to him—a "forlorn figure drinking ginger-ale with Peter Bourne." The editors of all these big papers asked Carter questions. They kidded about this Carter. Jimmy who?

Carter again was dynamite. He got who they were straight— (let's see, Tom Winship of *The Boston Globe*); talked to every editor there. "That little scoundrel won them over."

Patterson concluded his story of his education at the hands of Jimmy Carter: "Everytime I saw him I had to admire him more."

If the defiant outsider's assertive mastery be the basis for such admiration, President-elect Jimmy Carter, seeking to fill his Cabinet posts, was to encounter some of that same mastery himself from the other side.

A black leader, not well known but highly respected within the world of urban affairs, was asked to come to Plains for a conversation, obviously with the possibility of an appointment in view. He explained that he could not accept an appointment; the Carter people asked him to come anyway. He did. Carter talked to him alone, talked to him with Kirbo, Hamilton Jordan, and others in the room; talked to him alone again; pressed him once, pressed him twice, to accept a Cabinet post. The man declined, and declined again. He was willing to give advice. He wouldn't take that Cabinet post; he wouldn't take any other post.

At the end of the extended effort to persuade him, Carter asked: "What position *would* you like to hold?" This man answered: "President of the United States."

Carter smiled and ceased his importuning. Now *he* understood.

Patterson—to return to his story—was prepared for 1976. During his account of the "tough" campaign against Sanders, he looked across his desk at the Northern college professor and sometime member of Adlai Stevenson's staff who was interviewing him and said (I thought with a certain relish) "To go out and make nice speeches and *lose* is not Jimmy Carter's style."

We are a distance now from Lincoln's Second Inaugural. When I asked Jack Carter how the family had felt when his father became President he answered that they had taken it calmly. They had *expected* him to be elected.

Then he paused and smiled slightly. "Still," he said about Inauguration Day, "I'll admit that walkin' down Pennsylvania Avenue past those big buildings I did feel a little bit like we were Caesar comin' into a conquered town."

# 7

# A GOOD MAN IS
# HARD TO FIND

On the first Sunday Jimmy Carter was President of the United States he and his wife attended the couples class at the First Baptist Church on 16th Street in Washington. The teacher of that class, a pleasant life insurance executive from Tennessee named Fred Gregg, asked the class what story preceded the scheduled lesson. The President himself gave the answer: "The Good Samaritan." Mr. Gregg said: "Mr. President, you know the Bible real good. You help me out." After the class Gregg said: "There is nothing superficial about his Biblical knowledge. He knew that answer without even having studied the lesson."

This scene reminded me of an incident in a 1935 novel by Thornton Wilder called *Heaven's My Destination*, the best presentation in fiction I know of a particular kind of American and religious "good man." In the early pages its central character, an utterly earnest young Baptist, George Brush, seeing that the Annual Bible Question Bee is in progress in the First Baptist Church in the Texas town he is visiting, entered that contest and won first prize, "his particular triumph being the genealogical tables of King David."

Mr. Carter's particular triumphs extend well beyond either genealogical tables or the sequence of parables in the New Testament; nevertheless, one side of him repeatedly reminds a reader of the fictional character in Thornton Wilder's affectionate portrait.

The American achiever brings forth his accomplishments not only in the material world of peanut warehouses, million-dollar shelling machines, and nuclear submarines; not only by winning

Georgia Governor's races and Presidential primaries, but also in the less tangible realms of *moral* accomplishment, where the strenuously active individual will is to shape the self and the world into what they Ought To Be.

Mr. Brush, an earnest, foolish, principle-filled, exasperating, moving, comic, utterly serious "moral" man of the American provincial sort, intends to *do right* and right now. Why not the *best*? No mediocrity anywhere; I'll *never* lie to you; you can depend on it. He doesn't waste time, uses every minute; he has theories about what he ought to do in every field, which he applies forthwith with a simple directness, bringing to the world his principles and his Bible quotations, as though he were starting out in human society with a kind of moral equivalent of zero-based budgeting. Like Carter he reads, makes straight A's, does what he is supposed to do. He has that sectarian-American moralizing individualism that looks on the world as a free field for his improving deeds. He does have an ambitious ego; he says, "I didn't put myself through college for four years and go through a difficult religious conversion just to be like everybody else"; he writes in the margin of an article about Napoleon in the *Encyclopaedia Britannica*: "I am a great man, too—for good." One can picture a young Jimmy Carter doing that.

It is not hard to explain why this human type which looms large in American society has not been more often portrayed in the higher reaches of American literature. Americans who write books of literary distinction, especially recently, do not know anything about the world of George Brush and of the most conscientious deacons in the Plains Baptist Church. Earlier, when they did know, they were fleeing from it—to Greenwich Village or to Paris or somewhere exactly to escape from the annual Bible Question Bee and excessive knowledge of the genealogical tables of King David. The "interfering spirit of righteousness" in American religious culture has set on edge the teeth of most of the country's better writers, including many who write about politics for newspapers.

American writers of talent are more likely to produce *Elmer Gantry*, the far better-known but not better book, to which Wilder's book might be taken as a kind of implicit answer. In external ways Wilder's hero is very much like Elmer Gantry; muscular, disciplined, corn-fed, a successful athlete (or "ath-a-

lete," as Lewis would hear them say), a Baptist. They represented
the small town Bible-belt Protestants of our national history and
mythology. However while in the better-known book Sinclair
Lewis made Gantry an object of contemptuous satire, Wilder,
without altering the identifying objective facts, captures the
spirit of it in an amiable inward way, giving the thing a sizable
turn, and although showing his multitudinous faults—and what
Mr. Carter in a George Brushian way would call his "mistakes,"
which are many—makes Brush a sympathetic character.

I first noticed the parallel between the very real Jimmy Carter
and the fictional George Brush, somewhat ironically I suppose,
when I read the full text of the notorious *Playboy* interview.
Taken *in toto* it gives a *very* different effect from the famous
quoted snippets. I made a little list of some parallels, which have
now extended beyond that interview.

*Promises*.

Brush is a great list-maker, schedule-maker, promise-keeper,
full of self-improving resolutions. He was in Wellington, Oklaho-
ma, on his twenty-third birthday: "Tremendous were the good
resolutions adopted that morning. It was to be a great year."
Carter as candidate for the Georgia State Senate promised to read
through every bill he voted on; when he got to the Senate, he
says, he *did* it, even though it meant much early rising.

> *Carter* (to *Playboy*): I remember keeping a check list and
> every time I made a promise during the campaign, I wrote it
> down in a notebook. I believe I carried out every promise I
> made.

Carter had the "promises" that he made during his campaign
for the Presidency put down on paper—characteristically—in a
long compilation called (of course) "promises, promises," with
(this is an intriguing feature) gradations of the degree of his
commitment. Early in his term this document was an object of
curiosity and search by the press; a copy was held triumphantly
before the cameras one night by Ed Bradley of CBS.

Engage the will; commit the self by lists, promises, and resolutions; write them down; check them off. One of his aides says,
"Violating even the smallest promise bothers him." "Promises"
were made; "promises" are now to be fulfilled.

What's wrong with that? What's wrong is the expectation it arouses, the legalistic outlook it encourages, the disillusionment it leads to, and the picture of the self and the world it implies (freer and simpler than they are). It is hard enough in person-to-person relations to fulfill the most unequivocal oath; as the numbers of persons increase, the "gradations" of the oath-taking elaborate themselves, the meanings of words shift.

Carter regarded the relationship of his campaign to his government as a one-to-one link of promises made and then fulfilled. But the political relationship of candidate to the many institutions and the enormous population he will serve in an official capacity is mostly not susceptible to the simplicity of clear-cut personal promise. There are other actors. There is a limited capacity to deliver. It is hard enough just in individual relationships to achieve clear understanding so that the expectations on both sides are the same.

Politicians fail to do what some expect—think they have been "promised"—in great collective relationships, not because of a moral failure but because the actor does not have his hands on all the levers of action and is only one among many; and because the hearers are many and diverse, with many different nuances of understanding, listening, half-listening, interpreting, having the words interpreted by intermediaries. A deep cynicism in American culture about politicians has to do in part of course with allegedly "broken promises." But that tells as much about the public as about the politicians—perhaps even more about the complex relationship in which the many agents act.

I will balance the budget by 1980. I'll balance it if the appropriations that Congress makes allow me to. If the overriding demands of other promises don't prevent me from doing so. I will do it, I will balance the budget—if the GNP rises at a rate that will make that possible. Well, then, I will balance the budget in a *full employment* sense; there would be a budget that would be balanced *if* the economy were operating at full employment.

President Carter's shifting on this point is not a moral violation. But it would be better not to deal in the language of "promises."

### Not Lying.

George Brush is *very* careful about not lying, about telling the truth, even if it hurts. And something of what I have said above

applies to Carter's "I'll never lie to you." Well, most people,
particularly in the field of politics, would be disinclined to use the
word "never" even in intimate one-to-one personal relationships,
let alone in the enormously complex relations of politics. "I'll try
not to mislead you." The flatness of Carter's statement marks a
different temperament. Part of the problem is raising the issue in
the first place, and part rests with the words "lie" and "never":
lying and truth-telling are as simple sounding to the literal minded, and are as complicated in real life as is promising. "Never" is
one of those words the worldly wise don't use: it's absoluteness
asks for trouble. What followed from candidate Carter sometimes
was an exercise in fine-print reading (simple justice—you can
depend on it—"as revenues permit." Ah! Quite a qualification on
the promise—since revenues almost never do permit!).

Resolutions, lists of improving habits.

As one is to be bound absolutely to others by promises and
truths, so one binds oneself, pulls one's own will upward by
resolutions, regimens, planned lists of habits. Fix the self by
planning it, by regular practices. Such men, of course, have a
regimen. Brush regularly reads the Bible, keeps quotations from
Gandhi with him, and says his prayers even though it means that
other passengers on a pullman, seeing him do it, begin pelting
him with their shoes. Carter, reading the New Testament in
Spanish, was up to II Thessalonians by the time of the Indiana
primary, and cited Gandhi's list of seven sins in his eulogy of
Hubert Humphrey.

> Playboy: We've heard that you pray 25 times a day. Is that
> true?
> Carter: I've never counted, I've forgotten who asked me that,
> but I'd say that on an eventful day, you know, it's something
> like that.

The following could have come from Wilder's hero, from Ben
Franklin, from a Horatio Alger hero, from Boy's Life.

> There are certain habits of thinking which have a good effect
> upon health. If you think in the right way, you'll develop:
>   1. The habit of expecting to accomplish what you attempt.

2. The habit of expecting to like other people and to have them like you.

3. The habit of deciding quickly what you want to do, and doing it.

4. The habit of "sticking to it."

5. The habit of welcoming fearlessly all wholesome ideas and experiences [it appears that he first wrote "fearfully" and corrected it].

6. A person who wants to build good mental habits should avoid the idle daydream, should give up worry and anger, hatred and envy, should neither fear nor be ashamed of anything that is honest or purposeful.

It comes from Jimmy Carter. It is a document that he wrote when he was twelve, and which Miss Lillian handed to William Greider of *The Washington Post*.

Mr. Greider also quoted "Jimmy Carter's Health Report," given to him with a trusting lack of prudence or ceremony by Carter's mother: "Mrs. Carter did not exactly dote over the material—she handed a stack of old school papers to the visitor and promptly left the house to run errands." In the document the twelve-year-old Jimmy Carter wrote:

> In order that your brain may work well in school hours you must make good use of playtime. . . . Take happy thoughts to bed with you. . . . Correct posture helps the organs of your body do their work properly with less wasted effort. . . . The sloucher is likely to look upon himself as a failure. His posture may unconsciously reflect his own poor opinion of himself and pass this opinion on to others.

Mr. Greider adds:

> Jimmy did not slouch. He practiced deep breathing and chest-expanding exercises. He obviously did not see himself as one of life's future failures.

*Self-improvement, Self-reliance.*

George Brush reads *King Lear* every morning while shaving because he was told it was an excellent piece of literature. He keeps in shape of course. If he were not a pacifist he could beat up the fellows who taunt him; they are "all rotted out with tobacco and liquor."

Here is a passage from *Time* about Carter:

> Susan Clough types the musical program on a tidy series of yellow three-by-five cards and places them on the President's desk so that he can make mental notes of what he is hearing. Some of the music for this Wednesday: Bach's Toccata and Fugue in D minor, Verdi's *Otello*, Gounod's *Romeo et Juliette*, selections from Puccini and Mozart.
>
> Carter is an almost compulsive believer in such self-improvement. He has been studying the White House works of art. In February he asked White House Curator Clem Conger for historical details about all the objects in the Oval Office, which include an 18th century portrait of Benjamin Franklin by Jean-Baptiste Greuze, a Frederic Remington bronze, *Broncho Buster* (circa 1901), and the only known replica of Charles Willson Peale's portrait of George Washington, which is currently valued at $400,000 to $600,000. Carter recently stunned the curator of Washington's Corcoran Gallery of Art with his detailed knowledge of American artists. Thanks to a speed-reading course that he and his family just completed, the President now zips along at a rapid 1,200 words a minute. One night last week, as part of his final exam, he went through three entire books, including John Steinbeck's *Of Mice and Men*.

A moral man of this stripe also takes care of his own domestic needs—self-reliance.

> *Playboy* (in the middle of a discussion of foreign policy): Say, do you always do your own sewing? (This portion of the interview also took place aboard a plane. As he answered the interviewer's questions Carter had been sewing a rip in his jacket with a needle and thread he carried with him.)
> *Carter*: Uh-huh. (He bit off the thread with his teeth.)

*Frugality.*

Needless to say George Brush in Wilder's novel is an excellent book salesman who works hard, takes care of himself, does his chores, sells more books than any other salesman, and is so conscientious about his expense account that he is correct— although not correct about the motive—in believing that the president of the textbook company he works for himself reads over his expense accounts. "Brush's expense account statements were unlike any others ever received in the office. He recorded every nickel and expended a large amount of ingenuity in saving the firm's money. He never doubted that the great Mr. Caulkins examined his reports in person, and he was right. Mr. Caulkins not only read them; he took them home to his wife, and carried them about with him in his pocket to show his friends at the club."

As to Carter's frugality, Robert Shogan tells in his book *Promises to Keep*, an account of Carter's first one hundred days in office, the story of Rafshoon, who wears the same shirt size, bringing Carter a blue shirt for the nationally televised debate:

> "How much did you pay for it?" Carter asked.
> "Twenty dollars," Rafshoon said.
> "Twenty dollars?" Carter said indignantly. "I've never had a shirt for more than eight dollars."
> "He was really offended," said Rafshoon, who, when I talked to him, was still waiting for Carter to return either the shirt or the twenty dollars.

*Literal-mindedness.*

Subtlety, nuance, qualification, appropriation, casuistry, ambiguity lead down the slippery slope away from the good and right. The American Doer of Right sets tasks to himself that avoid those dangers. As this American is, or tries to be, resolute, so he is also literal in the complete fulfillment of his resolutions.

In *Why Not The Best?* the morally earnest American autobiographer explains (can it be a boast?) that when he set out to campaign for the Presidency he "studied the campaign platforms of all unsuccessful candidates for President since our electoral process began." Contemplate for a moment what that sentence says: this literal-minded Georgia Governor, striving to attain the great prize of the Presidential office, thereupon read dutifully through the platforms on which James G. Blaine, Alton B. Parker, and Alfred M. Landon went down to defeat. And not just those. It is characteristic that Mr. Carter said that he read *all* of those platforms, and that he did so "in order to avoid mistakes."

I believe that Mr. Carter's tendency to use absolutes, superlatives, exaggerations and quite literal, flat, unqualified statements is a reflection of his moralistic frame of mind. The President said

he felt Mr. Warnke was the best man in the country for the job—
"thoroughly and totally qualified" (*totally* qualified!). Griffin
Bell, he said, would be a "great" Attorney-General, ultimately
viewed as a "superlative choice"; the sum total of his rulings
would "withstand *any* scrutiny." Of Stanfield Turner of the CIA
he said: "I have never known a better military person" (*never!*).
"Totally," "completely," "superb," "superlative," "absolutely":
these words run through Carter's speech, sometimes doubled up.

At the announcement of her appointment, the Secretary of the
Commerce-designate, Jaunita Kreps, needled Carter about
this—about introducing her as the *best* choice, especially when
she and the world knew others had been asked; she needled him
gently also about the relative paucity of the "best" women. Plainly there are in the country 5,000 people—to pick a number—
including many women, who could do well in the job of Secretary
of Commerce or any other of the jobs in the Cabinet, including
Secretary of State. It is not the kind of thing that can be measured
by a single unequivocal superlative: by its human and political
nature, by its complexity and subtlety, it cannot be properly
judged by a single absolute standard.

Mr. Carter having created his Cabinet looked upon it and
called it, of course, "superb." The first Cabinet meeting was,
according to the man who appointed its members, "absolutely
superb and possibly unprecedented." (It would seem at least
enough to be superb without being absolutely superb.) The
Cabinet choices were also "superlative"; moreover in at least the
first two of his Cabinet choices—that is Secretary Vance and
OMB Director Lance—the appointments were not only "superlative" but Carter had "complete confidence" in these two men.
One would think confidence would be enough without its being
"complete." (The completeness of Mr. Carter's confidence in
Mr. Lance was affirmed not only in this moment at the outset of
Lance's governmental career but again at its end, when President
Carter unhappily accepted his resignation.)

And it is not appointees only in whom Mr. Carter's confidence
is "complete." At his press conference of May 27, 1977—for just
one example—at which he was defending the gradual U.S. withdrawal of troops from South Korea, he said, "We have also
*complete confidence* in the deep purpose of the South Koreans to
defend their own country." Later he said again that the South

Korean security has been brought about by "our *complete confidence* in the Republic of Korea and its ability, and a *complete awareness* on the part of the *rest of the world* that our own commitment is *firm*" (emphasis mine, although the emphatic language is his).

This use of such superlatives and exaggerations is a kind of verbal moral exertion: it is an effort to *push* the world, the hearers, perhaps oneself, up to the true, the beautiful, the good, the BEST, the completely superb, by words, like a preacher in a pulpit or one who is trying to arouse the will of others and of one's self by a proclamatory overreaching. We *can* do it. Why *don't* we? The will can be charged up to do what it ought to do by the pumping of words of sufficient elevation.

In his press conferences, at his best, as on many issues, foreign and domestic, Mr. Carter functions at a higher intellectual level than Presidents ordinarily do. One cannot help but contrast his detailed, knowledgeable, informative answers to questions to those of the first President under whom we had full access to press conference texts, Dwight Eisenhower (Ike would say, about some issue discussed daily in the newspapers: "They haven't told me about that"). But none of the others—including Kennedy—matches Carter in this regard: explaining the cruise missile-backfire bomber issue, or the competitive position of the U.S. steel industry, or the complexities of Palestinian representation at a Middle East conference. On such matters he has had no Presidential peer; he is more like a top aide who has all the facts than like most policy-makers who rely on others. He can be a kind of teacher to the nation, at that level, on complicated and weighty subjects.

But one might ask that he do the same sort of thing at the next level up, so important to him, the level of the purposes and moral realities. At that range he reverts to simplicity if not simplicism. One wishes he was as sophisticated about political ideas as he is about the concrete ingredients of specific issues of public policy.

· It is peculiarly fitting that the first shaking crisis of the fledgling Carter administration—its Bay of Pigs, so to speak—should have been the Bert Lance affair. A human drama of considerable moral complexity, it was itself in part caused, as President Carter said in the unusual press conference at which he accepted Lance's resignation, by the "high moral standards" he himself had set.

It was a drama in which the roughage of actual life bumped against the purity of the simple standards that go under the name of morality in this administration and in this culture.

(There certainly were aspects of the life of good Methodists Bert and Labelle Lance of "Butterfly Manna" that would remind a skeptical observer not of Wilder's naive hero but of the world Sinclair Lewis satirized in *Elmer Gantry*: from those who have been loaned much, much will be required.)

President Carter's treatment of the matter in that remarkable press conference was instructive: the words were the old unequivocal moralism, but the music was a regretful realism.

Characteristically Mr. Carter could not bring himself to admit that there was anything in Mr. Lance's behavior that was subject to censure. The affirmation of Mr. Lance's goodness and integrity rang through the whole press conference, with all the aforementioned superlatives: Bert Lance was a good man who did a good job at the OMB, who performed his duties "in a superlative way." "He's a good man"; "I know him without any doubt in my mind or heart to be a good and an honorable man . . . there is no doubt about Bert's being a man of complete integrity." (Not just integrity, but *complete* integrity.) As Carter regarded Lance as a man and as an administrator of the OMB, so he regarded Lance as a witness before the Senate committee: "He had to answer allegations and he did well. He told the truth." (He'll never lie to you?) "I thought Bert did a superb job Thursday, Friday, and Saturday in answering all the questions that had been leveled about him and against him." The standards to which government officials are to be held are still as high as ever. Characteristically President Carter admitted no qualification in those requirements either in the future or looking back to the way he had applied them to Bert Lance. He turned aside any efforts to be specific about points at issue in Lance's banking career. As a man, as a banker, as OMB director, and as witness before the Senate committee he was, according to President Carter's final press conference, morally umblemished, totally, superlatively, superbly, completely.

Nevertheless, Carter accepted his resignation.

Though the language was that of an absolute moral standard, which this man had in no way violated, the deed reflected the "limitation and fragmentation of all our human striving," to quote Carter's theologian Niebuhr. "There is none good, no not one," to quote another source. It was necessary to let this close friend go, even though it was humanly distressing, for reasons of the political good. The Jimmy Carter who appeared before the press and twice had to clear his throat because of the emotions of the moment was a human being trying to make sure that his friend left government service with minimum damage to his reputation and future. He was a realistic politician acknowledging the actual condition that it was hard to fit the post-Watergate standards for government officials to the free-wheeling banking practices in which Bert Lance had engaged. Through all the superlatives and absolutes and the insistence that nothing was wrong with Lance or with the Carter administration's interpretation of political morality there nevertheless ran a thread of adjustment to the world. It was in a sense the moment when the Carter administration rejoined the human race.

Mr. Carter plainly was a person standing by his friend, moved by his friend's plight, and admitting he had helped to cause it—a human Jimmy, not a stern moralist. The Carter administration could no longer effectively claim to be made of a categorically superior moral cloth, and that was just as well.

Although Wilder treats George Brush with amusement, and has almost everything he does as a result of his "principles" turn out differently from what he intended, and badly, and makes plain the severe limitation of his outlook, still Wilder's point of view on his young hero is quite different from that of Lewis toward Gantry. It is not disdainful. Wilder suggests that his character, in fact, has in him something of the author's own idealistic youth as a missionary's child. He respects something in Brush, and at the end he suggests that Brush may be learning to be wiser. The epigraph of the book is "of all forms of genius, goodness has the longest awkward age." Brush is a good man in a very awkward stage.

Popular American notions of "morality" have been locked into that awkward stage. Deriving mostly from what the free church Protestantism of the frontier did to Puritanism (by oversimplifying it); lacking therefore what a Catholic culture at its best may contain—not Ireland's, not Spain's, not that of the U.S. (then where?)—namely, grace, tradition, and intelligent casuistry, it sees the moral life as melodrama. I mention casuistry—a bad word to modern ears perhaps, but a term for part of what's missing: calibrated, discriminating reasoning. This much, yes; that much, no; this situation, yes; that, no (for these perennial reasons).

In this country where the revival tent followed the Puritan chapel we have dealt in the simplicity of literal commandments that are applicable only with difficulty to life in politics.

In the Protestant regions and especially in the regions where the free churches have held sway and an individualistic social philosophy has prevailed—that is to say in the provincial United States—a simple morality has had a central place. It would be the centerpiece of a Baptist church in the South. It would be what one would learn in the Baptist Young People's Union.

The mark of such a moral training is clear on Jimmy Carter, for good and ill. Namely, it is for the good in that the modern world, without such training, slips steadily into the morass of the amoral and immoral elimination of standards—better an oversimple morality than none. A stiff-necked moral simplicity is at least a corrective to cynicism and can be made effective symbolically.

But the faults of such morality are many. They coincide all too well with the older way we Americans thought about moral problems, before we faced the many-sided obligations and goods and evils in the modern world.

It leads then to a flipping back and forth between moralism and cynicism. If one's notion of what is right and good is absolute, perfect, and unadjustable, then one soon discovers that the actual world does not fit it; the flip side of moralism then is cynicism. There are no holding places, no terraced gradations of under-standing in a simple moralistic outlook. Persons less earnest than George Brush and Jimmy Carter fall therefore into the cynicism which is the companion to moralism in American culture. And never stronger than at present.

The list of absolute rules tends to fasten onto pieces and parts of life that have become heavily moralized, usually by a religious community, and to leave whole swatches of important areas of human living untouched. These lists of dos and don'ts—mostly of don'ts—are not the spur to a creative morality that looks at the possibilities of the world and its needs. To think of moral life as literal conformity to unqualified requirements—as lists, promises, and resolutions—implies a false picture of our actual life, and makes trouble.

Wiser thinkers about the political world have said that it is necessary to take account of the average deficiencies of mankind—not to assume but rather to take account of that persistent inclination of men and women to fall short of what would be "best." But this notion is un-American. From the nineteenth-century revivalist preacher to the twentieth-century teacher in Columbia Teachers College the American inclination has been in the other direction: what we *can* do.

The geniune striver, persistent, disciplined, shaping his life around his lists and promises and resolutions, has a hard time avoiding the thought that he is better than the drunkards and lechers in the boardinghouse, all these others that do not behave as he does. His day-to-day experience seems to confirm in him a premise of his own moral superiority. A subtler morality, in which pride is itself a deeper sin than the misdeeds of one's fellows, undercuts such a self-righteous inclination. But on the whole the literal simplicism of this moral outlook has not had that resource.

The self is to be "improved"—but the neighbor also.

Extending the norms of one's own life to the conduct of others is a universal human inclination. It is difficult indeed to discipline oneself to pursue any of the great goods, or avoid any of the evils, of living without imposing on one's fellows the obligation to do the same: a writer struggling mightily with his Fowler and his paragraphs grinds his teeth at the prose inflicted on him by TV commercials, newspapers, college students, and the Federal Register; a money-saving hard worker who remembers how he "scrimped and saved" has difficulty tolerating the blatant waste of governmental bureaucracy or twenty-dollar shirts; a chaste and monogamous Baptist deacon is inclined to recommend that those who are "living in sin" get married, and wandering fathers get reacquainted with their children; the teetotaling wives of frontier drunks want demon rum denied to *everybody* by law.

When he was campaigning in California during the primaries, Mr. Carter spoke to the California Senate and made a comment that may have been an oblique reference to Governor Jerry Brown's skeptical attitude toward the capacity of government and of society to *fix* the world. Carter said he wanted "an aggressive President who would put himself in the thick of the battle for a better America." Then he went on to make the following interesting statement:

> There are those who believe it is not worthwhile to try, that
> human nature never changes, that the human condition is
> fixed forever and that all struggle for human betterment is
> futile. I do not believe that. I believe that the essence of a
> worthwhile life is in the striving. I do not fear failure, but I do
> fear the resigned acceptance of what is mean or mediocre or
> wrong.

The answer is always to strive, to try harder, to give more effort, never to say that a good deal of life is a settling for what is possible under the circumstances.

There may not then be much room for the forgiving adjustment to others' limitations and failures. There is the danger of an implicit premise of one's own moral superiority. As Brush would have outbursts of self-righteousness, so Jimmy Carter's critics detect in him a tendency to take his own superiority both moral and intellectual as a given.

There is a moment in Wilder's book when George Brush, confused a little by the antagonism he seems to engender in his boardinghouse roommates asks (a very Brushian question) "What ought I to do?" He is given some sensible advice: "Get to be one of the fellas. Learn to drink, like anybody else. And leave other people's lives alone. Live and let live. Everybody likes to be let alone. And run around with the women. You're healthy, ain't ya? Enjoy life, see? You're going to be dead a long time, *believe* me." George Brush's response to this straightforward advice is of course a complete and indignant repudiation: "I'd rather be crazy all alone than sensible like you fellows are sensible."

*Sex and Marriage.*

Now I want to complicate the picture a little. If Carter sometimes seems to be George Brush, he is such a person after much more experience. And he has other qualities. And as I have said, the story of his emergence has to do not only with him but also with his puzzled interpreters. The press and the sophisticated urban community, including Washington, looking at such a person, may see more with the hostile eyes of Sinclair Lewis than with the amiable understanding of Thornton Wilder.

The subject by which to illustrate this point—or raise it at least—is the salient topic in the *Playboy* interview, sexual morality.

George Brush is of course an absolutist about sexual morality, to the point of absurdity. The evil that he would not do he did once, with a farmer's daughter, and he therefore feels bound to her forever. He searches for her; he finally finds her working in the Rising Sun Chop Suey Palace; insists that they marry, even though neither loves the other and she doesn't want to marry him. He feels he is required to by sexual ethics, and has in mind a dutiful program of producing the half dozen children he believes essential to the ideal American home. The marriage predictably is not happy. When his sister-in-law suggests a divorce he says, "Are you going to be like those big city folk, with such ideas?"

Carter's actual experience is very different from that of George Brush, to be sure, but the ethical point-of-view has strong similarities.

*Carter*: I'll have been away from Rosalynn for a few days and if I see her across an airport lobby, or across a street, I get just as excited as I did when I was, you know, 30 years younger.
*Playboy*: A lot of marriages are foundering these days. Why is yours so successful?
*Carter*: Well, I really love Rosalynn more now than I did when I married her. And I have loved no other women except her.
*Playboy*: . . . In San Francisco, you said you considered homosexuality a sin. What does that mean in political terms?
*Carter*: The issue of homosexuality always makes me nervous. It's obviously one of the major issues in San Francisco. I don't have any, you know, personal knowledge about homosexuality and I guess being a Baptist, that would contribute to a sense of being uneasy.
*Playboy*: Does it make you uneasy to discuss it simply as a political question?
*Carter*: No, it's more complicated than that. It's political, it's moral and it's strange territory for me. At home in Plains, we've had homosexuals in our community, our church. There's never been any sort of discrimination—some embarrassment but no animosity, no harassment. But to inject it into a public discussion on politics and how it conflicts with morality is a new experience for me.

At a Cabinet meeting early in his administration he told his new colleagues to maintain wholesome family relationships during their government tenure. "You should watch yourselves and keep your families together." He recommended exercise and off-the-job recreation. "I don't want your families breaking up because of your loyalty to me." (Parenthetically, in addition to the Brushian comedy of it this is quite an autobiographical interpretation of the relationships among high government officials.)

After he had been in office half a year there appeared an Associated Press story beginning: "Jimmy Carter is President of the United States, leader of the western world—and marriage counselor?" The story went on to say that he "touts" marriage and sometimes pushes his aides to give up single life for holy wedlock.

The wire service story says that Greg Schneiders, director of White House projects and his wife Marie "dated for five years." The subject of marriage came up in talks with Carter during campaign.

"It did not make any difference to us if we got married sooner or later," said Schneiders, "but Jimmy Carter and I finally agreed that sooner would be better than later. When Tim Kraft, Carter's appointments secretary, married in April, the President was so elated by the news that he gave Kraft more time than had been planned for his honeymoon."

A *Newsweek* story on "living together" a month later said: "Although staffers insist that Carter does not interfere with their personal lives, the fact is that a number of his aides have belatedly tied the knot—including Jack Watson, Greg Schneiders, Tim Kraft and Rex Granum, Federal Trade Commission head Mike Pertschuk and State Department official Richard Holbrooke. 'It does seem to defy the laws of probability,' admits one White House insider."

Now let me raise some question about these and other reports. Might one not say about this *Newsweek* list that it is as striking that Carter would have so many people around him who were living together without being married as the fact that they subsequently got hitched? A more strictly puritanical sort would not have had such a collection of "sinners" around him to begin with. The news reports about the life of his young assistants do not present them as paragons of Baptist virtue in the sexual field. In fact, there came a moment early in the administration when an

Episcopal priest who is also a newsman asked rather belligerently, to the merriment of the Washington press corps, a question of the President about the living arrangements and sexual morality of persons on his staff.

Carter's answer was genial and gentle, explaining that *one* part of the question was certainly correct (much laughter from the press) that he and Rosalynn were monogamous. He did not however propose to do anything about the allegations about his staff except to "pray for them." It was not a censorious or puritanical performance. Negative news stories in conservative newspapers came at Carter from the other direction, depicting him as one who tolerated promiscuity in his staff.

It was necessary to see and hear his famous remarks in the early weeks of the administration, about "living in sin" in order to capture their flavor. He made these remarks on a visit to HEW. Here's what he said: "Those of you who are living in sin, I hope you'll get married. Those of you who left your spouse, go home. Those of you who have forgotten your children's names, go home and get reacquainted."

The words certainly lend themselves to the interpretation that he was being "puritanical," censorious, the Baptist deacon applying his own moralism to other people's lives. But he made his remarks in a rather friendly, almost humorous way. He did not say or imply that anything other than one's own conscience would impinge on anyone's behavior.

There's a nice moment in Norman Mailer's *New York Times Magazine* story about Carter in which Mailer reports Carter learning about Mailer's four wives and multiple children, and saying "with all his humor in his eyes": "Good luck."

The repeated point of the *Playboy* interview, the point which led to Carter's notorious statements at the end, was that he was not what the interviewers thought him to be: a righteous, lawgiving, puritanical moralizer. He got himself in trouble with the *Playboy* interviewers exactly because he was trying to overcome their heavy stereotype about the attitudes he was supposed to hold.

Robert Sheer, the *Playboy* interviewer, kept coming back to this topic even after he'd been answered with an insistence that once provoked anger in Carter, and which suggests a heavy prejudice and stereotype in the interviewer.

And so I wonder about the report like the one written by Eleanor Randolph of *The Chicago Tribune* in an article in *Esquire* magazine for November, 1977, called "The Carter Complex." Among a number of negative items left over from the campaign summer about the Carters, there is reported this exchange involving Greg Schneiders and his girlfriend:

> Once, when Schneiders was trying to prepare Carter for a possible press-conference on adultery, Carter took the opportunity to remind Schneiders once again that he was "living in sin."
>
> "Well, if I have any questions on adultery, I will refer them to you," Carter told him.
>
> "That would be fine, sir, except that I'm not married, so technically I can't commit adultery," Schneiders replied.
>
> "Well, then," Carter continued, "if I have a question on fornication, I'll refer them to you."
>
> Schneiders insists that comments like this did not push him to the altar, but shortly after the election he and Marie got married. While they were on their honeymoon in the Caribbean, Schneiders learned that he would not get the appointments job but would be in the White House basement figuring out ways to keep Carter in touch with the people. It was not in any way a set-up.

Maybe it all happened that way and maybe there was a link between Schneiders's job and his living arrangements. But Schneiders is still working for Carter. His more visible difficulties had to do with his past financial life, not his marital arrangements; and one doesn't need to read very far in Randolph's article, good though it is, to see that it is written from a hostile premise. And one doesn't need to talk to very many Washington reporters to see that they are capable on this subject of unbendable stereotypes.

At a Washington restaurant early in the Carter days a friend of mine who is a White House reporter with a high social intelligence, but a dim view of Carter—a person not ordinarily given to conspiracy theories—told me darkly that he and his colleagues believed that there must be somebody in the Carter entourage *specifically charged* with checking up on the marital status of the administration people. I thought the conversation revealed more about the expectations and prejudices of his group of newspersons than about Carter. Later Mr. Hamilton Jordan was to rise in power in Carter's White House at the same time gossipists in the Washington press were reveling in his after-hours escapades.

Of course Carter is personally conservative and conventional on issues of sexual morality. But is not the more notable point his disinclination to impose his values on others? He has not reproduced the worst "interfering spirit of righteousness" which tries to make over the neighbors' morals—the outlook associated with the Anti-Saloon League and with the past history of Evangelical Protestantism. But a wary world of writers and observers seems to find that hard to believe, and seems still to take its cues on this point from H. L. Mencken.

If Carter has in him something of George Brush then Washington has many of Brush's boardinghouse roommates.

# 8

# Plan and Count; Count and Plan

A White House correspondent who does not like Carter said, as he glumly stirred his Bloody Mary with the celery stick at the Monocle restaurant on Capitol Hill, "Carter takes this *managerial* approach to government; he thinks everything can be solved by *managing*."

Where had this new President been to college? Where did he read political philosophy and history and literature, absorb the ideas and evelop the sensibility with which he would govern as leader of the free world? His college was Annapolis . . . whatever its merits, scarcely a center of the liberal arts.

Who was his hero? Hyman Rickover, admiral, engineer, bureaucracy-beater, the crusty maker of nuclear submarines, peremptory perfectionist. "He had a profound effect on my life, more perhaps than anyone except my parents." I asked a more recent Annapolis graduate who had gone on to a broader political and humanistic education how Rickover was regarded, and the answer was not reassuring. One phrase he used about Rickover was "total prima donna." Back in the 1950s I had read a book by Rickover in which he issued brusque orders to the American educational system to straighten itself out. Jimmy Carter himself said the following about Admiral Rickover: "He was unbelievably hardworking and competent and he demanded total dedication from his subordinates" (*total* dedication!).

Mr. Carter's campaign list of the alleged qualities of the American people was of course a kind of billiard shot—a way of saying indirectly that his opponents (tainted by association with Washington, with Insideness, with actual government) *lacked* these qualities, while he, the outsider, bound to "the people," possessed them. The list included not only words like "compassionate," "decent," "honest" and "filled with love," but also the word "competent," which made rather a metallic contrast with those other softer words.

If one asks what Jimmy Carter believes in—that is, what he holds to as a political philosophy—one receives a good deal of mumbling and vagueness as an answer. The word "populist" has only an intermittent application, fading in and out; "conservative" applies only in certain regards, and only some of the time; "liberal" applies perhaps even less ("The liberals are a waste of time," said his son Jack). Most of Mr. Carter's visceral commitments seem to be found not at the level of ideology but above it and below it: above it in the realm of moral affirmation; below it in the realm of managerial skill.

Here's the way Mr. Carter described himself in an interview when he was a candidate: "As President, I will start by giving management issues a high priority on my own schedule." About his appointees he said with chilling directness, "Those who cannot manage will not remain in office." Though there are no chapters on his economic or racial policies, and only the most general chapter on foreign policy, one whole chapter in his short autobiography is devoted to zero-based budgeting.

When he had received the nomination of his party to run for the nation's highest office, an office drenched in moral, historical, and cultural meaning for this nation and for mankind, what did he say on accepting that nomination? Well, he said many things, to be sure; he had typically, his list and his points, and one or two of them are more worthy of the moment than the sentence I will quote. But I think it is "fair" (to use one of his own words) to cite the following, as something close to his heart, a banner he held out to the troubled people: "As President, I want you to help me evolve an efficient, economical, purposeful and manageable government for our nation. I recognize the difficulty, but if I'm elected, it's going to be done!"

*The Wall Street Journal* article about him based on "dozens of interviews with upper and middle echelon figures in the administration" by that newspaper's reporters included this striking question and answer:

Does he have any vision?
Almost without exception the answer is no.

The qualities of mind that are associated with engineers and managers—the meticulously practical, inductive, fact-linked, down-to-earth, making-things-work-better outlook that carefully takes the world case-by-case to fix it in separable units, that plans everything and counts everything is—with all its great value at its "best"—still not the cast of mind that lifts the hearts of mankind or redefines the moral boundaries of the world. Vision, imagination, insight: these are not its strengths. The heart does not leap up as the parade goes by, with its banners reading "COMPE-TENCE!"

Carter's outlook in these matters has been examined, to our profit, in an article in *The Wilson Quarterly* (Winter, 1977) called "Jimmy Carter's Theory of Governing," by Jack Knott and Aaron Wildavsky. The authors described the aspect of Carter here discussed by saying that he had exhibited "a stronger belief in the *procedures* of governing than in the substance of policy . . . procedures about which he speaks with passion, determination and consistency." The two authors drew not only upon Carter's speeches and interviews, and his book, but also upon his experience as Governor of Georgia to demonstrate that "his concern is less with particular goals than with the need for goals, less with the content of policies than their ideal form—simplicity, uniformity, predictability, hierarchy, and comprehensiveness."

Make it predictable, uniform, simple; reorganize government into fewer units. "No candidate since Herbert Hoover, the Great Engineer, would have thought it important to talk to the public about so arcane a subject as zero-based budgeting, going so far as to include it in his five-minute television spots . . ."

The authors have little trouble identifying the faults in each of Carter's procedural principles. Take, for example, simplifying reorganization (they quote at the head of the article Alfred North Whitehead: "Seek simplicity and distrust it"). Assuming Carter to be right that the number of federal agencies is 1,900, then . . .

Reducing the number of agencies at the top of the hierarchy necessarily increases the number at the bottom. If there were only ten big departments each could have 190 sub-units, and if there were ten at each level, an issue would have to go through 19 bureaus before it was decided.

The criterion of *predictability* is particularly interesting. I remember how Rosalynn Carter's eyes flashed as she told assembled Hoosiers that under the current Washington bunch, businessmen and farmers didn't know what to count on: conditions weren't steady and predictable the way they would be when "Jimm-eh" took over. Well, within limited spheres one does wish for predictable government performance: one doesn't need much exposure to undertakings that are tied to the annual legislative budget cycle to deplore such avoidable idiocies as frantic spending at the end of a cycle and inability to plan for the next. Carter is not the first person to look for remedies for such avoidable unpredictable conduct. The question is whether he has his hands on the levers to correct it. Sometimes one heard in the pre-Presidential Carter managerialism the implication that the President is a kind of glorified national version of a city manager or chief executive officer of a corporation, who can make long-range plans that are sure and predictable without the interference of a Congress, a bureaucracy, the states, the citizenry and a thousand contingencies. Behind the idea of really *predictable* policies there stands the necessity of *control*.

Wildavsky and Knott point to the further difficulty—the social reality in a complicated world—that one man's predictability is another's unpredictability: if the rates for a governmental subsidy are *fixed* (predictable) to the receiver then they must *vary* (be unpredictable) with varying conditions for the taxpayer who pays them.

Predictability in the larger sense is not attainable or desirable in the great realm of history and freedom, of "politics," where a myriad of human choices and unanticipated snow storms make a future that cannot be known.

Tim Kraft, the President's appointments secretary, describes his boss as "a person who does not like surprises. He wants things planned and planned thoroughly, and he wants things to go as they've been planned." History and politics don't go as planned. However unsurprising the President's personal schedule may be—even there, for all the schedulings drawn up to the minute two weeks in advance, the imp of freedom must intervene and

Presidential trips to four continents be rather suddenly postponed—out in the drama of world affairs the possibilities of
prediction are severely limited, the more so as one leads, or as he
would rightly sometimes say, serves, a free country.

Two other characteristics of the President's outlook are closely
related to the penchant for the predictable-planned-controlled:
his counting and numbering, and his avid appetite for detail.

Numbers turn up everywhere, but nowhere more amusingly
than in those memos Hamilton Jordan wrote back during the
campaigns. (As Rickover shaped Carter so we may assume Carter, even more, shaped Jordan; he has done nothing else in his
adult life except work for Carter. "He learned his standards from
Jimmy," said one older Carter supporter in Georgia.)

During the primary campaign Jordan used something he called
"percentage of effort targeting":

> I have translated the 3,071 delegates to the national conven-
> tion . . . into points. In the equation which is developed, each
> delegate equals one point. Using this as a base and point of
> comparison, I have assigned a sequence factor of 1,569 points,
> on the premise that sequence of the primaries is one-half as
> important as the size factor.

This is taken from a Jordan memorandum quoted in Jules Witcover's *Marathon*.

> As 73 per cent of the convention delegates are selected by
> primary, I have allocated 73 per cent of the 1,569 points.
> 1,144—to the primary states, 27 per cent—425—to the non-
> primary states.

Jordan, says Witcover,

> then proceeded to allocate sequence points to the various key
> states: New Hampshire, the first primary, 150; Florida 125;
> Illinois . . . 100; and so on. Iowa, the first caucus state, was
> given 40 points.

It all sounded to me, I confess, like one of those Parker Brothers
board games that the family would try to play on Christmas
afternoon, usually losing some of the pieces. Jordan continued:

> The strategy factor is one half as important as the size factor. Consequently the strategy factor is assigned a numerical factor of 1,550, approximately half the number of delegates—1,320 points allocated to primary states and 230 to the nonprimary.

In our family I at least always had difficulty reading all the way through the instructions.

For the general election there was another such scheme:

> He started by assigning each state 1 point for each electoral vote it had, for a total of 538 points. Next he assigned half that amount for Democratic potential, and the same for need to campaign.
>
> The potential was determined by another rating system giving each state 1 point for each Democratic governor or U.S. senator; 1 point if its congressional (House) delegation had a Democratic majority; 1 point if both houses of the state legislature were Democratic; 2 points if the state gave more than 40 per cent of its vote to George McGovern in the 1972 presidential race.

And so on. For Jordan's "per cent of effort" plan he gave a numerical value to a day's campaigning by the principals as follows: Carter, 7; Mondale, 5; Rosalynn Carter, 4; Joan Mondale, 3; each Carter child, 1.

At a news briefing in September, 1976, Carter aides handed out a color-coded map and other documents showing that in the first week of formal campaigning, Carter, Mondale, their wives and children and children's wives—along with "Aunt Sissy" (Mrs. Emily Dolvin, sister of Carter's mother)—would visit 107 cities in thirty-seven states.

As with the Carter campaign, so with the Carter administration: count and plan; plan and count.

Charles Schultze, the economist, said of his boss that "He picks issues up quickly and has a mind for numbers." The propensity reaches beyond its natural province in the dismal science to the less likely realms of the arts. Roger Rosenblatt, discussing Carter's interest in the arts, said that when he was handed a complete set of de Maupassant "he remarked on the number of volumes."

As President he specified that he plays classical music from some fifty albums for eight to ten hours a day.

Meticulous attention to detail is both a personal characteristic and an expected norm for Jimmy Carter. He does it and he believes in it, and "meticulous" is one of his own words for it. All the writings about his Presidency, including his own, say that. All the observers attest to it. One of the complaints his staff have of him is that he attends to details he shouldn't take time for. As Governor of Georgia, Robert Shogan reports, he complained about the oversupply of bathroom tissue. This Commander-in-Chief of the armed forces was also the superintendent of the White House tennis courts: he required that he give his personal permission for their use. So also with the swimming pool. "The President shouldn't be spending his time deciding who gets to use the White House pool," complained one top Carter associate. "He spends hours on stuff like that. He loves detail." On the first trip to London he himself went over the list of people who would go and scratched some names, and made the decision that they should shift from Claridge's to the less expensive and less prestigious Britannia Hotel.

And these clearly vulnerable examples of attention to minutiae that a President of the United States should not deal with simply dramatize a habit of mind that is applied in other areas where the case may be more arguable. That President Carter does his homework, knows his stuff and has mastered the details is legend. Once he snapped at Jordan, when you've read as much on the subject as I have you'll have a right to an opinion. He does not need the prep sessions for press conferences that J.F.K. had, for example, with Ted Sorensen and others, because as he says he is reading all the time, preparing all the time.

Of this omnivorous appetite for detail, we may be permitted two parallel simultaneous, contradictory opinions.

It is a wasteful confusion of high policy with routine administration for the President to read the lowliest memoranda that subcabinet members wouldn't read. At that level the fact-work bias of the culture produces a fault even by its own criteria: in the vast Presidential domain there are too many memos even for the hardest working Jimmy Carter to supervise, so that to attend to some is to neglect others. And meanwhile matters of high policy also stretch beyond the reach of even Carter's hours.

There is a lack of historical imagination, of "policy" imagination, in the carrying up into the Presidential office the injunction

of Ben Franklin (or Poor Richard) and Hyman Rickover, that to do
things well one must attend to every detail oneself. Lincoln was a
poor administrator and a better model for a President.

There is another less obvious point on the negative side. It is
regularly said that all Presidents must learn, since there is no
training school. It is clear that Carter's limited experience makes
it especially necessary for him to learn (Washington, for all his
playing to the prejudice against it in the country, is a symbol and
repository of much experience and, despite the stereotypes, even
of much wisdom, especially in the years since World War II). But
how does this Georgia pupil, this too-old-fashioned and too-new-
fashioned American, interpret the learning he needs to do?
Facts. Meticulous study of details. Here this subject, there that
subject, case by case, separately. That's what America, land of
quiz kids and whiz kids, has thought the intelligence was for. But
is he—are we—learners in that deeper, more significant sense, in
which there is an overview and perhaps an alteration of values, an
enlarging of one's world view, by moving out into a larger world?
Philosophical, political, historical learning? Critical understanding? In other words, does all that mastery of fact alter values?
Does it enhance one's understanding of others' values—his or
ours (we use Carter as a pattern for the modern American, at
something like our best)? Does it deepen political and historical
understanding?

The self-assurance and self-containment present to the world a
closed system at that level: one learns facts; one learns about
others' attitudes—what Congressmen think of a rebate or tax at
the wellhead, what Senators think about the Panama Canal
treaties, etc.—in order to deal with these attitudes as pieces of
the intricate puzzle of accomplishment but not as sources of new
understanding. The American as manager lacks that political-
historical imagination and ability for self-criticism that allows him
to appreciate the perspective of others, and which marks the truly
political man.

Now for the positive side. Carter's patient and thorough absorption of *particulars* may make him, if not a prophet and
statesman, if not one who will leave a major moral deposit in the
conscience and intellect of his country, then perhaps something
else: a teacher of the facts about particular problems. We have to
pay attention to the tax on oil at wellhead, the SALT talks and the

cruise missile and the backfire bomber, the energy crisis, complicated and boring though they are. So says Carter, not from the bully pulpit (Theodore Roosevelt's phrase for the Presidency) but from the pedagogue's desk. Although he usually is not particularly effective in formal speeches, he can be very effective in press conferences, explaining the elements of a particular policy. If he is not likely to be a prophetic statesman who lifts the nation's political understanding he may sometimes be something else that is valuable, too, in its way: a teacher to the nation. The bully blackboard. It is a role the Puritans would have understood, and we understand, and not a bad one.

Given Carter's moral commitments, his selective and intermittent commitments to social justice, there might come out of his "competent" mastery of complexities a better leadership than some reformers, prophets, and visionaries would provide.

There is an American type of moral reformer lacking in the managerial virtues, who is therefore seriously deficient and vulnerable. Some specimens thereof have come out of the religious tradition and out of the tradition of moralizing politics with which Carter is affiliated. He does not, however, share their faults. He is no William Jennings Bryan, oratorically defending foolish positions.

The specific justification of the NATO alliance is being discussed in detail; an extremely impatient social gospel minister rises in unhappiness and disdain to say our role is not to settle questions of foreign policy, but to proclaim the moral ideal! Another social reforming minister is reported to have said to Henry Kissinger: "Our job is to proclaim that justice should roll down as waters; your job is to arrange the irrigation ditches." It is excessively convenient to deal only with the pure waters of justice, entirely apart from the shape of the irrigation ditches through which they must flow on the face of the actual earth.

Should President Carter prove to be a major President, it will be because he joins his moral earnestness with "tough, competent management" and the patience to attend to the irrigation ditches. It is possible that he will prove to be a better President than the Woodrow Wilson described by John Maynard Keynes— the spokesman for moral ideals who was all thumbs and boredom when it came to particulars. That would require, however, that he join his appetite for detail to a large moral and political understanding.

Now about "comprehensive" policies. Carter loves them. That the word "comprehensive" recurs as a modifier for the Carter proposals in every field is another facet of the striving, reaching cast of mind that produces the superlatives and exaggerations mentioned before. Alongside "superb" and "total," put "comprehensive" in the Carter lexicon. His tax reform is to be comprehensive. His energy program is comprehensive. (Indeed: "If it's not comprehensive, the American public will not accept it, the Congress will not act, and I will have failed.") Food prices? Farm price supports? "This is a matter that must be addressed in a comprehensive farm bill." Organized crime? Attorney General Bell is to present to the President "a comprehensive approach to the organized crime question." The welfare proposal is to be comprehensive. He seeks a comprehensive strategic arms limitation agreement and a comprehensive Middle East settlement.

Accompanying this ubiquitous comprehensiveness is an assertion of newness. He said of his welfare proposals, for example, that they represent a "complete, clear break" with the past.

Carter not only uses the word "comprehensive" about each of his policy proposals, and strives then to fulfill their sweeping promises. He makes an explicit defense of that way of doing political business—a way that is at odds with the outlook of most modern writers about administration, and most social scientists, who would defend "incrementalism" or "piecemeal engineering" against "wholistic"—i.e., comprehensive—efforts to make policy.

The heirs of John Dewey's pragmatism or instrumentalism, and the social scientists who have absorbed the thought-world of economics, with its "changes at the margin," and the public administrators and public policy people, regularly endorse step-by-step changes in public life, partly because there are "unintended side effects" one needs to observe, partly because small steps are more reversible, partly because they usually are politically possible. I remember sitting in the offices of the Secretary of HEW listening to a veteran of the long legislative history of the social security system down to the adding of Medicare and Medicaid telling the many small steps—the slices of salami—by which the modern benefit system had been built: if you can't do it this way, do it that way; if you can't get this much, get that much. Charles E. Lindblom wrote a famous article called "The Case for Muddling Through," and collaborated on a book in which the muddling through philosophy was defended under the less engaging title of "disjointed incrementalism." One argument for it is the limitation of human ability to know the future. You can't know everything. Your social policy will have effects you haven't anticipated. So move forward by attaching small "increments" to the world as it is: by half loaves, quarter loaves, small bites. One might expect the cautious mildly conservative Georgian to hold to some such view. Not so. He explicitly rejects it, at least theoretically. At two places in his autobiography he specifically rejects "incrementalism."

In the final chapter, full of peremptory commands to the world to straighten itself out to fit a Rickover/Carter sense of its proper order, he says of the changes to be made in Washington: "They cannot be made timidly or incrementally." ("Timidly" again.) Knott and Wildavsky quote his defense of the "comprehensive" as against the "incremental" approach:

> Most of the controversial issues that are not routinely well-addressed can only respond to a comprehensive approach. Incremental efforts to make basic changes are often foredoomed to failure because the special interest groups can benefit from the status quo, can focus their attention on the increments that most affect themselves, and the general public can't be made either interested or aware.

He expressed the same theory with reference to the reorganizing of government: "The most difficult thing to do is to reorganize incrementally." His commitment to "comprehensiveness" is thus a strategy: "If you try to do it one little tiny phase at a time, then all those who see their influence threatened will combine their efforts in a sort of secretive way." It is a strategy based on Carter's perception of the *power* arrangements in modern governments and societies. "They [these threatened ones] come out of their rat holes and they'll concentrate on undoing what you're trying to do." It is not a flattering picture of the opposition. "But if you are bold enough, comprehensive enough to rally the interest and support of the general electorate, then you can overcome that special interest type lobbying pressure." Comprehensiveness thus has as a part of its appeal to Carter, the drama and sweep that will attract the attention and support of the broad public: he and the aroused public with an untimid overall remaking of a whole field will route the "special interests" who come out of the "rat holes" to "work in the dark."

Carter may be more nearly correct—putting the melodrama aside—with respect to government reorganization than with respect to other fields. But the melodramatic formulation suggests already the counterarguments: "comprehensive" proposals are not necessarily true, good, or beautiful, serving the public interest simply because of their comprehensiveness. May not a proposal be comprehensive and still quite undesirable? Or "incremental"—i.e., small, related to one feature of policy only—and still good? And is the power-political strategy always as Carter describes it? Did Carter's energy proposal unite the beneficent public and scatter the special interests from their rat holes and dark places? Which category by the way describes the opponents of a higher gasoline tax? Comprehensiveness may as well unite your enemies as arouse your friendly public supporters; incremental salami-slicing may create a more favorable balance of power, because the "special interests" are fewer and negative effect upon them presumably smaller.

Is this statement, this idea, of Carter's true: "The comprehensive approach is inherently necessary to make controversial decisions." I suggest not—sometimes yes, sometimes no, not "inherently." His holding to that view derives, one would suppose, from (a) his experience with the Georgia legislature, where the special interest/public interest melodrama may coincide more nearly with reality than in the U.S. Congress; (b) his preoccupation with the sheer organizational issue, on which again it may have more consistent application than elsewhere—reorganizing government interesting the public, if it ever does, only if done with sweep; but (c) most of all, from his own temperament. This last would surely appear to be the main item: "comprehensive" is like "superb" and "total" and the "best," one of those striver-moralist high-reaching words and ideas to which the George Brushes of this world are drawn. On the morning that I write this Carter has announced a reorganizing of the Equal Opportunities agencies of the federal government—a reorganization that is, to be sure, "comprehensive."

The incrementalist-comprehensivist argument need not be decided in the abstract. Why a doctrinaire or an a priori decision? One's answer depends on varying circumstances. Carter's outlook has the merit of furnishing a counterweight against the doctrinaire incrementalism of much of the modern American policy science and public policy world. But often that world is right. Doesn't it depend upon the nature of the issue, the configuration of power, and—this seems very important, if a key is the arousal of the public—the timing? Lyndon Johnson seized the moment of the Selma march in 1965 to bring through Congress a Civil Rights Act more far-reaching in its effects, if not more "comprehensive," than even the act put on the books with all the intricate maneuvering and travail of the previous Spring. But at other times he sliced the bread. In the 1930s the moment came for the Wagner Act, which was more than a slice. But then some small slices are the start—later action adds bigger ones.

Knott and Wildavsky, illustrating the internal conflicts among Carter's principles of governing, write that comprehensiveness "in the sense of fundamental and inclusive change often contradicts predictability and simplicity." They illustrate this by reference to the food stamp program: "Fundamental changes, precisely because they are far-reaching, are unlikely to be predictable. That is how the food stamp program grew from an expected few hundred million dollars to more than $8 billion . . ." It is not exactly clear whether what Carter means by "comprehensive"—covering all the bases, all the parts and pieces of the policy's territory—is the same thing as "far-reaching" in the sense of radical. Are most of the elements in his energy proposals of 1977 "far-reaching?" Or is the "comprehensive" proposal a package of increments?

Despite his explicit commitment to "comprehensiveness" in each field of policy Carter exhibits the trait of most American pragmatic managers when it comes to either the links among fields or the philosophical underpinnings. *Time* magazine, in a lengthy discussion of his relationship to business and the economy after ten months, said "the President does tend to consider issues one by one." The magazine quotes a "senior Administration official": "Although he's a very fast learner he doesn't move easily from one concept to another. You can open one subject, and he'll quickly have it mastered. Then he'll master a second one. But he often doesn't see the relationship between the one and another, despite a really first class mind." A mind of a familiar American practical-technological type, we might add, not different really from the "incremental" people he seems on the surface to disagree with.

"Incrementalism" can be challenged in a different way from Carter's—for its disinclination to state larger philosophical and policy premises, or to engage in the larger argument about values. Pragmatic policy people, generally speaking, regard this as a waste of time if not actually dangerous (a certain amount of that social welfare salami-slicing is slipping things through on a presumably more conservative public that doesn't know what it's getting—it's not just "special interests" people who "work in the dark.") Carter, despite his Deaconship, Bible reading, and well-known devotion to Morality deals in that High Realm in such broad and simple terms as perhaps not really to differ much from the instrumentalist professional policy people. He's a manager, a product of technocratic ethos, too.

Modern effective technical management presumably does not ordinarily include the Rickover/Carter style of defiant inflexibility. Surely the canons of management in the modern organization world include injunctions to adjustment, flexibility, adaptability, learning what the situation is, and fitting one's ideas into the collaboration and dialogue with one's co-workers. But that doesn't describe Admiral Rickover, who has made a trademark of tactlessness. To describe Carter's values by the word "manager" may be misleading: he is not a product of the Harvard Business School, General Electric, or modern managerial training, but of his disciplinarian father in a small town; of Annapolis; of Admiral Rickover; of running his own small family-owned business; and of personal campaigning in a one-party state. These are not schools in the art of collaboration.

Carter's image as being "tough" and aggressive and buck-stopping and all that, and repeated statements by Carter people that *he* makes the decisions reach back behind modern organization life to the older, conservative theme of authority.

As with the "comprehensive" theme so with this one: it is the aspect of managing that is the more compatible with old-fashioned moralizing. Authority fits the picture of moral agency: clarity of moral responsibility. Comprehensiveness fits with the grand moral sweep of general principles and categorical imperatives.

When Mr. Carter had been in office a short time, ordering his day to the minute, issuing orders to his subordinates, and listening systematically to his fifty albums, there were many commentators who saw him now to be a "manager" *instead* of a "moralist." They set the later image *over against* and in *contrast* to the earlier: he was not a "Puritan" but rather an "engineer." I suggest however that we need not see these two deeply American images (Puritan or moralist; manager or engineer) as always opposed to each other. In some ways they are not. President Carter stands at the point of their intersection. He represents what is symbolized by each of those terms; he shows the ways that they overlap.

One may interpret the moralistic strain and the managerial efficiency strain in American culture as opposing tendencies, the former applied to the Americans' desire to DO GOOD and the latter representing his imperative to DO WELL (to make a million, achieve success, run a tight ship, be number one). The tapestry of our cultural history in fact might be woven around these two set in opposition to each other. When the managing is in the realm of commerce, the market, and money-making, and the moral impulse is social and altruistic, the two conflict. A great deal of American history revolves around that conflict.

But in other expressions the two are intertwined: for example, in the "philanthropic capitalist" and in the "practical idealist," phrases that describe what a great body of Americans would wish human beings to be.

As America's moralistic culture has cast up many kinds of moralizers, moralists, do-gooders, and idealists, so also America's technological culture has cast up many kinds of managers and administrators, practical and efficient persons meeting their payrolls and keeping their desks neat.

One manager is cautious, goes step-by-step. Another, in contrast, intends to be "comprehensive," and "long range." One kind of manager is adjustable, flexible, "other-directed," given to compromise, gets along by going along; another has a strong sense of the authoritative center of decisive action.

Carter, the second type in both cases, is also then more compatible with the moralizing remakers of the world. The moralist and the manager meet in their shared picture of a world swept clean to be remade by the energetic exertion of the individual will. (In theory, to be sure. In the event the comprehensivist and absolutist Carter may prove as flexible as a theoretical incrementalist.)

Mr. Carter, like Admiral Rickover, represents a combination of two major American clusters of value so interwoven as to be inextricable from each other: moral improvement and efficient management. "Incompetence" in their vocabulary is a term loaded with *moral* condemnation.

The moralizer of Mr. Carter's sort interprets the categorical imperative, the command to his will, as a claim on his total effort. If it should happen that he should fail in some high and worthy enterprise (and he does not undertake any other kind) then his response is to try harder, to keep trying. Persistence, resolution. "I'll make it up to you as President." Bumping against the world's complexity does not induce self-examination; the experience of the fragments and limits of all our efforts does not lead to rethinking or readjustment or wisdom; instead it prods still harder, a still harder try. Try, try again. And so it is with the managerial ethic in the Carter mode: include everything, do everything, work harder than everybody else. Enter every primary. Shake every hand. Cover every state. Every policy should be comprehensive. And include every area of policy in your effort. Hamilton Jordan said that Carter in his first year did not select from among the priorities in order to get some because his method was, in a basketball analogy, "the full court press." Try on the Middle East and the SALT talks and the Panama Canal and Welfare Reform and Tax Reform and Energy Policy and press on every player with total effort. (It is the nature of a full court press however that teams with good ball handlers and passing can score against it.)

One of his early supporters and associates says that Carter "likes people who have an engineer's or economist's cast of mind." (His appointees to Cabinet Level rank include five Ph.D.'s in economics, surely a record.)

If it is important to recognize the managerial virtues in their place it is equally important to recognize their subordination. It might be said that Carter is the sort of person who would make some President—some man of larger vision, eloquence, and historical understanding—an excellent chief-of-staff. It is not insignificant that he is, as Vice-President Mondale says, his own chief-of-staff: "His chief-of-staff is named Jimmy Carter. He is a guy with tremendous interest and capacity for detail himself."

If "competence" and making things "work better" are the sum of this talented administration, what intellectual deposit will it leave, in the intellectual and moral history of our country?

The moralizer and the manager are alike in their standing somewhat apart from the qualities that make for the highest political leadership. I mean "political" here in the deep and proper sense—a positive word, in the way that Americans don't use it. The moralizer (the conscientious man striving to fulfill the plain dictates of right and wrong) and the manager (the competent man trying to straighten out the world and make it efficient, predictable, and reorganized) share an implicit picture of human history and society that does not take fully into account the perennial ingredients of politics: conflicting interests, struggle for power, and differences in values among groups.

Both manager and moralist may assume that "interests" are automatically bad (special). They "work in the dark," says Jimmy Carter; he and "the people" stand against those "special" interests. Both may assume a world in which conflicts are intrusive and unnecessary, not a perennial fact of human life. Carter sometimes seems to imply that comprehensive, long range, tough planning and management will make conflicts of value and interest go away: "I hope that my normal, careful, methodical, scientific or planning approach to longer-range policies . . . would serve to remove those disharmonies long-before they reach the stage of actual implementation."

The United States has furnished the world with a great many more moralizers and managers than it has statesmen with a Burkian political wisdom, who see the fact of human freedom and hence variety casting up persistent differences in value, in taste, and certainly in interest, the last of which is not to be unequivocally denounced, and none of which are to be assumed away. It is of the essence of politics that people differ and that they will continue to differ. Wise statecraft-shaping policy takes that difference as a premise. Since people differ and are free, there are limits to the predictability and steadiness a government policy may achieve. Neither manager nor moralizer can fix the deep sources of change and difference, or the unpredictable developments rooted in the drama of human freedom in history.

George Kennan compared wise diplomacy—the analogy may apply also to domestic politics—to a gardener rather than to a carpenter. Much that happens is a result of actions outside his control to which he must wisely, carefully, alertly respond.

Both moralizers of the old-fashioned stripe, and engineers, scientists, planners and technicians of the newer stripe in American society have been criticized by political people for their expectation that the world can be built on straight lines. ·

The most interesting remark Jack Carter made to me, shortly after he said, "Dad's a perfectionist," and, "He is very linear," was a comment on that most familiar story of his father's, the story of the encounter with Rickover in which the Admiral asked Carter sternly why he hadn't done his "best" at Annapolis (the story that provided the title, used with another meaning by the Carter campaign, for Carter's book *Why Not the Best?*). Jack said: "Why not my best in my classes? Because there were other important things I had to do, that's why."

"I think," said the President's son, "that that Rickover story is dumb."

A legislative body, which by its nature cannot seek the "best," is at least as good a reflection of the political philosophy of a free society as the solitary executives, sitting alone with their burdens of decision in their oval offices. In the work of a board of aldermen, or a state legislature, or the parliaments of other democracies, and of the U.S. Congress, equals must face equals with sharply contrasting ideas of the better and the best, in something like deliberation—in an exchange, that includes not only the bargains of interests and balances of power but also some role for reason and conscience, for that capacity for "justice" without which democracy is not possible.

That interest and power are inextricably interwoven with reason and conscience in the many gaudy, messy, colorful tapestries of legislative enactment is not only inevitable but desirable. Values and interests on one side, and another side, and another, in differing mixtures, are forced to be dealt with. Sometimes their proponents even learn practically from each other. The opposition has its interests; sees what is good for the public in a different way; and knowing all the angles, we may alter our position.

The legislative body is the better symbol for democracy as an arrangement for reaching proximate solutions to insoluble problems. It is not yet clear whether Jimmy Carter has in him the genius for democratic politics in *that* sense. His "competence" may—in another example of the paradox of technical society (too narrow a drive for efficiency ends up being inefficient)—prove not to be "competent" in the intricate world of high policy. (Efficiency/competence/technical management makes exclusions and narrows focuses to achieve clear, isolated goals (the best); yet when what's excluded is of the essence of the activity, then apparent efficiency isn't efficient after all.)

A knowledgeable Washington critic of Carter, reading the crisp remarks quoted above about managerial efficiency, asked angrily, "Then why does he manage so badly?"

In his autobiography Carter lists his defects as he is considering whether to run for President. One of the defects he cites is his unwillingness to *compromise*. "A fault: I don't know how to compromise on any principle I believe is right." He quotes Ben Fortson, a Georgia politician, as having said he was "as stubborn as a Georgia mule." The way Carter writes this, and the way he concludes the point ("maybe this is a time, on matters of principle, for an absence of compromise") make his confession of it as a "fault" quite suspect. On the first page of *The Great Gatsby* Fitzgerald remarks about the careful editing of the confessions that young men make to each other. The faults confessed by Presidential candidates undergo an even more careful editing. Jimmy Carter, the confessing autobiographer, manages to turn his alleged fault into a virtue.

But given human freedom and given the differences among human beings—differences accentuated by our group life and by a big heterogeneous society—compromise is indeed a necessity and can indeed have its virtuous aspects. I recognize your difference from me and respect it and assume that, given its reality, I must accommodate myself to it in our shared life (in politics). If properly done, this is not a cause for reprobation but its opposite. Those who start with the world as it is and take the differences in interest and value among the groups as a given assume there will be surprises and no permanent, final "best" solutions. Yesterday's bests are today's problems.

The U.S. Government is not a nuclear submarine. Neither is it the Carter Warehouse business, where the measure of accomplishment was plainly shown in the accounts that Rosalynn Carter kept. The goods of government have different measures, more varied and less tangible; the limited ability of Americans to comprehend that difference is a recurrent fault, and a major source of the persistent cynicism about politics and government. It is said that we need more "business" in government; but government fills quite different human purposes (justice, freedom and order) from "business." In local politics it is said that there is no Republican or Democratic way to pave the streets—efficient paving is the only question. But there are questions about which streets, and whether to pave or save the money or to raise policemen's salaries, and those decisions cannot be answered by resort to the single goal of "efficiency"—or to any single goal comparable to the manager's account sheet or the nuclear engineer's functioning submarine. There is a vast field of considerations differing not only in complexity but in kind—values and interests compounded on each side of a contention. Ordinarily there is no "simple justice" on one side, with "special interests" on the other.

Knott and Wildavsky conclude their article with a couple of examples of the way Carter did learn, despite his managerial principles, from experience in Georgia. They commend his "energy, intelligence, and a demand for excellence," and his awareness of the importance of public confidence. In effect they say—I put the point now in my own way, for which they are not responsible—that Carter is too intelligent to be undone by his own mistaken managerial principles. Putting it another way, the Reinhold Niebuhr in him may win out over Admiral Rickover.

# 9

# THE RECUPERATING PRESIDENCY ?

The United States is a nation with a hefty load of social ideals but a comparatively flimsy cultural scaffolding upon which to support them. The office of the President, in the absence of other underpinnings, must do heavy symbolic service.

The United States is furthermore a nation whose heterogeneity, size, diversity, technological advancement, and newness require particularly strong staplings to link its many parts. Once again the cultural equipment available to the task is rather sparse, and the office of the President must perforce do much of the work.

It may be disproportionate for this immense, powerful, enormously variegated modern nation of two hundred fifteen million people to have placed as much of not only its power but also of its spiritual investment in one man, one office, as we have done, but there it is.

For old reasons and for new ones the President fills a space that is otherwise unoccupied, a space not only in the government but in the culture.

The older reasons have mostly to do with the absence of other centers of unity. Henry James wrote a famous paragraph about the deficiencies of the United States by the standards of Europe, for the purposes of a novelist's imagination, that may be adapted to this point. "No sovereign," he wrote, "no court, no personal loyalty, no aristocracy, no church, no clergy, no army, no diplomatic service, no country gentleman, no palaces, no castles, nor manors, nor old country houses, nor parsonages, nor thatched cottages, nor ivied ruins, no cathedrals, nor abbeys, nor little

Norman churches, no great universities nor public schools—no
Oxford, nor Eton, nor Harrow . . ."

An American of the present day, to be sure, will already have
objected to many items on this list—we do *so* have this or that
item of cultural equipment, or its equivalent (its superior!), if not
in Hawthorne's day, about which James was writing, then by
subsequent acquisition. And James's point was tangential to our
present interest: he dealt with the richness of a culture for literary
purposes, not the unity of the society for political purposes. But
these purposes are related, and, give or take an item, James's list
serves our point. We do not reach back to the days of those
abbeys, palaces, ivied ruins and cathedrals. Edmund Wilson
wrote of cities in the American middlewest, that they are built not
on the eighteenth century but on the flat land; a comparable new
beginning applies to the nation as a whole, built not on the
thirteenth century, or the fourth century, not on Charlemagne
and the Holy Roman Empire, or Constantine, or St. Augustine,
or St. Patrick, but on seventeenth-century Puritans breaking
away to build, as a city set upon a hill, a new and different society
on a new continent. We are, psychologically and institutionally,
what Seymour Martin Lipset called "the first new nation." The
Englishman Henry Fairlie wrote that we are a country "scribbled
into existence on a sheet of paper." Henry James' passage begins,
"No state, in the European sense of the word, and indeed barely a
specific national name." We were separated, diverse colonies; a
confederation; and then a federal union of states, retaining, in
spite of the centripetal and homogenizing forces of modernity,
local resistances to uniformity and centralism. One of Jimmy
Carter's achievements has been to blend a quite explicit and
ardent loyalty to the South as a region harmoniously with loyalty
to the United States.

We may add our own items to James's list. There is no London
or Paris. Neither New York nor Washington nor the two combined command nationwide allegiance as cities. If that Eastern
seaboard were to be sawed off and allowed to float out to sea, as a
major party's candidate proposed in 1964, then from that point of
view New York City should be allowed to sink first. The rest of
the country repeatedly assures the world that New York City is
*not* the United States, and reminds itself that that city is (or
rather was) at most a nice place to visit in which you wouldn't want

to live. New York City's financial woes exposed again the spiritual disengagement, the antagonism and disassociation much of the nation feels toward its greatest city. The son of the President of the United States, chatting amiably with his secret service detail outside a restaurant in Gainsville, Georgia, where we had just had a breakfast including grits and red-eye gravy, learned that one of the secret service was going to a wedding in New York City. He remarked, with genial sympathy, "Goin' up there and step in all that dog shit, huh?"

Although New York and Washington are often lumped as Eastern elite places there is also that separable alienation from Washington that did not hurt Mr. Carter in his rise to the presidency. As he neared the goal he claimed he hadn't been "anti-Washington" but that would be another of his claims that would have to be justified by the utmost casuistry; certainly the voting public heard what it took to be an anti-Washington theme. I remember that quintessential Jimmyist, Rosalynn Carter, energetically disdaining to a middlewestern audience all those people in Washington who've been there for years talking to each other, in contrast to the unsullied non-Washington purity of her Jimmy.

These disengagements from the major cities may be taken as indications of a larger set of disengagements: cultural, social, political, educational, religious.

The United States prides itself on the localism and diversity of its school system, with its multiplicity of school districts and local school boards struggling over biology textbooks and busing. Here there is nothing like that fabled French uniformity of curriculum with pupils—as it once was—from Àlgeria to Calais all reciting the same lesson. The United States has had local newspapers; *The New York Times*, though the "newspaper of record," is not—as one soon learns in Laramie or Winnebago—a *national* newspaper.

There is no Oxbridge. However much Harvard, Yale, and Princeton may want to present themselves as "national" universities, centers of training for leadership "in church and state," that Brahmin Ivy League taking-for-granted that the nation is rightly ordered when they are leading it is not accepted by those who are supposed to be led in Yuba City, Martinsville, or Americus. Once Yale would try to show its national character by

listing in the back of its catalogue the students from each state—
that son of the richest dentist in Elko, Nevada. But that did not
deceive the citizens of Elko; they perceive Yale to be not a center
of the nation but one of those snobbish Eastern places.

The most important of all the missing parts of our cultural
scaffolding are these three: no sovereign; no established church;
no unity of race or blood.

The constitution-makers scribbling us into national existence
on their pieces of paper combined in one office the Prime Minister and the King, the functioning partisan head of government
whose proposals and person are voted up and down in the political struggle on the one hand, and the head of state and focus of
suprapolitical unifying national loyalty on the other. The President makes the Thanksgiving proclamations, gives out medals of
freedom, greets boy scouts and victorious basketball teams, be-
stows his presence on awed and humble citizens, just like a King
or Queen. We mark our history by these Presidents as the English do with their Henrys and Georges, American school children filing out of second grade reciting names in sequence,
meaningless to them, Tyler, Polk, Taylor and Fillmore, Pierce,
Buchanan; our grandchildren will have the new sequence Nixon,
Ford, Carter, and will have to be careful not to forget Ford.

That we have no Church of England, no Archbishop of Canter-
bury, no Westminster Abbey is a more significant point than a
secular modern American may recognize. Citizens of this country
were startled when they saw Elizabeth crowned, to discover that
the Coronation was a religious ceremony, a ceremony of a Church
which however doddering and with however peculiar a beginning, fills a place in that nation's existence that is filled in some
way in all nations. When President Carter took his first trip to
Europe the pastor back home in the First Baptist Church at 16th
and O Streets in Washington remembered in his prayer that his
most notable parishioner was worshiping in Westminster Abbey,
in a way that showed some slight seepage even into this most
antiestablishmentarian of denominations in this antiroyal country
of the spirit of establishment and royalty.

The human impulses those institutions embody seep into any
nation, even this one that officially disavowed them. The universal social need for symbols of national unity and of its link to
ultimate mysteries clusters here, failing any alternative, around

the President. In a much-discussed article about "Civil Religion in America," by the sociologist of religion Robert Bellah, almost every quotation and illustration comes from or deals with a President: Washington, Jefferson, Kennedy, Lyndon Johnson, the Gettysburg Address and much else from Lincoln.

The need for tangible symbols of our national unity is increased by our heterogeneity: we lack the unity of kinship, of race, of "blood," as well as of religious belief. President Carter said at Notre Dame—a Southern Baptist at the Golden Dome of the Roman Catholic university—"In ancestry, religion, color, place of origin and cultural background, we Americans are as diverse a nation as the world has ever known." "No common mystique of blood or soil unites us," said the Southern Wasp President at the university built by Catholic immigrants. In a call-in show in California the President remarked—echoing F.D.R.'s famous greeting to the DAR—that "except for the Indians, we are all immigrants." The full range of the nation's "ethnic" and religious diversity had become truly present to the nation's consciousness only in the two decades before Mr. Carter took office; in years past the Wasp (before that term existed) had often thought of himself, and sometimes had been accepted by others, as more "American" than non-Wasps. No more. Catholic children of immigrants claim at least double the Americanism of the Protestant children of Puritans; Jews are a full part of what preachers not long ago got by with calling "this Christian country"; Buddhists may well outnumber adherents of the traditions of the Bible in sunbaked spots in California; religious exotica proliferate; the disabilities of vocal atheists in certain regards does not mean they are not numerous, in fact, and equal before the law.

Yet this nation, perhaps more than others, needs its tangible symbol of the link to what is valuable, lasting, and real, rising above the political struggles of the day. It needs such a gathering point of loyalty not only because the nation is heterogeneous, fissiparous, big, and still in a sense new, but also because to have some defining moral juices flowing, to have a "purpose" or "ideal," is built into our national being.

Gunnar Myrdal wrote in *An American Dilemma*, "It is a commonplace to point out the heterogeneity of the American nation and the swift succession of all sorts of changes in all its component parts . . . Still there is evidently a strong unity in this nation and a basic homogeneity and stability in its valuations."

He described what that unity and homogeneity consists of: "Americans of all national origins, classes, regions, creeds, and colors, have something in common: a social *ethos*, a political creed. It is difficult to avoid the judgment that this 'American Creed' is the cement in the structure of this great and disparate nation." Myrdal, as a Scandinavian social scientist, compared the cementing creed of this country to other countries: "America, compared to every other country in Western civilization, large or small, has the *most explicitly expressed* system of general ideals in reference to human interrelations. This body of ideals is more widely understood and appreciated than similar ideals are anywhere else . . . To be sure, the political creed of America is not very satisfactorily effectuated in actual social life. But as principles which *ought* to rule, the Creed has been made conscious to everyone in American society."

One may add that the nation's chief executive is perforce the prime candidate to serve as its continuing spokesman and interpreter. An abstract "creed," a set of social ideals and moral truths held in common, needs concrete symbols, and also spokesmen and interpreters. For Americans the most important voice and person to fulfill these roles has been, and is, the President of the United States.

Most of what I have said so far reaches back through American history. Modern developments add to the central suprapolitical cultural role—that of unifier and presumed moral spokesman— of the President. Modern life, modern technology, has centripetal and centrifugal effects: mobility, especially to the city; new means of transportation, communication, production. They whirl out of place and out of shape the old, the stable, the local, and the small: the local church, and the national churches, too, for that matter; Mom and Pop's celebrated corner grocery store; the buggy; the local school, the small college, the home-owned newspaper, the bookstore and even the book, the precinct captain, local party headquarters, the Board of Aldermen. CBS and Rupert Murdoch and General Dynamics and giant conglomerates and chains alter the country's moral flow chart. What do freshmen in a modern American college know about? Television. Mass culture. The name of the President, and his brother, as a part of mass culture.

Modernity—technology—furnishes that President with the new powers symbolized by the box in everyone's living room and by the little black box that someone carries for the President wherever he goes: television and nuclear weapons. Richard Nixon, through the television set, shared his maudlin farewell to his staff with the world, and was accompanied by the black box for nuclear retaliation even in the airplane as he crossed the country and the Presidential power passed to Gerald Ford (what if you had used the phone in the black box at one minute after twelve? asked David Frost. Oh, they would have said wrong number, replied Nixon).

Arthur Schlesinger, Jr., wrote: "By the early 1970's the American President had become on issues of war and peace the most absolute monarch (with the possible exception of Mao Tse-tung of China) among the great powers of the world."

Control of nuclear weaponry is but the pinnacle of a huge new structure of Presidential power and Presidential prestige—a penumbra of awe surrounding the office—built on the United States, twentieth-century emergence as a world power, and emergence after World War II as the Great Power, alone for a moment, thereafter in contest with the Soviet Union. "Leader of the free world," we began to call this awesome fellow with the box.

On the other box he appears in living color, in prime time, almost at his will, and tells us—millions of us at once—that the energy crisis is the moral equivalent of war and that Bert Lance is his friend. Soon we learn more about him than we know about our closest associates. Where Andrew Jackson was made the symbol for an age by the unconscious initiative and slow communication of the folk (in ballads, books, stories, newspaper accounts), Jimmy Carter, the first true television President, became a symbol quickly.

He showed a knack for the making of symbols and the cultural and moral role of the President. If Carter has flaws in fulfilling the Prime Minister's role—in relation to the nation's *conflict*—he demonstrated a greater sense of the Presidential role in relation to the nation's unity.

The period before Carter's election had been a troubled time

not only for the nation he was to lead but also for the office he was
to hold—a bad time for the country in part exactly because it had
been a bad time in and for the Presidential office.

Watergate, however else we describe it, had been distinctly a
Presidential collection of evils—"White House horrors," as no
less an authority than John Mitchell had said. And Mr. Nixon's
misdeeds did not stop with what we may call Watergate proper
but had had a wide scope—from sea to shining sea, from Key
Biscayne to San Clemente. As he kept pointing out, he was the
*President*: to borrow a phrase from the ballad "Frankie and
Johnny," he was our man, and he done us wrong. Watergate
represented not only a violation of the law; it represented a
violation of the spiritual and cultural investment of the American
people in the Presidential office. Mr. Carter, who certainly is
attuned to that cultural-spiritual wavelength, was able to respond
to the shame of the Presidency more effectively than other
candidates.

The Vietnam War was also a Presidential deed, or collection of
deeds—done by a series of Presidents, a series of mistaken policy
decisions by Presidents and their close advisors; then covered,
shaded, defended, extended, by a series of accompanying Presidential misdeeds. Each item in Mr. Carter's list of shameful
happenings, in the televised debates and on the hustings, was
traceable in the end to Presidents: not only Watergate and Vietnam but the foreign and domestic doings of the CIA and the FBI.
The President himself, or appointees responsible to him, ap-
proved covert actions in Chile, secret incursions into Cambodia,
Christmas bombings in North Vietnam, wire-tappings, income
tax harassments, "enemies" lists. When the Nixon defenders
would say, pouting, that *he* didn't *start* it, the *others* had done
what he had done, the half or quarter of the truth in that claim led
back still to other Presidents. The malaise of American life in that
pre-Carter time came in considerable part from that desk at
which Harry Truman had assured us the buck was to stop.

Professor Gregor Goethals of the Rhode Island School of De-
sign, a student of the rituals of public life, has noted the psychologically appropriate historical parentheses provided by the two
moments in recent history when the nation heard the Navy
hymn. This somber music was played in 1963 as the body of
President John F. Kennedy was brought down the Capitol steps

after having lain in state in the rotunda. It was heard next again when President-elect Jimmy Carter descended those same steps to be inaugurated President on January 20, 1977.

The bracketing of our national ills implied by that sequence may be unfair to the many-sided role of the complex figure of Lyndon Johnson and is too generous to John Kennedy, and perhaps to Dwight Eisenhower, in whose administrations seeds of some later troubles were sown (the lines are drawn here or here or here depending of course upon the way we identify the ills to be deplored). At the other end that bracketing is unfair to Gerald Ford. President Carter paid Mr. Ford a tribute of uncommon grace in his very first words as President at the high point of his Inauguration Day: "For myself and for our nation, I want to thank my predecessor for all that he has done to heal our land." That gracious gesture was itself an act of healing, and as a way to begin his address and his service as President could scarcely have been improved upon.

Nevertheless, though a decent man himself, Mr. Ford was tied to the degradation of the Presidency as Mr. Nixon's appointee. He had come into the office, doubly unelected, as the result of two successive and unique embarrassments in the nation's highest offices. He had defended Nixon, shared his policies, his party, his Cabinet, his staff, and had clinched the relationship by pardoning him. He was, moreover, a man of limited gifts. William V. Shannon of *The New York Times* adapted a biting phrase of Churchill's about Attlee to say that Mr. Ford "would have made a good mayor of Grand Rapids in a quiet year." If Mr. Ford had done much to "heal our land" it was nevertheless not inappropriate that the further healing be carried out by an abler President who did not have Mr. Ford's connection with the chief malefactor in the Presidential office.

Mr. Nixon was a peculiar American failure story, a grotesque and cautionary parody of a central American myth: he failed his way steadily from poor beginnings all the way to the White House and out again; he failed in his first "crisis" with his Checkers speech; failed his way through multiple campaign speeches about "Korea, corruption, and Communism"; failed his way upward, and showed there is room to fail at the top. One expression of his failure was his profligate borrowing for his own purpose of the moral capital of his office: with the American flag in one hand and a bust of Lincoln in the other, he would invoke "national security" for his petty doings and the "office of the Presidency" for his personal protection.

In the national worrying about the Presidency in the Nixon years the prevailing theme was impersonal, external, and institutional, having to do with the *power* of the Presidency, as against Congress especially, and also as against the other pieces of the American governmental system and parts of American society.

A second theme dealt with the conditions of the President's daily life. Mr. George Reedy's book *The Twilight of the Presidency* dealt with the isolation of the President, and with the impact of the Presidential court: cut off from reality by eager servants, spared bad news by the banishing of its bearers, every whim catered to, a President, with no equals around him, can allow his neuroses to flourish. The book's merit had been recognized already when it was published in 1970, well before the series of events that placed their daily strain on credulity beginning in March of 1973. But Watergate gave Mr. Reedy's book a new life.

The Nixon White House, as it turned out, was to exhibit in the most egregious form the disturbing tendencies Mr. Reedy had discerned in Mr. Johnson's administration and had generalized into his crepuscular theme. But first with Mr. Ford and then more clearly with Mr. Carter the "twilight" and "lengthening shadows" lifted.

Mr. Carter's view of the problem of the Presidency differed in emphasis from these others. By implication at least he dealt with the man at the center, and with his spiritual tie to the public. It was a personal and moral theme, in contrast to the institutional ones; he dealt with the link between the character of the man who fills the office and that of the people he leads. Mr. Carter, more plainly than other candidates, proposed in the old American moralist's way, to change the *character* of the man at the buck-stopping desk and thereby to stop the moral mischief done from it.

Whereas a considerable amount of literature in the Johnson-Nixon period had argued against the swelling of Presidential power and the Presidentializing of American life, President Carter—no man to suggest the diminution of an office he proposed to hold—did not make that argument. He did not promise that the President's office in his hands would be any less active, strong,

"aggressive" than it had been under other Presidents. Characteristically he said he would not be a "timid" President; he said he
would be "strong," and that there could be simultaneously a
"strong" President and a strong Congress. He did not say the
things that Eugene McCarthy said, evoking the picture of a
diffident President and a self-limiting, diminished Presidential
office. Neither did Carter emphasize the empowering and reforming of Congress as a check upon Presidential power. Carter
did not turn away from but rather used that impulse to make the
President the embodiment of the popular will.

The way Carter treated the unhappy condition of the office he
sought was neither to propose reforms to limit it nor explicitly to
denounce its defective occupants, but rather to shift the focus to
what had happened to the *nation*—only by implication as a result
of Presidential wickedness. The nation had been "hurt" (he did
not say by whom) and needed to be "healed" (the implication: by a
new Presidential healer). The American people had "lost" something "precious" that should be restored (the transparent implication: by a President—Carter himself—who would be the re-
storer). Where much of the discussion had assumed a public
afraid of the President's power, Mr. Carter's themes assumed
instead a public ashamed of the President's behavior. The nation,
he said, felt "shame"; he proposed to "make us proud again."

The nation had been "hurt"; it was "shamed"; something had
been "lost." Leaders did these things; government did these
things; and we were now ashamed and hurt, and a new President
was to come back and make us proud and to rediscover what had
been lost.

Though he made this starkly moral interpretation of the events
of the recent past, candidate Carter did not ordinarily specify the
acts or agents. No doubt in all of this there was some calculation.
He did not condemn Richard Nixon very often by name; he did
not condemn Mr. Ford's pardon, as many in his party thought he
should. When in the early stages of the general election campaign
he did refer to the "Nixon-Ford administration," tying Ford to
Nixon, this was widely felt to be out of character and damaging to
him.

The nation had "lost" something precious, for which it was now
searching. The nation's "hurt" should be healed and pride in
government restored. This something lost was mislaid by leaders,

but still retained and waiting for recovery, by the people—good, competent, decent, and filled with love—led by a leader whose qualities corresponded to their own.

Leaders, unspecified, had done misdeeds; government, without being particular about which or whose, had hurt, shamed, and misled us. Now government was to be restored to the conditions that existed before these things were done. Carter's rather melodramatic neo-Wilsonian way of interpreting events (people good; leaders bad) preserved a sense of the wrongs done without insisting that blame for doing the wrongs be assigned with specificity.

The many gestures of his early months in office that were called "symbols" were in considerable part marks of contrast to the Presidency at its low point under Nixon and Johnson. Where Nixon had expensive seats, fat cats and limousines, Carter had cheap seats, common people, buses, and a walk with his family down Pennsylvania Avenue. Carter sold the yacht *Sequoia* (while Mr. Nixon in the Frost interviews was explaining, characteristically, that the Russian leader's yacht was *much* more plush). President Carter set his cousin Hugh to an exercise in what Meg Greenfield called "perkicide" (killing perquisites) for the White House staff, and did much pompicide too. No "Hail to the Chief" for this President's entrances.

President Carter's post-Watergate themes were moral, personal, cultural, and symbolic, rather than legal, political, and institutional . . . certainly rather than partisan or ideological. Already before the general election campaign a Carter worker said I should have heard Carter talking there in the courtyard of Colony Square (the new Atlanta development in which Carter's headquarters were located). He quietly told the staff what the election meant: "I don't want to go hear that Jimmy Carter again," said one worker; one fan, "I don't want to cry anymore." Again at St. Simon Island as President-elect he talked with a quiet sobriety to the Cabinet designates about the higher moral meaning of the common task upon which they were all about to embark. And he did the same with the White House staff. Before taking office he gave his staff what they report to have been a deeply moving talk, insisting with quiet passion that they—we—*must* succeed, *must* set an example, because the nation, having suffered "two failed Presidencies," could not stand another.

One can picture this unusual man from south Georgia making quite a scar upon the American earth, and not only by the criteria the political community employs—that is, the legislation he initiates and manages to have enacted, the crises he copes with, and the policies his administration pursues.

Despite his very "American" limitations, or even because of them, President Carter has qualifications to help rebuild the nation's moral scaffolding.

Some said constrain the President; he said link the President to the people. Some said change the Presidency; he said change the President.

II

When President Carter gave the Commencement Address at Notre Dame it was the valedictorian who produced the afternoon's most memorable phrase. Speaking to his fellow students as they went out into the world, into their various jobs, duties, and walks of life, he remarked: "Not all of us can be peanut farmers from Georgia."

When the honored students were asked to stand, one of those receiving highest honors held up a sign saying, "Need Job."

The peanut farmer from Georgia who has a job was of course the last of the honored guests to enter the convention center— the building in which Adrian Dantley and Austin Carr scored baskets for Notre Dame. (The College of Science graduates at one point in the solemn ceremony began shouting "DE-fense. DE-fense!") Carter showed that he was still a one-on-one politician. As he marched into the center with the President of the university, Theodore Hesburgh, at the end of the academic procession, preceded by the faculty and honored guests, he began, despite his mortar board, his black robe, the formal procession and the solemnity of the occasion in which he was participating, to work the crowd. He shook hands on this side and that with the seniors.

Father Hesburgh, introducing the President, said that Carter is "the first President that I can remember" who has "put front and center justice and liberty for all here and around the world." An American President, in Carter's time, needs not only to exemplify personal rectitude but also to revive the sense that the nation has an exemplary role, too: that it represents ideals of universal application. So Jimmy Carter did, with the human rights theme. It was as much for the restoration of national self-respect as for its international consequences.

When Carter came out to speak at Notre Dame he was showered with peanuts, a few of which he threw back into the crowd. He said that throwing peanuts was a new trend that he did not "deplore, because the more that are thrown or consumed, the higher the price goes."

He also told a joke he attributed to Charles Kirbo. (It seemed to be a joke then going around because I had heard it before that week.) A drunk charged with being drunk and setting a bed on fire gave as his defense that he had indeed been drunk but that the bed had been on fire when he got into it.

The speech, one of the few major speeches of Carter's first year, was a review of his foreign policy outlook, with human rights as the main theme. Some hard-line folk did not like the shift of emphasis from cold war opposition to the communist power to the relationship among rich and poor nations. The human rights theme itself was undergoing muted public criticism and some official qualification. Secretary of State Vance had made a speech at the end of April in Athens, Georgia, which had stated the careful reservations a diplomat would want to apply to so abstract a moral principle in the immense variety of life in international politics.

Carter himself reaffirmed the principle and linked it to the moral substance of the American nation: "We are confident that democracy's example will be compelling."

It brought memories now to hear him at this Roman Catholic center repudiating the older perverse sort of "anti-communism." "Being confident for our own future" (the nation's *confidence* was another repeated theme) "we are now free of that inordinate fear of communism which once led us to embrace any dictator who joined us in our fear."

There was a most interesting passage about words and ideas in the political world. After a reaffirmation of "America's commitment to human rights as the fundamental tenet of our foreign policy" Carter said "we live in a world that is imperfect and will always be imperfect—a world that is complex and will always be complex. I understand fully the limits of moral suasion. I have no illusion that changes will come easily or soon. But I also believe that it is a mistake to undervalue the power of words and of the ideas that words embody."

This engineer and manager in the White House referred to that passage in his conversation with Harvey Shapiro in a way that made one believe it was more than a speech-writer's insertion. One would hope that he would take his own advice, and not undervalue the power of words (not merely slogans) and of the ideas that words embody. Actually, as Carter has the opportunity to reformulate domestic ideology, breaking the old conservative/liberal definitions that go back to the New Deal, so also he has the opportunity to break the realist/idealist debate in foreign policy as it took form first in the interwar period and then, magnified, during the Cold War.

His illustrations in South Bend were these: "In our own history, that power [of words and ideas] has ranged from Thomas Paine's 'Common Sense' to Martin Luther King, Jr.'s, 'I Have a Dream.' Not only was there an implicit repudiation of the ghost of Joe McCarthy but also explicit praise by a devout Baptist in a Roman Catholic university for Tom Paine (Theodore Roosevelt called Paine, 'a filthy little atheist'). And there was another endorsement of the black Georgia activist by the white Georgia conservative.

"In the life of the human spirit," President Carter said, "words *are* actions—much more so than many of us may realize who live in countries where freedom of expression is taken for granted.

"The leaders of totalitarian countries understand this very well. The proof is that words are precisely the action for which dissidents in those countries are being persecuted."

At the end of his speech he made, as is his wont, a list of points. Carter said:

> Let me conclude. Our policy is based upon an historical vision of America's role; it is derived from a larger view of global change; it is rooted in our moral values.

In the text as released to the press this phrase stopped there. When the President delivered the speech, however, he added, extemporaneously and characteristically, after "our moral values," the phrase "which never change!"

They never change. That's important to him. There is an "unchanging center around which our lives can function," for Jimmy Carter, as for the Puritan strain of which he is a modern embodiment, for the evangelical strain that grew in part out of Puritanism, and for an older America.

# PART III

# HOW SWEET
# THE SOUND

# 10

## THE FAMILIAR
## STRANGENESS OF
## THE BIBLE BELT

President Carter is an active, visible, explicit, praying, Bible-class-teaching Southern Baptist deacon, and "born again" besides. Interpretations of him that make that fact the ruling feature are already, as the Bible says in another connection, legion. Nevertheless the Christianity that President Carter professes is very different from, say, Dostoevsky's metaphysical torment; or Jane Austen's gentle English deference to serious matters; or G.K. Chesterton's belligerent Catholic orthodoxy; or the almost sacramental solidarity with all of suffering humanity of George Bernanos' country priest. Although it differs also from many among the proliferating two hundred American varieties of Christianity, Mr. Carter's evangelistic Southern Baptist belief gathers up much that is central and distinctive here, as would not be true of any other country in what used to be called Christendom. In other words the Christian religion Mr. Carter professes is very much in an American version.

It goes so far inside the core of the culture as it used to be that it is puzzling to the culture that has grown a long way out from that core. It goes so deep into the old root as to be remote from the modern proliferating branches. The evangelical free church Protestant Christianity professed by Jimmy Carter was once the dominant religious influence, and almost the dominant cultural influence, in the nation of which he is President. That was a long time ago.

The religious life of the South is now indeed distinctive, and a primary cause and expression of the regional distinctiveness, but it is a distinction achieved in large part by holding fast to what the whole nation once was. The "different" religious life of the South is therefore not the difference of Zen Buddhists, astrology cults, Hari Krishna people, the Great I Am, or the multitudinous cults of Southern California. It is strangely familiar, a reminder of a past that still has its remnants, memories, and aftereffects.

Southern religion, for all the puzzlement and entertainment it provided to Northern reporters, is no polar opposite to the North or to the country as a whole. It includes many of the national characteristics. One finds in this religious realm in particular the paradox of the Puritan from Georgia: the older characteristics of the Union preserved under glass in the heart of the Confederacy, while the nation as a whole diluted or abandoned them.

Once the nation as a whole was predominately Protestant; today the South still is. Once the nation as a whole struck European observers as more seriously religious than their home country; today the South does. Once the dominant flavor of the whole nation's religious life was evangelistic, free church, Biblical; today the South's is.

The preservation came about in the following way, if I may telescope a great deal of history.

The colonies were overwhelmingly Protestant, and their being so was a prime reason for their existence. The United States is, as H. Richard Niebuhr, brother of Reinhold Niebuhr, put it, the land of "constructive Protestantism." It is the place where Protestant Christianity, which in Europe was a protest against a long-established Roman Catholicism, had now a chance to build a society from the ground up on its own principles. As Louis Hartz wrote that the United States has no feudal past, and therefore is the land where political liberalism was the foundation instead of the embattled resistance, so one may say the same in the religious field: no Catholic past; Protestantism on the ground floor. But movements of protest (like "liberation" movements today) do have difficulty providing constructive principles; their forte is dynamism and change, not the building of foundations. Some of our American difficulties, down to the present day, stem from that limitation.

And it wasn't the whole of Protestantism that came here; it was Calvinism and the sects. It was, that is, the left side of the Reformation represented by the Puritan movement in England. Every step the Christian religion took on its way (so to speak) from Rome to the Plains Baptist Church was a step in the direction of separation and individualism.

Reformation Protestantism affirmed the "priesthood of all believers" (misunderstood by modern political reporters scribbling in their notebooks as Jimmy Carter talked as the *sainthood* of all believers: hardly that!). That was a powerful move away from the great collectivity of the Roman Catholic church toward the distinct and separated individual: every man his own priest. The Puritans in England wanted to carry that further, by purifying the national church, the Church of England, with a more serious personal, purified, Biblical, unadorned religion. And the *separatists* among the Puritans wanted to carry that so far as to disentangle themselves altogether from any *national* church structure: quite a move in those days. The Pilgrims were separatists; the Puritans who came to Massachusetts Bay at least wanted separation from England. And then Roger Williams separated himself from those separatists, first briefly to be a Baptist and to found the first Baptist church in this country in Providence, and then to go on beyond that into the realm of unaffiliated seeking.

As the religious history of this country developed, separationist and revivalistic Baptists carried the gospel out into the Southern frontier, as to Sumter County, Georgia. They represented the most individualistic wing of one of the most individualistic denominations of the most individualistic part of the heritage of Biblical religion.

Though this country is built on those Founding Fathers and their scrap of paper, it is also built, emotionally, culturally, popularly, on the two clusters of religious revivals in which that religion flourished and grew, the events that are called by historians the "awakenings." Before the Revolution, around 1740, there was the Great Awakening whose best-known leaders were Jonathan Edwards and the English evangelist George Whitfield. This was a shaping event for the generation that fought the Revolution and founded the country; it was called by H. Richard Niebuhr our "national conversion." Whereas the deistic enlightenment furnished the intelligentsia and the generals for the American Revolution, the Great Awakening furnished the foot soldiers.

Then in the early nineteenth century there came a second wave, called the Second Great Awakening, which, though it began in the Northeast, spread out to the Western and Southern frontiers. It featured camp meetings and revivals: a direct appeal to ordinary people's emotions with which the sedate older churches were uncomfortable.

The Baptists and the Methodists were *not* uncomfortable with such an appeal. At the time of the Revolution, Presbyterians and Congregationalists, Episcopalians and Quakers were the largest religious groups; by the time of the Civil War, Baptists and Methodists had passed them all in numbers of members. They remain to this day the largest Protestant religious groups, and are overwhelmingly dominant in the South. (Earl, Jimmy, Hugh and Alton Carter were or are Baptists; Daddy King is a Baptist, as of course was his son; Lillian Gordy and her father Jim Jack Gordy, Rosalynn Smith, and Bert and LaBelle Lance were or are Methodists.) The Southern black population is overwhelmingly Baptist and Methodist (including varieties of separate denominations); in the 1960's, nine out of ten Southern black church members were Protestant, six of ten Baptist. Baptists and Methodists combined represent over 80% of the white religious affiliation in six Southern states, over seventy per cent in five others. If one adds the closely related denominations, the Presbyterians and Disciples (Lyndon Johnson was a member of The Disciples of Christ) the proportions go up to over 90%. The South is not really religiously "pluralistic"; it is instead very much an exaggerated version of the condition of the whole country beyond the seaboard in the pre-Civil War days.

The explanations of the North/South difference in religion begin of course with the War. Differing attitudes toward slavery in the 1840's and 1850's split the Protestant churches on sectional lines: *Southern* Baptists, *Southern* Presbyterians, *Southern* Methodists came into being as separate denominations.

And the waves of immigration from 1840 to 1920 that brought very large numbers of Roman Catholics, and also Jews and Lutherans and others, to the North, touched the South only slightly. The South remained an unethnic biracial unmelting pot.

I was feeling uncomfortable in Colony Square, just before Carter's election, with what seemed to me a lack of appreciation of the composition of the modern Democratic Party. When one Georgia Democratic leader and Carter supporter tried to tell me that the 159 counties of Georgia were a microcosm of the country

I couldn't believe he believed it. To one whose sense of the party, and the country, comes from Connecticut and an industrial city, the Georgians lacked an internalized understanding of Catholic America (as something more than a problem on abortion), of Jewish America, of the Northern city ghettos, of the labor unions. I remembered what Robert Kennedy was supposed to have said about Oregon: "How can you campaign here? There are no *ethnics!*"

The South was poor, rural, defeated; native white and black. W. J. Cash wrote that what the average Southerner required was "a faith as simple and emotional as himself." Behind the barrier of Southern distinctiveness and isolation the evangelical Protestantism that once marked the country as a whole was preserved, grew, and reciprocally influenced and was influenced by the regional culture. A contemporary historian, Carl Degler, writes: "Today . . . the South is the most Protestant region of the country . . . Both systematic public-opinion polls and impressionistic evidence concur in concluding that the South is the most religious region of the country and, further, that the character of its Protestantism is traditional and conservative . . . Religion helps to set the South apart from the nation not only because it is conservative, but also because it is taken seriously by Southerners."

All this religious history still has its echoes not only in Plains and in Jimmy Carter but in American culture as a whole.

In the days when Jimmy Carter was starting out on life's pathway, making straight A's (except for one C in music) in the Plains Elementary School, the United States was still, culturally speaking, a "Protestant" country; it had not yet become, as it was to do while he was learning about nuclear submarines in the 1940's and early 1950's, a three-faith Protestant-Catholic-Jewish country, nor yet what it is now, an indescribable conglomeration.

The other major religious groupings have been flavored by the surrounding Protestant culture. The Irish Puritanism of one strand of Roman Catholicism, for example, has been reinforced by a Puritan ingredient in American Protestant culture; and reform Judaism is often hard to distinguish from liberal Protestantism. The secular beliefs in this country have been influenced by the surrounding Protestant culture (it does make a difference what church you are staying away from or rebelling against). One can tell that John Dewey's particular brand of nonreligion—of instrumentalism with a "common faith" in democracy and science—goes back to the Congregational Churches of New England.

Protestant individualism is symbolized in the very name of the Baptists, and in their central practice. They were rebaptizers: the baptizing of infants was not sufficient or sacramentally efficacious. Believers join the church at the age of adult comprehension and adult decision—that is, not by being brought by their parents willy-nilly through the accident of their birth and of their parents' religion, but rather by their own separate, distinct individual decision (that's the theory). Jimmy Carter was baptized when he was eleven in Plains. When later in life he and his family joined the First Baptist Church at 16th and O Streets in Washington his daughter Amy, aged nine, was baptized. (Though his wife came forward to join the church, Jeff Carter stayed behind in the pew.) We may be permitted to surmise that both Jimmy and Amy were influenced by the parents, just as they would have been within the Roman Catholic Church or the Church of England. Nevertheless their sharp sense of separated individual self-consciousness that is symbolized by adult baptism was cemented into the foundations of America. Americans provided Max Weber the most pungent historical example of the effect of the individualizing attitude of the Protestant Reformation upon economic activity: the Protestant girls on jobs were more quickly able to comprehend the advantage to them of a piecework method of payment in which hard work would be individually rewarded.

On October 9, 1955, the Invocation at the Plains Baptist Church was given by Jimmy Carter; the men who attended the Brotherhood conference in Savannah on November 14 included Jimmy Carter and Clarence Dodson; those who "graciously consented to serve as census captains" in the church census of February 26, 1956, included Jimmy Carter; the faculty for the Vacation Bible School in June of 1956 included Mrs. Rosalynn Carter, who taught Girls' Handwork to the Juniors (Mrs. Walter Spann—i.e., Gloria Carter—taught "Character Stories" to the Intermediates); on August 26, 1956, Circle Five of the Women's Missionary Society met in the Fellowship Hall with Mrs. Jimmy Carter as hostess.

The church bulletins for subsequent years regularly contain

more of the same: Mrs. Rosalynn Carter often a teacher or superintendent in Vacation Bible School, usually for the Juniors; repeatedly hostess to the Women's Missionary Society; a donor of flowers; hostess at dinner for the revival. "I don't ever remember askin' Rosalynn to do anything that she wouldn't do," says the widow of the pastor of the church from 1955 to 1967, Mrs. Ethel Harris. "She took her turn keeping the nursery on Sunday morning just like everybody else."

Jimmy Carter was often an usher, and sometimes in charge of the ushers—including during the month of November, 1966, during which he was defeated in a Governor's race of which no mention is made in the bulletins of the church. He was the Chairman of the Children's Home Car Committee, and reported on it often; he taught the Juniors "Studies in Amos"; he was (often) a leader for "cottage prayer meetings" that preceded the annual spring revival; he led prayer services; he was thanked for the asphalt tile in the nursery and another time for two truckloads of gravel around the church entrances. On December 3, 1961, it was reported that as Chairman of the Children's Home Car Committee the fiscally conservative nation's future chief executive had raised $1,003.11. "Jimmy and Rosalynn didn't just do the jobs that get publicity," says Mrs. Harris. "They did the jobs that needed to be done."

Jimmy Carter was a leader in the "Brotherhood" painting of the "pastorium," as it is called, while Mrs. Harris's husband was ill and being treated at Duke. With "Brother Bob" Harris, Jimmy Carter helped to build a "Friendship Campground." Brother Bob furnished the pastoral leadership; Jimmy Carter, with his political connections, was able to get the bulldozers to clear the site. Jimmy Carter took his turn, as the world now knows, teaching Sunday School, and served as head of the "Brotherhood" for thirty-four churches.

"Jackie" Carter, the oldest child appears also in the later bulletins. He was speaker for "student night at Christmas" on Christmas, 1966. Mrs. Harris taught Chip and Jeff in Sunday School; they were "sweet little boys, very bright, very smart." If it was necessary though, she "could always count on the Carters to discipline the boys if there was any mischief."

I asked Jack about the influence of those years in the Plains Baptist Church, in the bulletins of which he sometimes appeared. I thought it might have been a powerful influence and one that might fit my theories about his daddy. He exploded that in a hurry.

"I think it tells the whole story that when I was a senior in high school I won a trip to a Governor's conference and all the years in the Plains Baptist Church fell away before that conference was over."

I knew from others that Jack in his youth had had attacks of doubts and troubled conversations with clergymen.

"How did it happen that your father never had those questionings that you did?" I asked.

"How do you know he didn't?"

The most striking of Jimmy Carter's voluntary undertakings for the church came not long after his defeat for Governor of Georgia and his service as Chairman of the Ushers for the Plains Baptist Church in November, 1966—not long after the celebrated talk in the woods with his sister Ruth and his religious rejuvenation. It is not your ordinary Presidential candidate at this historical moment who has volunteered as an adult for the sort of "pioneer mission work" evangelical trip up North that Jimmy Carter undertook in 1967.

Carter gave an account of his being asked to make such trips in a speech to Disciples of Christ laymen at Lafayette, Indiana, in June, 1976. Though the speech came in the middle of the campaign season Carter had promised Charles Kirbo a year earlier that he would do it. (Kirbo is an active member of the Disciples.) When I tried to get a copy of this speech from the Carter press headquarters in the summer of 1976 I was told rather abruptly, almost with embarrassment, that they only kept politically significant speeches, and this wasn't one of them.

Here is what Carter said, as transcribed from a tape:

> I was asked to go by my church on what we call pioneer mission work where we leave our businesses for a week or two, go to areas in the nation, maybe in our own state or in other states. We have a procedure by which through telephone calls we identify families within which there are no church members at all and then we get laymen to go into those communities to visit those families. We try to see about a hundred families per week. It's a very exciting thing and a very difficult thing to do.

Carter then told more effectively than he did in his book about the nudging that helped him volunteer:

> And when I was asked to do this for the first time I said, "I don't have any time. I've got to get my crops planted." And the Brotherhood leader said, "When do you get through planting your crop?" And I said, "Well, I won't get my crop planted until probably the middle of May." And he said, "Well, we happen to have a group going to Pennsylvania about the first of June." [Laughter]

Doing good, for the quintessential American, means lots of volunteer activities of that kind and lots of joining; extending the way things are done in church out into the town. Jimmy Carter joined the Lions International, of which he rose to be district governor; the Certified Seed Growers (perhaps this is different—a "special interest" group!); and a Great Books reading group in Americus. He was elected to the school board and came to serve as its chairman, making him vulnerable to subsequent criticisms because it was then still segregated.

Politics in that environment seems yet another version of this same approach to the world, with the same assumptions about society and man and morals, about offering oneself for service to do good. Though his grandfather and father and mother had been active politically, Carter's political activity seems to also be an extension of that churchly sort of doing "good." In the conversation he had with a pastor when he embarked on his political career, he defended his entry into this allegedly "dirty" arena—defended it specifically against the alternative of going into the ministry—by a typically Carterian reference to numbers: how would you like to be a pastor for eighty thousand people? (A newspaper critic of Carter, reading this story, objected because, he said, it was a favorite theme of Jody, Ham, *et al*, in the summer of 1976: the flacks were working overtime to convince the press that it was true. Maybe so. I don't doubt that there is a lot more fuel in Carter's political ambition than his evangelical desire to do Christian deeds. But the more interesting point is the confusion of appraisals between this man and me: I am not *praising* Carter for the sectarian-Baptist-Bible belt ingredient in his politics. My intention is to be analytical; my appraisal, based on experience, includes at least as much of a negative as of a positive judgment.)

The way the Carters and their followers undertook their political campaign had the flavor of this heritage. From 1966 to 1970 the Sunday meetings of Carter supporters around the state were something like a religious meeting. The campaigning was person-to-person, an every-member canvas or evangelistic tour. "We felt like missionaries," said a woman who was one of the main campaigners. "I never felt like supporting anybody like I supported him. We did it with missionary zeal because he stood for something good." Missionary zeal—but what was the gospel? When I asked others about this good woman's politics or ideology I got only vagueness in reply: *Jimmy* was the gospel, or Jimmy's axiomatic goodness. At one point in our conversation the same woman said, revealingly, "They [the Carters] are just real good people, just like us. He [Carter] is just like us." That is, to be sure, not an uncommon way to arrive at one's political judgments (he's good, just like us); and it isn't limited to the Protestant middle class of the South. But it does have rather severe shortcomings.

On the day before the election, Parks Rusk, Dean Rusk's brother, told proudly of his part in devising the "hi-neighbor" campaign. Neighbors and friends of Jimmy's would knock on doors telling voters—*testifying* to voters, from personal experience—of his moral worth—not of his ideology, or his policies, but of his "integrity." Rusk related how neighbors and friends told other neighbors that this man they knew personally was a "man of staunch character, a family man, a churchman, a businessman, a civic worker—staunch all the way. He had *remarkable* across-the-board credentials." (Mr. Rusk enthusiastically poured out all of this anachronistic material to me on Monday, November 1, the day before a giant, modern, mass-organized election for the President of the United States, leader of the free world, commander-in-chief of a nuclear power, might or might not be won by his hi-neighbor candidate.) From that hi-neighbor idea grew the peanut brigades, with their trips North. Whether these Georgia neighbors were as effective in the huge general election as they had been in New Hampshire certainly would be questioned by some Northern Democratic Party leaders.

When the peanut brigades' staunch neighbor got to be President he proposed, and his Georgia friends endorsed, a "People-to-People" exchange program, matching American states with states and provinces abroad, like one he had participated in as Governor. He and his friends from home were enthusiastic. Other Governors, State Department people, and diplomats did not appear to share that enthusiasm. A State Department person said: "When you try to work that out with the federal government on a large scale . . . it's not easy."

Voluntarism and individualism are symbolized by "conversion," by the revival meeting, by missionary activities. Change your heart, your life. Change it at a particular moment—a time and place you can identify. Be born again. Society, history, the complex of institutions drop away leaving the solitary individual in his isolated moment. These churches, at the extreme, jump straight from the Bible to nineteenth- or twentieth-century America, implying that all the intervening centuries of Western history are sort of a mistake. "Historylessness" is one of their main characteristics, according to religious historian Sidney Mead. These revival-based American free churches on the frontier tend to be ahistorical, noninstitutional, nonintellectual (it's the *heart* before the intellect).

In the summer of 1976, political reporters were settled in Americus, in what one of them unkindly described as "a sleazy little crossroads motel," puzzling about the unusual politician over in Plains. The journalist chosen to be the pool reporter for the Men's Bible Class on one Sunday was William V. Shannon of *The New York Times*, a practicing and knowledgeable Roman Catholic who was later to be appointed by Carter as Ambassador to Ireland. Shannon's report of his morning among the Baptists, though carefully respectful, included a rather Romish surprise at the thinness of it all. He didn't quite know what to make of informal conversation about the Bible by the laymen in the Bible class, or the extemporaneous prayers and the rather formless flavor of the service itself—no vestments, no altar, no sacraments, no priest, no liturgy, no recitation of the creed, no form, no climax in the objective act of the mass. Just Georgia people singing a little and talking a little.

It is indeed formless by the measure of the Roman Mother Church of form, and from that fact comes much of the cultural influence: not objective, traditional, institutionalized, doctrinally elaborate communal form, but subjective individual experience. The "saving" of the individual soul.

Mr. Carter, like some thirty million other Americans, is an evangelical. The center of the evangelical movement is conversion. The center of conversion is a turning about of the heart and will at an identifiable moment. It is not only individualism but an enthusiastic individualism. That core idea—the conversion of individuals—though prominent throughout the New Testament and hence in Christianity in general is extracted in this American setting from among a great many other elements in Christianity (tradition, sacrament, liturgy, creed, the priest), and made the center and almost the whole of religious life. From that conversionist focus come the awakenings and revivals and missionary efforts that mark American Christianity.

A person is able to *decide*, with "decisions" dramatized in the revival meeting. He or she is converted, born again. *Voluntary* activities are undertaken by an act of will; missionary and evangelistic activities, undertaken by the free choice of the evangelists, appeal for the free decision of the evangelized.

And this religious culture is of course quite moralistic. Once more it is focused on the individual will: change your conduct. Do good. Do what is right. A variant of it produces George Brush. To an outsider the application of moral ideas can seem to be quite selective, as in the strictures against Demon Rum, dancing, playing cards. But the implicit effect on the society can be a great deal broader than these narrow and explicit prohibitions. The religious outlook implies a social philosophy, and the marks of it are still visible on a people to whom the Brotherhood conferences, Vacation Bible Schools, and missionary circles of the Plains Baptist Church are totally unfamiliar.

There was a time when visitors from other countries—Tocqueville, for example, coming from France in the 1830's and Lord Bryce coming from England in the 1880's—remarked with a certain surprise on the peculiar and central connections of religion with democratic institutions in America—religion of a particular shape and kind. In their bemused discovery of its importance and their puzzled effort to make out its nature and effects they somewhat resembled the members of the national political press gathered there in the Best Western Motel in Americus in 1976, undertaking the same task with respect to Jimmy Carter

and the Men's Bible Class at the Plains Baptist Church. Tocqueville and Bryce may have had more background.

"Upon my arrival in the United States," wrote Tocqueville,
"the religious aspect was the first thing that struck my attention;
and the longer I stayed there the more did perceive the great
political consequences resulting from this state of things, to
which I was unaccustomed. In France I had almost always seen
the spirit of religion and the spirit of freedom pursuing courses
diametrically opposed to each other; but in America I found they
were intimately united, and that they reigned in common cause
over the same country." Religion "reigned," though, only by a
voluntary adherence, and by an indirect effect upon government,
that was compatible with the spirit of freedom: "The real authority of religion was increased by a state of things which diminished its apparent force." A state of things, that is, in which
church and state are separated, religions are entirely voluntary,
and the influence upon politics and government is informal and
indirect.

Tocqueville, struck by an arrangement peculiar to him as a
French Roman Catholic, quizzed people about how it worked,
much as the Northerners quizzed deacons and Pastor Edwards in
Plains, and wary non-Baptists quizzed Jimmy Carter in New
Jersey. "Religion in America," wrote Tocqueville, as a result of
his researches, "takes no direct part in the government of society,
but nevertheless it must be regarded as the foremost of the
political institutions in that country, for if it does not impart a
taste for freedom it facilitates the use of free institutions." Those
votes of the congregation of the Plains Baptist Church over the
admitting of the Reverend Mr. Clennon King, the rather bizarre
black minister who applied for membership, with suspect timing,
on the Sunday before the election, may not have been in their
content and early result altogether edifying but they did demonstrate that each Baptist church makes its own rules, and by
internally democratic procedures.

Tocqueville was struck by the unanimous opinion that freely
held religious conviction was fundamental to democracy: "I do
not know whether all Americans have a sincere faith in their
religion, for who can search the human heart? But I am certain
that they hold it to be indispensable to the maintenance of
republican institutions." Every American, of all classes and par-

ties, held that view. It is not held any longer, today, but the shadow and memory of it reaches down to Jimmy Carter's Presidency.

Americans worked out a peculiar combination, from the point of view of Europe—from the point of view of most of the nations of the world—in which a separation between church and state and strictly voluntary membership and support of churches, on the one hand, were combined with wide religious membership and influence, including a permeation of the culture and an indirect influence on government. Voluntarily professed religious belief of this kind was held to be stronger, more real, more efficacious in shaping character than any automatic traditional religion that used the coercive power of the state as an ally. The reason Americans felt—as in the quotation from Tocqueville— religious belief to be the necessary foundation of republican institutions is that such free institutions require, to work right, the shaping of character, or morality, of civic virtue in the citizenry.

It has often been said that whereas Thomas Jefferson wanted church and state to be separate in order to protect the state from the church, Roger Williams wanted them separate in order to protect the church from the state. Using coercion, tying up with state power, damages the spiritual essence of true religion.

The Baptists were originally a "sect." That means choosing purity and withdrawal from society, rather than the universal, inclusive embrace of society and state that the "Church" sought. Puritans wanted to purify the Church of England; *separatist* Puritans did not want there even to *be* a Church of England—a national church (a big step); and *re*baptizers wanted individuals making *adult* decisions. Methodists wanted to bring rigor, seriousness, and simplicity to the Church of England. In every case they appealed to the poorer citizens, to people without power.

The individualistic sects set themselves apart from the heavy institutions of the social order. They were withdrawing from a corrupt collective world, with its institutions of power and coercion, in order to achieve a purity that could only be achieved by that withdrawal. They emphasized an individual's moral life and not the problems and responsibilities of the magistrate—in the earliest days Baptists did not expect to be magistrates. They were sects that found being a part of the government, with its use of the instrument of power, incompatible with the Christian life. The ethos of the free church Protestant world, and especially that of the Baptists that comes down to us in our own day, derives from that: antigovernmental, anti-institutional, antisocial.

The religious traditions that come out of this background have therefore not had to develop either the institutional forms or the intellectual discriminations to relate the high claims of the religion they profess to the difficult world of power, of politics and economics.

What happened in the United States, and most particularly with Southern Baptists in the South, is that this hitherto sect became a *de facto* church. Ironically the Baptists often have the power position their forebears explicitly and on principle rejected: they become a central religious institution with secular power. The Plains Baptist Church is the dominant institution in that little town. Southern Baptist Churches are dominant forces in towns bigger than Plains: Mark Twain once described Waco, Texas, as one tall tower surrounded entirely by Baptists. Dr. Criswell, the Dallas minister of the largest Southern Baptist Church in the world, endorsed Gerald Ford over Jimmy Carter in something of a political-religious media event that television covered extensively. He is a man who is not without influence and obviously not without his desire to affect the course of government. We have groups that are sects in their outlook but churches in their actual position, providing, among other things, a region's power elite, a Governor, a director of Office of Management and Budget, a President of The United States.

The Methodists and the Baptists and the Disciples of Christ have scrambled to develop the categories of understanding for participation in the responsibilities of a modern powerful nation. But it has been a scramble. Rabbi Louis Finkelstein once said when asked what guidance Judaism could give for a Jew in a position of executive power like Herbert Lehman, then the Governor of New York, replied, after some thought, "It was never expected that a Jew would be Governor of New York." So it is also in a sense with Baptists.

This religious culture has many values. It is good at producing the direct act of personal generosity, the voluntary donation of one's time or money to help "someone in need," the friendliness and cheerful giving that foreign observers note as an American characteristic. It can rouse human energies for a clear cut "moral" purpose—for a crusade, for a short-term enterprise with an unmistakably good and concrete purpose (electing Jimmy Carter looked that way to the peanut brigade). It can arouse enthusiasm and change people. The characteristic contributions have been the rousing of the sentiments of generosity, "morality," reform.

But it has not been notable for inculcating wisdom, depth, continuing responsibility in the difficult secular world of power. It has not been notable, in other words, for bringing its valuable simplicities into the service of a better politics.

# 11

## BLESSED ASSURANCE
## COMES TO
## WASHINGTON

Mary McCarthy wrote a sentence in her *Memories of a Catholic Girlhood* that Reinhold Niebuhr liked and quoted, with a laugh: "Religion is a good thing for good people and a bad thing for bad people." Fanatics and egotists may be made worse; gentle, generous people may be reinforced in their good qualities. Maybe so. But the sentence is shorthand, and a very fractional truth, an oversimplification that a fuller treatment would qualify to the point almost of obliteration. In a view too complex to put into such shorthand—most especially in Niebuhr's own elaborated view—"good" and "bad" are seen to be mixed in varying proportions in everybody, religious or not. (Niebuhr, to the consternation of many religious folk, kept resisting ideas that put the "sanctified," "saved," "converted" into some categorically superior position.) And if the notion of "good" and "bad" people be retained, one may observe that the McCarthy rule doesn't always hold. Religion of some flat, literal, us-against-them kind can have a bad effect upon people who would otherwise be humane, and religion of a better kind can soften and improve the Scrooges of this world, the bad people, the proud and selfish people. At least religious folk have believed this last point, with some supporting evidence.

Jimmy Carter may be a subtle addition to that evidence. Whereas the conservative and evangelical Protestant world he comes out of seems to a not very sympathetic observer to produce many examples of the potentially decent people made worse by a narrow and rigid religious nurture—made closed-minded, censorious, bigoted—Carter just might be someone on whom the effect was the other way around. This is a thin patch of ice, I know, where one skates near bad taste and presumption. As Tocqueville said, "Who can know the human heart?" But let me put the hypothesis.

In pockets of the old-time religion on the American continent many potentially gentle, self-effacing, good-hearted people turn into absolutists holding insistently to rigid formulae when their religious belief is touched. That's been drummed into them. Carter on the other hand is "by nature," as Herman Melville might say, a very proud man, exacting, not very tolerant of human frailty, a man who certainly has an element of rigidity in his make-up; he has a strong ego and an enormous, not-too-fastidious ambition. There are versions of the Christian religion that could just put all of that into overdrive. But Carter's appropriation of religion is evidently not of that sort. It is in fact flexible, self-critical, in accord with a better expression of his religious tradition, in which it checks and challenges rather than reinforces such qualities.

Carter's companion in theological discussion, William Gunter, was asked by Nicholas Horrock of *The New York Times*, before the world knew Jimmy Carter very well, to give a one-sentence characterization of his friend. Judge Gunter (as he then was) produced the following: "Jimmy Carter is a pragmatic intellectual whose religious faith gives him a modicum of humility." The word "modicum" is interesting, as is Judge Gunter's decision to include a reference to the problem of humility in so short a statement. In private, Gunter, whose admiration for Carter is immense, said that Carter would be a cocky, mean s.o.b. without his religious faith. That faith makes him know he may be wrong. He *has* admitted bein' wrong!

One can understand why the Judge felt it necessary to make this last point explicit. One view of Carter goes like this: "I think that it has become clear that he brings to the job his own values . . . and he does not have much use for other people's values. He operates less on consensus than other Presidents have."

Or this: Carter "seems never to be willing to compromise or accept advice. He is reluctant to admit that it is possible for him to make a mistake."

Or this: "He's one hundred per cent right and everyone else is one hundred per cent wrong, and he's the President and we have to do it his way."

These are statements by businessmen quoted in *Time* after Carter had been President for nine months. It is the view of him some newsmen kept telling us was held by many in Georgia.

Admirers of Carter certainly do not deny that he is self-confident and sure of himself. Everyone you talk to about Carter, everything you read about him, makes that point. A sub-Cabinet officer and a Democratic Party activist who was an early Carter supporter among liberals in the North, said to me—for just one typical example—"*Never* in my life have I met anybody who is as sure of himself, as self-confident. That's what struck me when I first met him."

The first thing Republican Congressman John Anderson said when I asked about Carter was that he is "a very self-confident man."

A related quality is ascribed also to Rosalynn Carter. A White House staff person said: "They are very *secure* people for this day and age, the most secure people I know."

Sometimes, among those who do not like him, there is a more negative word than "self-confidence." I tried a version of it on his oldest son: some people found Carter "cocky." Jack Carter, making a careful distinction, denied that this word applied to his father. "He isn't by nature a cocky person." I looked over at Carter's daughter-in-law, Judy Langford Carter, whom I had already learned had perceptions of her own and a willingness to express them. "Well," she said, smiling slightly and pausing, "it's a fine line. He *is* awfully self-assured. *Awfully* self-confident."

At the same time, they both insisted, he is very self-critical.

Self-assurance, security, self-confidence, cockiness, arrogance: friend and foe, family and the outside observers, critics and supporters agree that there is a quality in Carter that one or another of these words describes. He is not a man troubled by self-doubt, anguish, dark nights of the soul. He is not one who presents to the world a picture of that standard modern condition, the self in trouble with itself.

One of Carter's staff members in Washington and one of his earliest supporters in Chicago both worked through the circumstances of his life step-by-step to explain these qualities: he was a first child; had a secure, two-parent home; an ambitious mother and a disciplinarian, able father. His childhood environment was manageable; he was easily a leader in school, got straight A's; was the smartest person in his own hometown. There were Annapolis and Hyman Rickover. He returned to his hometown, where as businessman, civic leader, political leader, he was and is "used to being smarter than all the people around him" (this from the aide in Washington).

Carter seems to want to give this self-confident, secure picture of himself. No, he doesn't wake up at night. He would fall asleep quickly before the debates without any sleeping pill. He'll do his best and then not worry about it afterward. He's confident that he can do the job. He looks forward to each day's work. If he does his best then he is at ease. He says so often, so readily, so explicitly, that he is at ease, happy, secure, confident, and that he enjoys his work, that one might almost suspect a deliberate effort to present himself to the world modeled after the active-positive Presidents in James David Barker's *Presidential Character*, a book Carter has read and praised. Some might wonder whether he protests too much.

The negative side of these qualities, this strong ego, might well be pride, ruthless ambition, self-righteousness. Carter's appropriation of Christianity features the themes that go in the other direction: humility, forgiveness, "service."

He is not only knowledgable about Bible texts but also has a grasp of their inner meaning. One instance of this, perhaps ironically, appeared in the last section of the notorious *Playboy* interview.

Although that interview covered an enormous range of subjects, it kept coming back to *Playboy's* home territory, sex, and the fear of what a religious man would say or do or imply regarding that subject ("makes us feel guilty," said interviewer Robert Scheer on the "Today" show, pouting a little). The *Playboy* interviewers, down in Plains that last time, about to leave, mentioned yet again "people who are uneasy about [Carter's] religious beliefs" and the possibility that he would be a "rigid, unbending President." Carter answered them one more time, referred to his church and his Sunday school and gave a better exposition of the polity of the Baptist Church than most laymen could give.

Then, gathering homiletical steam, he launched into his argument to persuade them that his religious beliefs wouldn't make him coercively puritanical, self-righteous, or censorious. On the contrary—those beliefs teach the opposite lesson: humility, forgiveness, judging not that one be not judged. Carter gave an extemporaneous version of the parable of the Pharisee and the Publican which is certainly a *locus classicus* in the history of the West for the present point. The Pharisee says "I thank thee that I am not as other men"; the Publican says, "Be merciful to me, a sinner." Which one, Jesus asked rhetorically, was "justified." One of the markings Carter made in June Bingham's biography of Niebuhr, *Courage to Change*, referred to this parable as applied to the church: the church "stands in constant danger of itself becoming the Anti-Christ, since it is tempted, like the Pharisee, to say in prayer, 'I thank thee Lord that I am not like other institutions.' "

Carter gave his interlocuters from *Playboy* an informed exposition of the best subpart of the complicated Christian doctrine—the part about forgiveness and humility. Maybe Woodrow Wilson or Theodore Roosevelt—two religiously literate Presidents—have some passages like these somewhere, but given their characteristics, I doubt it. Certainly it was not their main note. They exemplified the righteous, moralizing, law-giving side of the Biblical heritage, the side that worried the *Playboy* interviewers. There has always been another, more profound side, which keeps getting obscured in the practice of churches and of church people. In modern times, affected somewhat I believe by a seepage of ideas from great currents of modern secular thought (Marx, Freud, science, relativism), distinguished theologians like Niebuhr and Tillich have come down with force on the side of humility, forgiveness, nonabsoluteness, the limitations of human perception about the right and the good. Carter has absorbed that and characteristically made a personal application of it. It is objectionable—"sinful"—to claim finality for our point of view or goodness for ourselves. To illustrate this point Carter used what would have been another good choice if the world hadn't been listening, a passage that would be quite appropriate in Sunday school, or anywhere else had there been no commercial press waiting to misunderstand it and to dramatize it to the public. Carter's illustration of his more general point is the perfectionist remark of Jesus that appears in Matthew 5:28, in the collection of sayings that is called The Sermon on the Mount. It is set in the context of a series of sayings about the new way that Jesus interprets the old law: in a more radical and inward way. I suppose, given the public response, one could say wistfully that Carter should have chosen for his illustration the saying about "you shall not swear falsely," or "you shall not kill." But Carter instead took the saying about adultery and, like an earnest Sunday school teacher, applied it to himself. He was trying hard to make his point to these interviewers. Because no person can fulfill so high a demand (not to lust even "in the heart"), we must be "saved" not by moral performance but by "grace"—by God's forgiveness. The standard is raised to the level of the impossible, and the believer is cast back, therefore, into contrition about himself and nonjudgmental forgiveness toward others. That was the point Carter was making—not really anything at all about lust, adultery or sex. The teaching he was trying, with winsome naiveté, to explain goes back to the heart of the Protestant Reformation, to Luther—that of justification by grace alone. It goes back before that to Augustine, and before that to Paul, and before that—here we are again—back to the teachings of Jesus in Matthew 5. In other words, to the very core of Christianity.

Carter's sound rendering of the best of Christian teaching was carried to the vast public in a distorted and selective way with the text of one paragraph rolling across the screen on the *Today* program while the two *Playboy* interviewers milked the publicity. Headlines featured "lust" and "adultery." It was evident that many commentators and reporters didn't even know that Carter had been applying a sentence from the New Testament; they seemed never to have heard of or read the fifth chapter of Matthew, although one would be hard put to find a piece of writing of comparable length more fundamental to the history of the West. One got the impression from some of the furor that Carter had gratuitously volunteered some comments about his lustiness. News stories concentrated on two phrases that Carter used. Columnists, reporters, politicians, cartoonists and editorial writers criticized Carter for the phrases and for giving the interview to *Playboy*: he wasn't prudent, calculating, smart in his own interest. They were shocked-by-proxy—shocked, not in their own right, but on behalf of their picture of little old ladies in Dubuque whom they assumed would be shocked.

I leave aside that exhausted discussion of whether he should
have given the interview to that magazine; I guess it's clear he
shouldn't have, but if one can get by that issue, and look at the
interview itself, it was quite an impressive document.

Anyone who has been interviewed by a newsperson with
biases, stereotypes, and a limited understanding of the subject,
knows how frustrating that can be. The interviewee comes out
distorted by the limitations of the interviewer. Thus one wire
service reporter asked Carter whether he believed in the literal
words of the Bible, whether "sin originated with a serpent." On
another occasion he was asked, of course, about Jonah and the
whale. What is Carter supposed to do with that sort of thing? As to
the matter of the serpent he said, "I can't disavow it. I have no
way of knowing." Then, grinning, he said, "I don't believe the
earth has four corners, that it's square," as described in the Bible.
"The Bible is obviously written in allegories," he said.

There is an unsympathetic and unknowing contingent that
wants to fasten the word "fundamentalist" onto Carter, along
with the stereotypes it brings. This is a major example of that
phenomenon of the unfriendly interpreter, who himself needs to
be interpreted, and of the reciprocity of antagonisms, discussed
earlier.

But Carter, however eager some may be to call him by the
name (epithet, to them), is not a fundamentalist. Southern Baptists in general overcame the fundamentalist controversy; Mrs.
Harris disavows the label; Gunter scoffs at the image it applies to
Carter. A careful examination of his position in context led the
religious historian E. Brooks Holifield to say bluntly, "He's not a
Fundamentalist." Anybody who knows that territory can tell
from exposure to Carter's religious outlook that he's a long way
from the reaction against modernity that fundamentalism represented.

What is his attitude toward the Bible? A dutiful parishioner and
Sunday school goer like Jimmy Carter certainly does learn it, read
it repeatedly, study it.

I refer again to Mary McCarthy's *Memoirs of a Catholic Girlhood*. Looking back somewhat patronizingly from her superior
adult repudiation of that childhood she does nevertheless say
this: at least being brought up in a devout Catholic home taught
you some important ingredients for the understanding of the

history of our civilization—the names of the saints, who they were and why they were saints, for example. A Bible-based Protestant church cannot claim as much perhaps but at least there is the Bible.

There's a moment in Randall Jarrell's funny novel *Pictures from an Institution* when the visiting poet asks what one can assume that the students all have read and is told by the English professor, "There *is* no book that one can assume that all our students have read." The narrator—speaking clearly for Jarrell— observes that in such a sentence more than in the march of armies one could hear the sound of the fall of civilization.

Well, if there is a book that should be the point of unifying reference for the civilization of which we are still a part, it would be that collection of books, poems, narratives, histories, preachers' manuals, and letters gathered together across centuries first by the Jewish world and then by the Christian sect within Judaism into what now appears in the drawer of a hotel room desk as *The Holy Bible*.

What we hear Carter getting from it is not the indiscriminate recitation of the genealogical tables of King David or the bloodthirsty tales from the book of Judges, or imaginative numerology from the book of Revelation but rather the kernel of the story as it has been assimilated by the Christian Church.

People in the classes that he takes his turn teaching say he's better than others at bringing out the meaning of the passages he deals with. He does strike a critical note, even a kind of relativizing note (not a word he would accept), that certainly is incompatible with the rigidities of literalism. (He has said, "I don't believe everything in the Bible to be literally true. I don't think the earth was created in seven days as we know days now and I reserve the right to make my own interpretation.")

Robert Shogan records in his book *Promises to Keep* Carter's teaching of a Sunday school class at the First Baptist Church in Washington after he was President. He asked the class what the Bible is. He received a series of metaphorical answers—"A law, a road map, a letter from God, an almanac, a description of what God is like." Finally, Shogan reports, Carter provided his own definition: "A debate between God and man, God and woman, over the laws of God, a constant interchange between God and human beings in which we struggle to justify ourselves." Whatever you may make of that, it isn't the sort of thing that one can hear in old-fashioned churchly settings, that the Bible is "the literal word of God"; it isn't what many orthodox Christians who are not necessarily fundamentalist would say. It mirrors instead the more problematic view some theologians of the twentieth century have reflected. Carter marked this passage from Niebuhr: "For we are made to be in dialogue not only with ourselves but also with our fellows, and ultimately with God. The Bible, in fact, is the record, not of a monologue on the part of God or man, but of a spirited exchange between them."

The complex view that sees the Bible as an exchange between man and God is one evidence that Carter doesn't fit the stereotype of the fundamentalist. Another is the quotation that Carter continually uses from Tillich: "Religion is a search." Carter often follows his Tillich quotation with the remark that when you've stopped searching you've stopped believing, which is a liberated view from the perspective of the literalistic Rock of Gibraltar kind of biblical Christianity. There are those who insist on certain fundamentals that have to be believed, and believed in precisely stated formulae. Not Carter. In June Bingham's book Carter underlined this sentence: "We must never confuse our fragmentary apprehension of the truth with the truth itself." It was not usual for the old-time religion to admit that it had only a fragmentary apprehension of the truth, and even less self-critically to remind itself of that fragmentariness.

When candidate Jimmy Carter was talking to Bill Moyers on the 4th of July, 1976, he remarked that the interview that they had done—Moyers's "Conversation with Jimmy Carter" on the Public Broadcasting System in May—had been the best thing to come out of the campaign.

At a party in New York during the party convention in August a pretty woman whom Moyers had not met until that day—Ruth Carter Stapleton, as it turned out—made her way through the crush of the crowd in order to tell him how much her brother liked that interview.

Carter, as it seemed, had had an especially grueling day, and at the end of it did not want to go to the studio to do this television interview. Gregg Schneiders, his aide, insisted that a promise had been made and that he had to do it. Carter went to the studio, exhausted and grumpy. When he started talking to Moyers about the South, and netting fish, and his religious beliefs, however, he found his exhaustion leaving him and he enjoyed himself and had a memorable conversation. He felt rapport with Moyers and felt that the interview was more important than most of the things he did. Ruth Stapleton wanted Moyers to know that.

On an evening five months later, in the White House, Rosalynn went over and sat in Jimmy's lap ("just like two twenty-year-olds" according to a visitor) and they talked about the campaign and election. Rosalynn said that just not enough people got to *know* Jimmy.

They talked about what helped. Jimmy said that Rosalynn's appearance on *Meet the Press* was the *FINEST* thing he had ever seen, the best thing of that kind ever. She beamed. A visitor said that Jimmy's interview with Bill Moyers was the best of *its* kind. She beamed again, the two "sitting like kids together in a chair."

Not everybody agreed about the Moyers interview. Some found such a public discussion of private religious views distasteful. David Broder used a passage from the Moyers interview as a sample of Carter's overweening self-confidence. Moyers, as Broder quoted him, asked Carter whether he ever had any doubts, and Carter answered, "I can't think of any."

I had missed the Moyers program when it was telecast, and therefore made a trip over to the offices of WNET on the Westside of New York City in order to view it all by myself in a booth. (The transcript alone does not give the full effect.)

I found that, despite my respect for Broder, and my agreement with the general point that Carter is loaded to the brim with self-confidence, that I would not press that interpretation of the exchange on the Moyers tape. The question from Moyers came very suddenly, without warning: "Do you ever have any doubts?" (In a way it was more revealing of Moyers than Carter.) Here's the complete exchange:

> *Moyers:* Do you ever have any doubts? People say to me, "Jimmy Carter appears to be so full of certainty and conviction in a time when, as Gabriel said in *Green Pastures*, 'Everything that's loose is coming, everything that's tied together is turning loose, coming loose.'" Do you ever have any doubts? About yourself, about God, about life?
> *Carter:* I can't think of any, you know.

(That's where Broder stopped quoting. The effect on the program wasn't the same as the effect in print. And Carter, having knocked down the line drive, then began to field it.)

> Obviously I don't know all of the answers to the philosophical questions and theological questions that—you know, the questions that are contrived. But the things that I haven't been able to answer in a theory of supposition, I just accept them and go on. The things that I can't influence or change.
>
> I do have, obviously, many doubts about the best way to answer a question or how to alleviate a concern or how to meet a need. Or to how—how to create in my own life a more meaningful purpose and to let my life be expanded in my heart and mind. So doubts about the best avenue to take among many options is a kind of doubt. That is a constant presence with me. But doubt about my faith? No. Doubt about my purpose in life? I don't have any doubts about that.

Despite his not having resolved all the ultimate questions he had made a decision about where he stood on them—surely a respectable position.

At another point Moyers, again rather suddenly, asked a question that, again, your ordinary interviewer would not have asked, "What do you think we're on earth for?" Carter answered with a capsule statement that included the so-called great commandment: "To love God with all your heart and soul and mind, and love yourself. I try to take that condensation of the Christian theology and let it be something through which I search for a meaningful existence."

There are wide differences in sensibility and taste in these matters, of course. To those who find this sentimental and who find Carter's chapter in his autobiography about "the person in front of you" (love the person in front of you at any given moment) inadequate, especially for political understanding, I would suggest at least that if one is going to err, this is the direction in which to err. It is certainly not the direction from which the worst effects of religion have come. And on the whole, by the standards of the thick strands of sentimentality that run through American Protestantism, Carter's expression of the kernel of the religious belief does not err badly in that direction.

What does one object to in religious "sentimentality"? Herman Melville wrote that Christianity is "a volume bound in rose leaves, clasped with violets, and by the beaks of hummingbirds printed with peach juice on the leaves of lilies." An editor at *Harper's* in the nineteenth century, receiving one of the very popular religious novels, wrote across the first page in large letters "FUDGE." The problem with sentimentality is the waste and misuse of powerful human emotions. It is the evoking of those emotions—the words and images that describe them—with inadequate intellectual control, for inadequate purpose, with inadequate links to life. Carter's expression of potentially sentimental points usually does not leave the slightly sick feeling that one can have after the syrup of sentimental religion. Why not? Because behind Carter's expression of these themes there is control, there is more intellectual discipline, perhaps more serious practical application.

Carter, as I say, can state accurately central themes of Christianity, as understood in particular by the Protestant Reformation: "By accepting God's grace, something we don't deserve, yet we get."

This core belief, properly understood, with its possible psychological power, goes beyond the usual form of either liberal Christianity or conservative Christianity as they have often appeared in this country. Both in their different ways are moralistic, and this Reformation idea isn't. Antecedent to any moral performance, any earning, any *quid pro quo* relationship to ultimate powers by doing good, there is a "gift" freely offered every day.

Kandy Stroud took her tape recorder to two sessions of the Men's Bible Class in Plains once when Carter was teaching early during the primaries, and another time just after his nomination. She presents what she heard in her book *How Jimmy Won*:

> Quite often if you go into a Baptist church in an average town, certainly in the South, you find a social and economic elite. We're the ones who are kind of the prominent people in town, and we have a tendency—all of us, certainly I have myself—to think because I have been accepted by God . . . I have a tendency to think I'm better than other people, that surely God must have recognized my worth and my goodness and therefore wanted me because I'm better than others.
> But we're saved through what? Grace.

> Grace means a gift, a gift of God. Through what? Through
> faith. In whom? Christ. We're saved by grace through faith in
> Christ. And when we have that faith, along with it should come
> humility. Christ more than anything else talked about pride
> and deplored pride. Because He saw that when we think we're
> better than anyone else we almost automatically are separated
> from others. When His disciples struggled over who's going to
> sit at your right hand, who's going to sit at your left hand, who's
> going to be highest when we all go to heaven? Christ said the
> greatest among you are what? Servants.

Carter understands the territory, and generally articulates it at
something like its best.

When Carter's staff persuaded him not to use a biblical quotation in his inaugural address—a passage from the Old Testament
about healing that seemed to them to sound self-righteous—he
substituted the familiar passage from Micah: "What doth the
Lord require of thee O man but to do justly and to love mercy,
and to walk humbly with thy God." A religiously literate friend of
Carter's who was at the White House in March after the inauguration was called upon by the President to say grace at dinner. This
man's custom is to draw upon verses from the Bible in the first
part of the grace. He began, "What doth the Lord require of thee
O man . . ." and repeated the verse from Micah before asking a
blessing of the meal of the evening. In the middle of the conversation at dinner the President remarked to his guest: "I liked the
blessing you said."

Carter makes an explicit application of the central Christian
ideas to a believer's security. To the Indianapolis congregation he
used the analogy of his own "daddy" (not many Presidential
candidates, or other modern, adult American males would speak
in that way). His "daddy" when he was young was always there
and would pick him up and take care of him if he needed it.

Carter told the Disciples of Christ in Lafayette that Christian
belief gives "an unchanging core around which our lives can
function. And that's an enormous benefit to us and a tremendous
blessing."

That phrase "an unchanging core around which our lives can
function" seems representative of the man.

Though Carter is obviously well read in the Bible and has read
some contemporary theology, he does not show an interest in

theological or religious quibbles. For him the main points are settled and he's living on the basis of these settled points rather than examining and reexamining and speculating about them. Norman Mailer's effort to extract a discussion about Kierkegaard from him ran up against Carter's limited interest in that sort of thing, quotations from Kierkegaard in his writing notwithstanding.

One may see in Carter's decision to line himself up with received tradition a kind of spiritual economy.

He is not a man tortured by doubts. He said to Moyers, "I don't worry about it too much any more. I used to when I was a college sophomore, and we used to debate for hours and hours why we're here, who made us, where we shall go, what's our purpose." But not anymore. That is the sort of thing one did when one was a sophomore. A decision is made and one operates then on that basis. Meaning no disrespect one could say it is the kind of religious faith that might appeal to an engineer or naval commander's practical mind. This is to be the end point. Let's decide it and go from there.

In fact there is an aspect of his dutiful staying with the belief in which he is born that partakes of the security that he then describes. One can almost say that the bright, linear, focused young man made a kind of willed decision to hold to the belief of his parents and his upbringing without much question and not to stir around about it.

From that "unchanging core" comes an acceptance, a lack of fear of death. Robert Sheer—who asked *every*thing—asked him about the assassination of Presidents. Carter answered:

> Well, in the first place, I'm not afraid of death. In the second place, it's the same commitment I made when I volunteered to go into the submarine force. I accepted a certain degree of danger when I made the original decision, then I didn't worry about it anymore. It wasn't something that preyed on my mind; it wasn't something I had to reassess every five minutes. There is a certain element of danger in running for President, borne out by statistics on the number of Presidents who have been attacked, but I have to say frankly that it's something I never worry about.

Although Carter isn't afraid of it, he does refer, typically, to the *statistics* on attacks on Presidents.

Sheer returned to the first part of his answer: why does he not fear death:

> It's part of my religious belief, I just look at death as not a threat. It's inevitable, and I have an assurance of eternal life. There is no feeling on my part that I *have* to be President, or that I *have* to live, or that I'm immune to danger. It's just that the termination of my physical life is relatively insignificant in my concept of overall existence. I don't say that in a mysterious way: I recognize the possibility of assassination. But I guess everybody recognized the possibility of other forms of death— automobile accidents, airplane accidents, cancer. I just don't worry.

Kandy Stroud asked him, teasingly she says, if he was prepared for the "Second Coming." Carter gave a serious reply: "I'm ready. I have no fear. I'm not afraid of dying."

In the interview with Bill Moyers there is a similar comment:

> You know, I'm not afraid to see my life ended. I feel like every day is meaningful. I don't have any fear at all of death.

When conservative American Christianity presents the idea of grace it often does so in a smug way: we have something you don't have. I don't sense any of that in Carter's religious outlook, even though he personally has a self-confessed inclination to distinguish himself sharply from most other people. He doesn't have the kind of trumping-your-ace Christian belief that's not hard to find elsewhere.

In none of these longer records of his religious ideas (Stroud twice, Shogan, *Playboy*, Moyers) is the tone at all smug. So it was also in the Second Christian Church and in Lafayette. In *Courage to Change* he chose to mark the following passage from Niebuhr:

> Unless a person has some initial faith in God's forgiveness, he is unlikely to face up to the depth of sin in himself: and unless he faces up to the depth of sin in himself, he is unlikely to feel the repentance which can result in God's forgiveness and the grace of a "new life."

A reader who balks at the religious language may nevertheless see that this is not a paragraph that would appeal either to complacent church folk or to the world's "winners" as presented in the success books: it does not promote being number one, getting power, getting to the top. There is a core of self-criticism in that quotation, and self-criticism set into symbols of what is ultimate.

# 12

## A MAN WHO READ NIEBUHR

Once when I was young I took down from a shelf a book called *Moral Man and Immoral Society*, by Reinhold Niebuhr, and on first looking into it I was stunned to find so much truth written right there on the page. Then felt I more or less like some watcher of the skies when a new planet swims into his ken, or (somewhat) like stout Cortez when with eagle eyes he stared at the Pacific— and all his men looked at each other with a wild surmise—silent, upon a peak in Darien. I was later to learn that a reading of Mr. Niebuhr had something of the same effect on Georgia State Senator Jimmy Carter. His way of formulating the point, in some contrast to the poem of Keats that I have been quoting, went as follows: "That's the most amazin' thing I've ever read."

Because I, too, came out of a Protestant religious environment remote from cosmopolitan centers, and had an interest in politics, and felt—I impute this now to Mr. Carter, joining him to me in this feeling—that churchly homilies generally speaking did not get these two (the Christian religion and politics) put together right, and yet that that connection for all its faulty, bollixed, mixed-up, wrongheaded usual treatment is still a giant magnet of a subject—almost as powerful a subject as there is—I therefore conclude, despite the skeptics, that Mr. Carter's reading and appreciation of, and learning a lot from, Reinhold Niebuhr may be real. As they say on those religions programs on television, I believe. I believe that the affinity between Carter and Niebuhr is authentic and important.

I will explain in a moment how I come to this belief—it is not really an act of blind faith. And I will also explain why it matters. There are those, of course, who ask why anyone should care particularly whether Mr. Carter is or is not affected by this particular writer. My answer is that it has to do with Carter's fundamentals, and the link those might have with the country's.

But first as to the skeptics. They are many. One Niebuhr scholar—a man who voted for Carter, and is not necessarily critical of him otherwise—said rather irreverently of the President of the United States (but if you call yourself Jimmy, what can you expect?): "This guy doesn't sound very Niebuhrian to *me*." Vernon Jordan, holding his hands apart to indicate two widely separated, contrasting symbols, said once, shaking his head, "Niebuhr and The Plains Baptist Sunday School. Can you believe that?" Evidently he couldn't.

Jimmy Carter's widely known—some would say widely advertised—interest in Reinhold Niebuhr has been greeted with a steady rain of doubt almost from the moment Mr. Carter stuck his head out into the contemporary political weather. When in his autobiography he quoted as epigraphs—one, two, three, in an unlikely triple play—Reinhold Niebuhr, Bob Dylan, and Dylan Thomas—there were those who regarded that stunning combination as a transparently calculated distribution for propaganda purposes—the nasal Mr. Dylan for the yearning, bouncing young; Dylan Thomas for the culturally literate, some of them perhaps still bouncing slightly too; and Reinhold Niebuhr for the religiously literate and the politically philosophical. Quite a trio.

And—well-distributed triple plays aside—there are doubts today about *any* politician's learned references. The quotations with which a modern politician decorates his addresses are assumed by the skeptics and the cynics in the press (the two categories, some would say, exhaust the field) to have passed straight from the speech writer's copy of *Bartlett's Familiar Quotations* through the speech text and the politician's mouth out again into the ears of the audience, without stopping to be intellectually digested at any point along the way. Theodore Sorensen was known to carry a copy of Bartlett's on speechwriting trips; John F. Kennedy's speeches would often show the result. The wicked Englishman Henry Fairlie wrote, about the Kennedy days: "One can well understand how, in the impoverished intellectual and cultural life of Washington, it was taken as a marvel that a politician could quote some lines of W. B. Yeats or pronounce the name of Aristotle. There may not have been books on the New Frontier, but there were books of quotations." Carter at least must have quarried his Niebuhr sentence himself. The sentence is: "The sad duty of politics is to establish justice in a sinful world." He couldn't find *that* in any book of quotations, nor is it likely that Jody Powell found it for him.

Nevertheless it was assumed by many to be the mere decoration and bait that politicians use, an assumption that experience with modern political speechwriting encourages. I was startled in another Presidential campaign when a senior speechwriter made a rather sweeping request for a quotation from the Bible. It was to be used in a speech in Harlem.

"A quotation saying what?"

"Anything. It doesn't matter."

Apparently all that was needed was a speech-ending rumble of the sound of Biblical music, without regard to meaning. Such experiences experiences do not encourage excessively earnest study of learned quotations and references made by politicians in the texts of their speeches.

In Mr. Carter's own case—to continue the list of reasons for the aforementioned skepticism—there had been among the items in Hamilton Jordan's famous "prescient" memorandum of 1972, spelling out step one—step two—step three how to achieve the Presidency (a calculating document in the extreme), the recommendation that Mr. Carter, at the right stage, deliberately lay on some heavyweights. Was then the adroit reference to Niebuhr just a calculated act in the meticulous Carter-Jordan plan?

Remembering Jordan's penchant for point systems, one could imagine a day when Mr. Jordan might have asked: "How many points would it be worth to quote Reinhold Niebuhr?"

Another line of skepticism—and this one certainly has a point—holds that Carter has such a different kind of a mind from Niebuhr's as to make them very ill-suited intellectual companions. Where Carter is thorough, clear, accurate, analytical, down-to-earth, inductive, and as his son Jack says "very linear"; the practical straight-thinking, perhaps rather rigid "Yankee" who gets things done and is not given to flights of imagination, Niebuhr on the other hand, though not quite the Germanic thinker of the cloudland, was nevertheless intellectually powerful, complex, inexact, undefinitional, inclined toward irony, ambiguity, and contradiction. He was not, like Carter, concrete and factually minded. He once wrote on a student paper the impatient injunction: "Seek significant generalizations!" He certainly did that himself. On the other hand, where Carter is driven to those unguarded exaggerations, superlatives, and absolutes—"a *superb* Cabinet!" "A welfare plan that is a *complete* break with the past!" "*Complete* confidence in Bert Lance!"—Niebuhr was, at his higher intellectual level, qualified, unabsolute, unsuperlative. His book *The Irony of American History* might be described as one long criticism of our national self-exaggeration. Niebuhr was a thinker who held contraries together, in tension, in his mind, in a way that would give an engineer or a manager the fidgets. He was not careful and definitional but set down what he had to say in a rush, leaving the reader to follow as best he could. A young Jewish theologian remarked after a day-long session that this Niebuhr was less interested in precise and systematic definition than anybody of comparable eminence he had ever met. Carter can sit for *hours*, the dutiful student of detail, listening to Brzezinsky briefings; "He *loves* that," says his daughter-in-law Judy. Niebuhr on the other hand, could scarcely sit still to hear himself talk, let alone anybody else, and certainly not for hours of detail on a subject the intellectual meat of which he had already caught in the first sentence. I have this memory of him going out the door, leaving meetings, with parting shots, over at least three decades. A man who worked on Carter's campaign staff, who is knowledgeable about Niebuhr, and is now part of the administration, shook his head in disbelief when I first asked about this connection: "They really are very different kinds of minds."

Moreover some reporters—among them the scrupulous and intelligent Elizabeth Drew of *The New Yorker*—had wondered in print why Carter always used exactly the same Niebuhr quotation; perhaps the absolute grand total in his supply kit was one.

And it could be said of that quotation—here I add something of my own to this catalogue of reservations—that it was not necessarily the distinctive note of Niebuhr. With the stress on the *sadness*, the *duty*, and the *sinful* world, that Niebuhr sentence could almost have come from any sober-sided politically minded representative of the Calvinist-Reformed-Puritan traditions. Perhaps with the word "sinful" secularized, it could have been provided by a "realistic" political writer of our American past—by a founding father like John Adams or James Madison. It could come from any of the folk who are always explaining that men are not angels; that politicians must not assume a way but rather must take for granted the nonangelic and self-interested character of human beings in the aggregate; that interest, power, and conflict are not accidental and occasional but essential and constant elements of "politics."

None of this is news, although it may sound like it in amazing-grace/born-again surroundings, featuring individual conversions, in a more innocent Protestant smalltown America. Niebuhr on this point—the realistic foundations of politics—was to an extent simply the mediator of older European and American realistic themes.

American leaders since World War II have understandably wanted to hear these older themes of *statecraft*, about the "responsible use of power"; about "hard choices"; about politics being the art of the "possible"; about the "grey" areas, without sharp moral lines; about the "sad" duty and the "sinful" world. Sometimes one could detect in the voice of these balance-of-power politicians a kind of furrowed-browed self-sympathy as, suffering servants, they presented themselves as caught (oh, woe!) in the awesome (!) responsibility and "sad" duty of these hard choices.

Niebuhr was, indeed, a significant modern American spokesman for the realistic "sad duty" point of view. Dean Acheson used as the title of a book of his early Cold War speeches a phrase from Niebuhr: *The Pattern of Responsibility*. Several members of the State Department's policy planning staff in its important years 1946-50 read Niebuhr; George Kennan called him "the Father of us all"—i.e., all of us American realists. But the point of view is a very old one and by no means unique to him. What made Niebuhr distinctive was not this realism but the American and Christian idealism he combined with it. He was at once as realistic as the realists and as idealistic as the idealists, differing from each by his commitment to the other; he was a both/and man, with combinations—"tensions"—that looked (appropriately, given his own language) ironical, even paradoxical. But the foundation was "social justice" as a surrogate for "love" in collective life. Niebuhr had worked out his realistic ideas in another, earlier context than these postwar diplomatists; he was later to be, as some of them were not and Carter was not, an early and vigorous opponent of the Vietnam War. If you divide the ideological world into those whose first instinct is to resist change in the direction of greater equality, and those whose first instinct is to promote it, Niebuhr for all his realism was in the latter group. The "sad duty" "sinful world" themes—true enough in their place—were not primary for him.

The more serious questioning of Carter's link to Reinhold Niebuhr, of course, has to do with their respective view of "man," of the goodness or otherwise of human beings, and specifically the American people. The shorthand would be: Niebuhr, pessimist; Carter, optimist. Carter's main campaign theme, that the government ought to be as compassionate and decent and honest and chock full o' downright goodness as the American people appears to run directly contrary to Niebuhr's view of man, and especially of man as taken in huge lumps like the "American people"; human beings are "fallen," "sinful," self-interested, inclined to self-love, proud—and pride is the core of "sin." Niebuhr is seen (rightly, as far as it goes) to have been a theologian who tried to resuscitate the ancient Christian doctrine of sin and to apply it especially to groups, to the collective. The individual characteristics of the human person are aggravated when human beings are gathered together either in organized groups (they have little or no conscience, and no self-restraining capacity) such as the giant economic interests and nations—which exhibit these tendencies in the extreme—or in latent groups like the social and economic classes. One human being can rise above his egotism and his self-interest, sometimes even to the height of self-sacrifice and forgiveness of an enemy—but one cannot expect that in the politics of large groups of human beings. Politics must be founded on the realities of the common deficiencies of mankind. The American people (*any* people) therefore, would not be an entity whose "goodness," "decency" "compassion" and fullness of love one would continually extol.

When Harvey Shapiro of *The New York Times Book Review* interviewed the President in May of 1977, he pressed him on this point, and more than once: doesn't the title of your book *A Government As Good As Its People* run counter to the Niebuhr quote; doesn't it clash with the darker view of man as "fallen"? Isn't there a conflict between his theme (Mr. Carter grants that it is his theme)—the goodness and compassion and honesty of the average American—and the theologians and somber Southern novelists Carter reads and quotes? "It's a rather smiling view of America, and of its people that comes through in the book," said Mr. Shapiro. "[It] runs somewhat counter to Southern writers who see man as fallen. And if one thinks of Government as in part an instrument to help man protect himself from his own base nature, from his own egotistic sin, I don't see that reflected in your book." It is an obvious point, a point that appears repeatedly, especially in any conversation about Carter and Niebuhr but also about the Southern novelists with a Calvinist ingredient, or about Puritanism. A scholar, in argument against some material in these pages, contrasted (I oversimplify) the frowning, perhaps, scowling, Puritan with the benign, smiling Carter. On Inauguration Day a Democratic politician, better read than most, who had held several state offices and once ran for Governor in his state, by then perforce a Carter supporter, looked at me in disbelief when I mentioned this theme. "Niebuhr would have taken all that stuff of Jimmy's about the goodness of the people," he said, "and torn it to shreds."

So now how can these contradictions be explained? Or if not explained, then qualified, modified, corrected?

I shall call to that purpose a text from a suitable source for our present subject, *The Confessions of St. Augustine*. Augustine, who with the understanding of his times, assumed that Moses wrote all the first five books of the Bible, noticed how widely the interpretations varied: one man says Moses meant this; another man says Moses meant that; another man says Moses meant still another thing. But, asked Augustine, why can't it be in such profound writings as these that all of these interpreters have *some* part of the truth. A profound writer may cast light not like a window but like a prism, in many directions, and may be seen differently from different angles. St. Augustine then said, in his own right: "I certainly—and I fearlessly declare it from my heart—were I to write anything to have the highest authority, should prefer so to write, that whatever of truth anyone might apprehend concerning these matters, my words should re-echo, rather than that I should set down one true opinion so clearly as that I should exclude the rest . . ."

Well, St. Augustine certainly did achieve that fruitful rich prismatic ambiguity, and so did Reinhold Niebuhr. And one of those who saw something important in the prism of Reinhold Niebuhr is now the President of the United States.

As there is more than one side of Niebuhr, so there is also to Carter. If, as is often said, Mr. Carter is complicated, and no simple figure to interpret, then the same is true, multiplied, of Reinhold Niebuhr.

Though stereotypes of the two men could be set in direct opposition to each other, in the more complex reality they have a considerable overlap.

Niebuhr is usually thought of as a tutor in realism to social idealists. He may also be an instructor in social justice to religious conservatives. For Carter he must have been at least a reinforcement.

Niebuhr had the credentials. A religiously conservative Southern Baptist deacon could take social ideas from Niebuhr that he would not take from an antireligious radical. Underneath Niebuhr's social philosophy there are the everlasting arms of Christian belief; he is biblical; he gives off the sound of orthodoxy (one word for him and his group—a word he didn't like—was "neo-orthodox").

And his understanding of the role of institutions and the continuities of social life—the quasi conservatism of his underlying social outlook—helped to make him acceptable. He has the ingredients on the one side of his religious and cultural conservatism that make more palatable the social and economic progressivism on the other. In other words, given his complexity, he can have differing relationships to people coming at him from different backgrounds.

Though popular treatments labeled Niebuhr a "pessimist," he wasn't a pessimist about man or about life. We had an exchange about that one day and he settled (one might have predicted) for the word "ambivalent." As a Christian preacher and moralist he did not have that final pessimism of the really dark gloomy folk of the modern age; he had an ultimate hope.

That doesn't mean, however, that he had any *immediate* earthly hope that the world would be made beautiful by science and progress. He was of course a consistent critic of the idea of inevitable progress, and of any theory that located the root cause of evil anywhere except in man himself (in malleable institutions, for instance) or that assumed that that root cause can be finally eliminated in this life. It continues "to the end of time"—the perennial human struggle.

Niebuhr's greatest paragraph, which James Reston has quoted in his column more than once, appears in *The Irony of American History*:

> Nothing that is worth doing can be achieved in our lifetime; therefore we must be saved by hope. Nothing which is true or beautiful or good makes complete sense in any immediate context of history; therefore we must be saved by faith. Nothing we do, however virtuous, can be accomplished alone; therefore we are saved by love. No virtuous act is quite as virtuous from the standpoint of our friend or foe as it is from our standpoint. Therefore we must be saved by the final form of love which is forgiveness.

Niebuhr's belief embraces a combination of tendencies that go further in opposing directions than his opponents'. He was more "hopeful" fundamentally and profoundly with a hope reaching "beyond history"; and at the same time he was unflinching in looking at the evils of the actual human life—as for example looking the gross evil of Nazism squarely in the eye, and early, and seeing that it was an abomination that had to be fought. It couldn't be conference-tabled away, set aside by sermons on brotherhood or by pretending it was somebody else's problem, or by saying it would be nice if we had a gathering where all the leaders of the world got their feet under the table and sort of talked things out and had square dancing in the evening. He was also of course against the optimism that appeared in some social scientists who thought they could fix things with a sufficient supply of questionnaires, foundation grants, and behavioral manipulations.

In Niebuhr there are always tensions between two or more things held simultaneously. Human beings are in his view both better fundamentally and worse in actual practice than prevailing modern views would see them to be; in his lingo there is a high estimate of human stature in the concept of the "image of God," but a low estimate of human "virtue" in man as sinner in actual practice.

The relevance of this old Biblical-Christian talk to the present subject is that Niebuhr's view of man includes a profound positive element, even though the realistic and negative element is much more widely advertised. He kept insisting that in every situation there is a higher possibility for love, justice, forgiveness. As he is at once more realistic than the realists and more idealistic than the idealists, so he is also at once nearly as optimistic as the optimists at the same time he is nearly as pessimistic as the pessimists. Well, that's a Niebuhrian sentence, or an effort at one, to try to get across the point that these things are combined, simultaneously present, not separable.

Niebuhr is not a pessimist about man as is, for example, Thomas Hobbes. Hobbes is the figure whom a lot of contemporary American political scientists jump up and down in happiness to discover when they are forced to work their way through the classic texts, because Hobbes presents the picture of an unequivocally self-interested human being. Man left in ordinary state would always seek only his own interest and if there weren't any government to keep him in check would be engaged in the "war of all against all" and life would be—one of the most familiar quotations out of the history of political thinking—"solitary, poor, nasty, brutish, and short." Niebuhr's view is *not* like that. He does not hold that a human being always and only prefers his self-interest—the view that the freshmen tries to defend in the first day of an introductory ethics course, putting St. Francis, John Dillinger, Abraham Lincoln, and Adolf Hitler on the same plane, because each got his kicks in his own way. Niebuhr, the Christian theologian, is of course a critic of this "reductionism" that would shrink man to some bundle of self-interested drives.

It surely is not misinterpreting him to underline—in the right context, when one is arguing with a pessimistic and reductionistic and cynical world—the first part of that parallel statement of the foundation of democracy: "Man's capacity for justice makes democracy possible; man's inclination to injustice makes democracy necessary." (That is Niebuhr's best-known sentence and was marked by Jimmy Carter's pen both times it appears in June Bingham's book.) Niebuhr did indeed believe that human beings have an expandable capacity for justice, or else democratic society would not be possible.

Now about the relevance of all of this to President Carter. I said Niebuhr was complicated, and that Carter in his different role in

the world is complicated too; and that their complications overlap. They have the same ingredients. Taking Carter as a whole,
one finds a Christian politician whose human realism, whose
taking account of the realities of life—the "sad" realities if you
will—is necessary in order to try to achieve that surrogate in
politics for Christian love, social justice. Not so far from Niebuhr.
In his acceptance speech in Madison Square Garden Carter
described the troops he was about to lead into political battle as
follows: "We have emerged idealists without illusions, realists
who still know the old dreams of justice and liberty . . ." In his
speech to the United Nations in March after he became President, he said "we can only improve this world if we are realistic
about its complexities."

When Harvey Shapiro asked President Carter whether he saw
the conflict described above (between his government-as-good-
as-people theme and the "fallen" man writers), the President
responded with an interestingly flat and unequivocal denial: "No,
I don't." He understood the question; it was clear; it was repeated; he is an intelligent man. His plain answer was: I see no
such conflict. Mr. Carter located the celebrated goodness more
in the realm of possibility and aspiration than of fact: "A government as good as they (the American people) are *or would like to
be.*" And he noted the timing: at the time of his campaign the
betrayals and disappointments (Watergate, Vietnam, Nixon, the
CIA, the FBI) called for a reminder of the possible and remembered goodness in the people that ought to be in the government.

There is in Carter's answer to Shapiro a slightly Niebuhr-like
"tension" between the ultimate, impossible ideal, and the
realities: the original "inspiration" of the founding American
truth "stays there," he said, even though ugly recent events
contrast with it. "I think the people still have a hunger for a
concept of their own government that they can admire and cherish and which inspired them. There's been a derogation of that
concept and that vision of what government stands for. And
during my own campaign I saw a need, and still see a need, for the
government to restore itself to its former vision."

Mr. Carter did grant the more sober themes: "Niebuhr does
say that there is inherent selfishness, or failure, callousness,
pride—they exist." But he believed the moment called for another emphasis: "There comes a time in a crisis when the superb

qualities of human beings in a collective fashion are evoked in a religious concept or in a governmental structure that transcends the mundane commitments of people. It stands there then as a reminder of what people can do." Carter is a product, in part, of the sectarian heritage of the Southern Baptist world; and, in part, of the soft-sell evangelism—the benign evangelism—that has developed in recent years. His Gift-of-Inner-Healing sister Ruth certainly is a *long* way from Reinhold Niebuhr's view of mankind as "sinner." And Jimmy Carter, subject to these influences, is some distance away, too. A scholar of religion, Nels Nielsen of Rice University, has written:

> The term "evangelical" comes closer to defining Carter's position than others. Reference to the political theories developed in Neo-Orthodoxy alone, does not explain his political participation. Carter has never adopted its drastic view of the all-pervasiveness and inevitability of sin. Had he done so, he would be a different type of political activist. Reinhold Niebuhr, for example, repeatedly criticizes the sectarian and Baptist traditions. His all-inclusive doctrine of original sin has not been emphasized by Carter.

Given theological differences, the following statement by Mr. Carter still is not too bad a layman's softened version of Niebuhr: ". . . there's an almost perfect concept expressed in the Christian ethic, that there's an ultimate pattern for government, but the struggle to reach it is always unsuccessful. The perfect standard is one that human beings don't quite reach, but we try to."

Niebuhr wasn't as "pessimistic" about man, nor is Carter as "optimistic," as the surface criticism holds.


II


"I've studied Niebuhr for a long time," President Carter told Shapiro in the Oval Office. "I always wanted to meet him. I've had some correspondence with his wife. I was broken up three or four years ago when I read that he had died, because he was one of the people in the United States that someday I wanted to meet."

This note of regret at having missed the chance to meet Niebuhr, and the wistful attraction, recurs.

In his important speech to the National Press Club on February 9, 1973, for example, Governor Carter referred to Niebuhr as "a theologian whom I have really cared for in my life, who died last year, who was quite intrigued with the relationship between politics and Christianity." "Quite intrigued" is nice.

One of the books Carter was reading during the campaign year was *Justice and Mercy*, a posthumous collection of Niebuhr's prayers and sermons edited by Mrs. Niebuhr.

When President Carter appointed a committee to screen candidates for the controversial—as it turned out—position of director of the National Endowment for the Humanities, he named to the five-person group both Niebuhr's daughter, Elizabeth Sifton, an editor at Viking Press, and Niebuhr's biographer, June Bingham.

During the four years when he lived in Atlanta as Governor of Georgia, Mr. Carter attended the Baptist church nearest to the Governor's mansion, called the Northside Baptist Church. The man who was then the youth pastor of that church, Mr. Tony Calloway, who heard Carter often in Bible class and in other church gatherings, says that Carter did talk about Niebuhr a lot and that he used Niebuhrian themes. It was "more than just a layman's knowledge." "I heard lots of Niebuhr coming through."

I have my own report on this topic, secondhand but convincing. In July of 1976 I made a pilgrimage by Delta Airlines to Atlanta—the first of many—to explore this subject (Carter and Niebuhr) with a prime expert, William B. Gunter of Gainsville and Atlanta, who was then a Justice of the Georgia Supreme Court by Carter's appointment. Judge Gunter told me that he and Carter became friends in the winter of 1964-65, when they served together on a committee to revise the Democratic Party rules in the state of Georgia.

"Although I'm a lawyer," said Mr. Gunter, "my *hobby* is theology. I am an amateur theologian." When Carter, who shared Gunter's interest in theology, visited him at his home in Gainsville he looked at Gunter's library of two hundred volumes of Niebuhr, Barth, Bonhoeffer, and the like, and made the following memorable remark: "Your *Bible* books are more than the whole library at Plains!"

Niebuhr had had a great influence on Gunter, as my own extended conversation with him and a glance at his bookshelves attest. Of Niebuhr's books, Gunter says, "I read 'em all—*Irony, Moral Man and Immoral Society, Leaves*, all of 'em."

Jimmy and I "started talkin' about all this"—about Christianity and politics, and about Reinhold Niebuhr and what he had to say.

Mr. Gunter thereupon selected a book called *Reinhold Niebuhr on Politics* to give to Carter. This book is a systematic arrangement of Reinhold Niebuhr's thought on politics, edited by two political scientists (Harry Davis of Beloit College and Robert Good, who is now President of Denison University) young scholars at the beginning of their career when they did the pasting and organizing in the late 1950's.

I remember receiving mimeographed copies of the manuscript with a request for comment from Mr. Good, an old friend and colleague in political and intellectual enterprises, as they were putting it together. I later used the book itself in many classes, irreverently reducing its name on course syllabi to the initials RNOP.

It can be a little startling as life goes along to discover someone or something known in a younger and lesser stage appearing now in some important historical setting. I remember at the time of the Bay of Pigs a distinguished older woman at a dinner table in Santa Barbara making the following remark about Richard Bissell of the CIA, the Chief of the Cuban invasion operation: "Imagine! Dicky Bissell invading Cuba!" I had something of the same feeling about Ted Sorensen. Imagine Ted Sorensen, once playing Ping-Pong at the tables in the University of Nebraska YMCA, helping now to decide the world's fate, more or less, in the Cuban missile crisis. So, at a lesser level and a further remove: remembering now that dog-eared mimeographed copy and the request for comments, and hundreds of often-puzzled faces of students with those course syllabi: imagine the President of the United States reading RNOP!

Davis and Good give Niebuhr's political thought a system and arrangement that Niebuhr himself would never have given to it. "I regarded RNOP as the best *condensed* statement of Niebuhr's political thought," said Bill Gunter. Two weeks after Gunter gave Carter the copy of RNOP Carter called him and said "that's the most amazin' thing I've ever read."

It may have been the most amazin' thing he'd read, but alas there is a sad little story about it.

It seems that Mr. Good, the co-editor of RNOP, reading in *Time* magazine in 1976 that candidate Jimmy Carter regarded the book very highly, indeed to the point of its being his "political Bible," was moved, as any man might be in such a circumstance, to communicate with the candidate. (Mr. Good, a Democrat, was appointed by President Johnson to be America's first Ambassador to Zambia.)

He selected for presentation to this Democratic candidate and admirer of his book not just an ordinary copy of RNOP but the one that he had presented to his own father, who had since died. This copy of the book was filled with markings, clippings, and Niebuhr memorabilia contributed by the son and the father, so that it had become, to Mr. Good, quite a valuable item. Mr. Good wrote what he describes as a "rather sentimental" letter to the man who, as it appeared, would probably be President, expressing his gratification at the high opinion Mr. Carter was reported to hold of the book. And he presented Mr. Carter with a copy that meant a great deal to the giver, with the hope that it would become a part of Carter's personal library.

Time passed. The reader will have guessed the outcome of this little tale. There came one day in the mail to Mr. Good from the Carter-Mondale headquarters a form letter of that bureaucratic subnumber intended for gifts of books. The printed letter, putatively signed by "Jimmy Carter" but with an ink that would not smear, carried the information that as candidate he could not accept any present. Should he be elected President the book would eventually go to the Presidential library; in the event of his defeat it would be sent to "some school in need of books." Sincerely yours.

Plainly this could happen to any candidate. It does demonstrate that Jimmy Carter, the candidate of compassion and love, with his unique and intimate relationship to the people and his very strong admiration for Reinhold Niebuhr and for Davis and Good's book, had not fully communicated all of these qualities to the lower echelons of the staff who managed the in-coming mail. One may be permitted to wonder a bit about a candidate who would employ a staff member as insensitive and dumb as that.

### III

Nevertheless, mishandled gifts of books aside, Carter is one of many who has read Niebuhr to the benefit of his understanding. There is a kinship of understanding between the two men. Of course President Carter is not one of those disciples who can reproduce Niebuhr's phrases. The country is better off without that.

But he does share the main outline: Christian realism, realism in the service of social justice, social intelligence in the service of "love."

Niebuhr's writing was done in the setting of an argument against opponents. It was, at a high level, polemical and oblique. He was leaning against errors in the atmosphere that he wanted to correct. He was therefore not like St. Thomas or Aristotle or a modern analytic philosopher, dealing in calm tranquility with the ideas he wanted to treat in their isolated, pure, and eternal form. Instead he was making general statements to affect a quite particular contemporary setting—a particular set of attitudes. He did battle on many fronts but his chief opponent was the soft, harmonistic, gooey, naive, do-goodish outlook of the social idealism of which he himself had been a product not because he *disagreed* with the objective of social justice, but because he *agreed* with it. He wanted to make the effort to achieve those objectives more effective. He wanted the children of light—the social idealists—to borrow some of the wisdom of the children of darkness—the cynics who knew all about power and interest and man's inclination to love himself—in order that the former might be more effective.

Niebuhr was teaching political intelligence to a community that by and large didn't have it. He was saying to social idealists— look at the realities of power and interest that resist the ideals you seek. Moreover, notice that power and self-interest are complicated. They affect not only the "bad" people you are fighting but your own side as well—your own self. To deal with the realities of the world one must be politically wise—borrow the wisdom of a serpent while being as harmless as a dove.

Carter's career and his speeches and his book reflect those same themes: Christianity related to politics; love as the motive for social justice; realistic political skill in the service of justice.

Mr. Carter's actual performance as a politician and a President presents the ambiguity and debatable mixture—depending, to be sure, on the opinion of the appraiser—to be found in any actual political figure. While even his admirers grant certain faults—stubbornness, pride, rigidity—even his detractors usually grant other positive characteristics, in accord with the present point. He can be politically skillful, not only in obtaining his own advancement, but in the interests of larger purposes; in the interest, let us say, of moral ends as he conceives them. He has exhibited (sometimes) a sense of the moment and of the public— of how far to go and when to act that is one mark of the skillful politician or statesman.

The objective in politics is not to exhibit the *purity* of one's own position, how much purer it is than anyone else's (a "utopian" or moralistic error Niebuhr denounced) but rather to bring others along—to shape action and policy to improve the real situation.

Many American public figures with a strong church connection or a heavy identification with something moral or ideal lack political intelligence—lack, that is, knowledge of the real conditions, and of the limitations of their fellow men, and for that matter of themselves. They have often, in one variety of the American moralistic species, a strong belief in exhortation and in sudden changes of heart. Often, too, there is such a sharp right/ wrong set of absolutes as to narrow the vision of the unsharp, unabsolute, messy and complicated reality. "You Englishmen!" wrote George Bernard Shaw once (what he said applies doubly to Americans), "You look upon the world as a moral gymnasium in which to exercise your principles! Bend your efforts to your neighbor's need and that will be principle enough!" A long-time Washington official—a reader and admirer of Niebuhr—used to compare the moralists and idealists to cheerleaders who simply shout, "We want a touchdown!" while quarterbacks have to calculate what down it is, where they are on the field, the dangers of an interception—the realities and limited objectives. (FDR used this analogy once, and Ike when President disapproved of it.) Carter, for all his being a Deacon and reading the Bible and being a post-Watergate leader setting forth high moral standards, by no means fits the pure model of the politically unintelligent moralist or utopian. On the contrary: he has in him, whether effectively combined or not, something like the combination Niebuhr taught, which links a sophisticated morality to intelligence.

Any list of instances in which Carter has exhibited such a pragmatic idealism will be, of course, subject to partisan and ideological dispute; we judge these matters according to our prejudices. His admirers would have difficulty claiming that he showed forth such skill in the matter of Bert Lance, or in his response (hurt feelings) to the criticisms of his administration by black leaders during his first summer. But on the other hand a sympathetic interpreter at least can find a continuing thread of examples of the combination mentioned above. The stating of high moral purpose, for example, is not to be abjured but is to be timed right. Carter did seize the *kairos* ("the right time," the action fitting the fullness of the moment as Paul Tillich, one of his theological mentors, might put it, both in the first moment of his term as Governor, when he stated flatly that the day for racial discrimination is over, and in his first moment as President, when he thanked his predecessor for all that he had done to heal our land. (Tillich was taken once to a baseball game. He asked in Teutonic bewilderment why there was all the shouting suddenly in the seventh inning, and was told: "The second baseman fulfilled the *kairos.*") As to his skill in reading the situation, Wildavsky and Knott, in their article on "Jimmy Carter's Theory of Governing" cite instances from his days as Governor in which he learned from and adapted effectively to circumstances: on busing in Atlanta and on the handling of racial disturbances in the state. Some readers will agree that he showed good timing and a combination of political savvy and moral purpose in his handling of the pardon/amnesty for Vietnam protesters (maybe including his wooden insistence on a verbal distinction between those words— certainly including the time and place of his policy speech, to the VFW); the care and result of his choice of Walter Mondale to be the Vice-Presidential nominee; his preparing of the ground for the decision against the B-1 bomber (and the decision itself, and its clarity); his proposed welfare reform forcing the constituencies that had destroyed the Nixon welfare effort to stew in the possibility of severe limitation, underlining *work* to conservatives and *public service* jobs to liberals, increasing the amount of money proposed to be spent when he had to, and combining ingredients to make it more palatable to the constituencies than was thought possible on that subject, his use of his first year to force the nation to face the energy crisis, his role in the search for Middle East peace and the SALT negotiations.

I believe there is an important parallel between what Carter calls "special interests" and the "socially prominent," and what Niebuhr called "collective egotism" and "ideological taint." What these terms mean (vulgarized) is: you think differently if you are rich. Where you sit in the boat sharply affects your attitude about which way it tips. The team you are playing on or rooting for has a predictable effect upon your opinion about close calls. All this, true enough of an individual (one tennis player), is magnified in the collective (the masses in Ohio State or Notre Dame football stadia, for whom no call against the home team is ever right). That's "collective egotism," and it applies with added force to economic interest groups where more than a game is at stake— and even more to classes and to nations (a supposedly grown-up nation, the United States, as late as the Carter administration, could still get exercised as a child playing king of the mountain about its *rights* to the Panama Canal).

Niebuhr learned from Marx and/or life in Henry Ford's De-troit about the "ideology" of the classes, most powerfully the "privileged" classes. They not only want to have every referee's call go their way and to hold their favored position in the boat; they invent rationalizations to show that all this is right, true, and beautiful. Your "social location" has a marked influence on the way you think about society—and if you won't grant that it is so about you by yourself, listen to the prevailing tone of your social group. Niebuhr softened the hard line of Marx, for whom, in popular reading at least, economic class virtually determines social thought, into the much less rigid notion of the "ideological taint" on everybody's thought—from self-love, especially collec-tive self-love. Our social ideas are "tainted" by who we are, where we are socially. And we rationalize the use of power to protect our interests. He tied it back into resuscitated Christian doctrine on the one side and into realistic radical-reform politics on the other.

Now here's a layman's translation:

> When we get a few powerful men, whether it be me or
> someone else, it's almost human nature to expect that person
> to manipulate government to his own benefit and the benefit

of his friends, and to rationalize it and say, what's good for me
is good for my community.

That was Governor Jimmy Carter speaking to the Georgia
Municipal Association in 1971.

I detect many such traces in Carter. He has a particular resistance to "special interest" groups that may be more rigid and a
little different from Niebuhr's, but it has a resemblance. He can
make a distinction between his membership in the Certified Seed
Growers, which represent an economic interest, and the school
board or library board, which are not the same. Critics might
charge that he believes that, as President of all the people, he has
a unique, almost mystical relation to them, and believes himself
in that role, to be uniquely free of "ideological taint." Defenders
might answer that, for all his pride, there are repeated notes of
humility and self-criticism and confession in Carter.

And now about the "socially prominent." Carter has been
called a "populist," and with some historical reason. He did bid
for, and gain, the votes of many white "populists," if such they
be, who voted for Wallace. A reviewer of his book of speeches,
*A Government As Good As Its People*, noting how often he referred to the "socially prominent," associated that repeated
reference with Wallace, with envy, with the politics of resentment.

I have now a very important correction to make for all those
who share that perception of Carter: most of his references to the
"socially prominent" are in direct contrast to Wallace's; they are
to *himself* and *people like himself*. Many others are to the people
he is talking to. Carter is *not* the consistent voice of the resentful
lower middle class—not by a long shot. Where Wallace is attacking *other* people Carter is criticizing his own. His theme is
usually not envy or resentment but collective self-criticism. I
heard that theme first in the Second Christian Church in Indianapolis—his talk made *very* clear that he had advantages that
blacks and poor whites don't. It was very clear in his famous 1974
Law Day speech: "I'm part of it," he said. And it is unmistakable
in his remarkable outburst (too little reported), early in the
general election campaign, at a party of well-fixed Hollywood
people given by Warren Beatty:

> If *we* make a mistake, the chances are we won't actually go to prison, and if we don't like the public-school system, we put our kids in private schools.

Notice how he uses *we*; he is one of the privileged himself.

> When the tax structure is modified, which Congress does almost every year, you can rest assured that powerful people who are well organized, who have good lawyers, who have lobbyists in the Capitol in Washington—they don't get cheated. But there are millions of people in this country who do get cheated, and they are the very ones who can't afford it.

That may be populism and resentment, but not in his own behalf.

> I can go a mile from my house, and there are people there who are very poor, and when they get sick it's almost impossible for them to get a doctor. In the county where I am from, we don't have a doctor, a dentist, a pharmacist, a registered nurse, and people who live there who are very poor have no access to preventive health care.

Finally, notice how he attacks his own audience:

> So, I say, public servants like me and Jerry Brown and others have a special responsibility to bypass the big shots, including *you and people like you*, and make a concerted effort to understand people who are poor, black, speak a foreign language, who are not well educated, who are inarticulate, who are stymied, who have some monumental problem.

That is scarcely the style of George Wallace.

I think what Carter represents is less the politics of resentment than a Niebuhrian politics of the self-critical struggle for justice.

Let me add another theme which seems to me still farther from the melodrama of the ordinary populist or moral crusader, and characteristic instead of a more profound outlook.

When in the last days of the campaign the Plains church suddenly had that brouhaha over racial discrimination, Carter— with the election on the line really—talked to Andrew Young and decided what he would say. (He was in Sacramento, as it happened, at a press conference.) He didn't strike the note of indignant condemnation, of denunciation, or proclaim that he would resign. Instead he said: "I can't resign from the human race because there's discrimination . . . and I don't intend to resign from my own church because there's discrimination. I think my best possible approach is to stay with the church to try to change the attitude which I abhor." "I can't resign from the human race"—I am identified with it, a member of it, share its faults though I resist them in myself and others, and am not your surface moralizer speaking.

On November 21, back home in Plains after the election was over and he had won, he led the church in prayer urging everyone to "love other human beings as ourselves . . ." and beseeching that "the wounds be healed rapidly." "There is no one among us who is better than another; we are all sinful in Your sight," he prayed.

That Carter was perceived to be a simple moralizer was partly his own fault no doubt—the result of the bold bright crayon colored slogans an unknown candidate needed to use to become known, and also of the particular coloring Carter found congenial and productive in the post-Watergate atmosphere. Perhaps he then deserved the unholy glee of columnists and editorialists (ha! ha! "the man who invented ethics") when the Bert Lance affair made the colors seem to run and fade.

But the simplifications of modern publicity were at fault in this, too. The public, and therefore the press, does not have the categories to handle much complexity, especially about "morality." Whenever one encounters Carter at length or in quiet seriousness—in the *Playboy* interview, the Moyers interview, the ruminative remarks in the Shapiro interview about Dylan Thomas's line "Hands have no tears to flow," or in his Bible school teaching—he does not appear the simple or self-righteous moralizer he was pictured to be: far from it. He is then seen to be a reflective representative of a much subtler and more critical ethic which separates itself exactly from such moralizing simplicity and righteousness. The themes that run throughout are not any righteous thunderings but humility, love, forgiveness, grace. It seems to me quite striking, given the picture some have of

Carter, that he should have taken out his pen and marked in the margin of June Bingham's book this quotation from Niebuhr:

> The Church is a curiously mixed body consisting of those who have never been shaken in their self-esteem and self-righteousness . . . and of true Christians who live by "a broken spirit and a contrite heart." Whether we belong to this latter group, which makes up the true but invisible Church, no one but God can know.

## IV

Mrs. Bingham's book was published in 1961, as "An Introduction to the Life and Thought of Reinhold Niebuhr." Its title, *Courage to Change*, comes from this prayer:

> O God, Give us serenity to accept what cannot be changed, courage to change what should be changed, and wisdom to distinguish the one from the other.

The prayer, Mrs. Bingham explains, "was composed by Reinhold Niebuhr in 1934 when he preached occasionally in the small church near his summer home in Heath, Massachusetts. After the service, Howard Chandler Robbins, a summer neighbor, asked for a copy. He is reported to have been handed the original, with words to the following effect: "Here, take the prayer, I have no further use for it." Other people, it is clear, have felt differently. Robbins published it as part of a pamphlet the following year. Since then it has been adopted as the motto of Alcoholics Anonymous; the USO distributed millions of copies to servicemen during World War II; the National Council of Churches has reprinted it; and even today it is used commercially on Christmas cards.

After the election, at a dinner sponsored by the Congressional Democratic Study Group, Congressman Jonathan Bingham of New York, Mrs. Bingham's husband, took her over to President-elect Carter's table. Carter remarked immediately that he knew her book—that he had read it, and underlined it. Congressman Bingham started to explain how they had first met Niebuhr on a train (an incident with which Mrs. Bingham's book begins). "I know," said Carter, "I've read the book."

Carter had used a Niebuhrian sentence about love and justice in his acceptance speech. Congressman Bingham, happy to have recognized the source of the sentence, said to the President-elect, "That was Niebuhr, wasn't it?"

"Of course," Carter answered.

After the Inauguration, Congressman and Mrs. Bingham came through a White House reception line. Usually the Congressman shakes hands first and introduces his wife; when the Binghams came through the line, the new President embraced Mrs. Bingham while Rosalynn looked on. Carter explained then that this was June Bingham, the author of the book on Niebuhr that he often mentioned. He told them that it was one of a handful of personal books that he brought from Plains to supplement the White House library.

Carter's fifty-seven marks and underlinings in Mrs. Bingham's book are certainly not whimsical. They identify sentences, words, and longer quotations that go to the two centers of Niebuhr's own thinking, love and justice on the one hand; pride, power, and interest on the other.

Toward the end of the book Mrs. Bingham is explaining that Niebuhr recognized in the young of the 1950's the need not to temper idealism but to arouse social conscience. To them he says "there must be a passion for justice." Carter underlined that sentence. On an earlier page he underlined the sentence that Americans need to remember that "justice is as important as liberty," in a world of rich and poor nations.

Carter marked this central Niebuhrian thesis:

> The large group is incapable of agape or selfless love . . . nations have less power of self-transcendence. (p. 175)

The highest norm for any large group is therefore justice, although there is always the ideal possibility that justice may be raised to a higher level by love.

". . . love must be translated into justice in order to be effective" (p. 15)—a possible source of the sentence in Carter's acceptance speech.

". . . justice must be the instrument of love." (p. 139).

Carter also underlined passages containing the thesis—the un-Baptist thesis one might almost say—of *Moral Man and Immoral Society* and of *The Nature and Destiny of Man*. Here are some that he marked:

> Man cannot love himself inordinately without pretending that it is not his, but a universal interest, which he is supporting. (p. 143)

> Everyone knows that the mob is likely to be less moral than the individual. [Any large group] . . . is also likely to be less moral than the individual. (p. 173)

> The paradox is that patriotism transmutes individual unselfishness into national egoism. (p. 174)

> Most of the evil is done by good people who do not know that they are not good. (p. 149)

What does it matter whether there is any affinity between Carter and Niebuhr? To answer I call again upon eminent sources, and I need another chapter.

# 13

## LOVE AND JUSTICE IN POLITICS

One day in 1960 John Courtney Murray, the most distinguished American Catholic thinker of recent decades, made a graciously favorable remark to Niebuhr, who might be described as his Protestant counterpart. The remark was all the more striking because Father Murray was not the sort of man to pay a compliment lightly. He was a rather austere Jesuit, and at the moment he made the generous comment he was looming like some dark ambiguous symbol in a Bergman movie against the sunlit windows opening onto the Pacific. Niebuhr, an arm paralyzed, sat lively, talking, laughing, on the other side of the table.

As the two most eminent members of the fund for the Republic's project on "Religion in a Free Society" in the late 1950's and early 1960's, they sparred with each other in an amiable, respectful wariness. Niebuhr took soft jabs at what seemed to him the rigid rationalism of the historic natural law position Father Murray defended. Father Murray, for his part, would strike a blow against the "ambiguists" who find the world strewn with "predicaments" and "ironies" expressed only in "paradoxes." He wrote an essay during this period that, though it dealt with foreign policy, obviously had other applications—and though no one was named, a rather clear target.

> The ambiguist rightly puts emphasis on the complexity of the situations with which foreign policy has to deal. . . . But does the fact of complexity justify the vocabulary of description or the monotonous moral verdict? It is as if a surgeon in the midst of a gastronenterostomy were to say that the highly complex situation in front of him is so full of paradox ("The patient is at

once receiving blood and losing it"), and irony ("Half a
stomach will be better than a whole one") and dilemmas ("Not
too much, nor too little, anesthesia") that all surgical solutions
are necessarily ambiguous. Complicated situations, surgical or
moral, are merely complicated. It is for the statesman, as for
the surgeon, to master the complications and minister as best
he can to the health of the body, politic or physical. The work
may be done deftly or clumsily, intelligently or stupidly, with
variant degrees of success or failure; but why call it in either
case "ambiguous"?

Father Murray obviously felt that the role of a thinker should
*not* be to declare about a complicated situation that all of this is
ambiguous, ironical, or paradoxical, but rather, exactly, to set to
work to clarify it. An engineer and naval officer, incidentally,
might have a similar reaction.

So Father Murray was certainly no uncritical fan of Niebuhr's.
Nevertheless one day in Santa Barbara when the subject was
"intellectual history" (the subjects were immense) Murray said,
in a sudden graceful gesture, "Reinie, the rest of us *talk* about
intellectual history, you have *made* it . . ."

Niebuhr had indeed made intellectual history, and was to add
still further chapters to intellectual history before his death in
1971. He kept pecking at his typewriter through fifty-five years of
American history and world events, from before America's entry
into World War I almost to America's withdrawal from Vietnam.
Now in the late 1970s there comes on the scene, at the pinnacle of
power, a man who has read him, admired him, and wishes he
could have met him.

What Father Murray doubtless had in mind was Niebuhr's
large influence, particularly in the 1930's, 1940's, and 1950's, on
the minds of important American political and religious leaders:
he punctured sentimental Protestant liberalism, revived a
tougher-minded Christian socialism, became a most formidable
opponent of pacifism and isolationism as the Nazi threat grew and
of world federalism after the war; he led many intellectuals away
from Stalinism and Communism; helped to found the ADA and
the Liberal Party and to shape the realistic anticommunist American liberalism of the postwar era, as well as the "responsible,"
"realist" outlook in American foreign policy as the nation became
a world power. There is a much longer list of items than this.

I want to carry Father Murray's remark further. Niebuhr may
be taken as at least a symbol if not a maker of intellectual history,
on a still larger stage—the drama of the continual reshaping of the
moral underpinnings of this nation. He was at once a recoverer of
the usable past and very much its critic.

First, take the Social Gospel Movement that flourished in the
time and the world of his youth. It was the prime movement for—
shall we say?—"linkage" within American Protestantism between Christianity and the Good Society, and between both of
these and the United States of America. It was the late nineteenth
century and the early twentieth century, optimistic, activist, do-
goodish effort (quite vulnerable but still important—"liberat-
ing," as we now say, in its time) to apply "the teachings of Jesus"
to the remaking of the world—to "bringing in" the "kingdom of
God on earth." Niebuhr broke with it, and sharply criticized both
its theology and its politics. How then was he at all a representative of it? By having his interests shaped by it and by preserving
the link of religion to social justice.

Niebuhr carried on its application of the Christian religion to
the political world, and the central place for love and justice in the
interpretation of what Christianity was all about. In that sense he
was continuing the social gospel; at the same time he was a severe
and unremitting critic of its utopianism and sentimentality. He
was at once the greatest representative and the most effective
critic of the Social Gospel Movement.

Next, take Puritanism. Self-criticism was *not* a characteristic
theme of this Puritanism; it *is* a characteristic theme in Reinhold
Niebuhr. "Love," especially as applied to politics and government, was not a primary theme of Puritanism; it is, with all the
layers of qualification, such a theme in Reinhold Niebuhr. A
wariness about righteousness and fanaticism was not a feature of
Puritanism, which indeed inclined to those characteristics itself;
a constant wariness exactly of those qualities is central to the
thought of Reinhold Niebuhr.

At the same time he advanced the Puritan strand because he
defended the relationship of the Christian religion to the practical world, and saw that relationship as purposeful, active, moral, historical, political. There was neither in the Puritans nor in
Reinhold Niebuhr any flight from the world, any mysticism that
escapes from this world into another, any fancy yellow book

estheticism or anything of the sleeping-waking cultures of the East, nor any solipsistic or hedonistic individualism, nor any shoulder-shrugging fatalism or sighing meaninglessness. There was instead the proclamation that the world was ruled by a purposeful moral arbiter—thundered by Puritan preachers; and restated with a tremendous asterisk of national and religious self-criticism, grace and forgiveness, by Reinhold Niebuhr. And rescued thereby.

Finally, Niebuhr was also at once the most effective propagator as well as a powerful critic of the expression of the whole of the Christian religion in the modern American world. Niebuhr defended Christianity to the disdainful modern intellectuals—gave it a hearing again. He had an influence growing through the 1930's and into the 1940's that caused Sidney Hook and others to make a counterattack against a so-called "failure of nerve" (i.e., a falling back into religion).

Once more Niebuhr was at the same time rescuer and critic. He opened the antique formulae of the Christian religion to a twentieth-century meaning. The stale air of a rather enclosed Christianity, in this country a largely bourgeois Christianity, had the cleansing effect of the critical, relativizing mind. Niebuhr was able to take a good deal of the modern relativism and skepticism up into a reformulated Christianity while reviving its orthodox formulae. He rejected the sort of thing that the older liberals did, trying to mate religion and science in a happy modern marriage. He created instead a critical and dialectical outlook in which the Christianity he affirmed was continually corrected by wisdom from the modern nonreligious world, and yet was also correcting it.

And these three layers of the refurbished Biblical religion of the West represent a recovery of national roots—but a recovery that is also a continuing revision.

Niebuhr had his faults, of substance as well as style (those of style spring at a reader from every page). He was repetitious; he was not careful; he dashed off articles between breakfast and lunch; he didn't get the facts right; he put things in formulae and kept repeating the formulae; in his inexactitude he gave aid and comfort to some positions he wouldn't himself have espoused. Moreover the politics and the theology and the ethics he espoused are all subject to dispute by learned colleagues—a great deal of such correction has been going on. It may be that "love" should not be thought of in as rigorously altruistic, selfless terms as Niebuhr does. Setting up "love" as altruism and noncoercion, selfless, unprudential, absolute may make it even more impossible than it need be, and may neglect the shared and collaborative ingredients in our communal life. Niebuhr didn't write enough about the nature of community, nor did he understand well enough the role of law in society, especially in his early period. A long list of such criticisms, as they used to say on the radio, is available on request. But this is not the place to cite them. In the end he remains the most important political moralist in the twentieth century's most powerful country.


II


Now for another source: another nominee of the Democratic Party for the Presidency, the late Hubert Humphrey. (One could triangulate Niebuhr for the uninitiated by his relation to the last three Democratic nominees: Humphrey was an old friend and liberal comrade in arms going back to the founding of the ADA, until they took opposite positions about the Vietnam war; George McGovern is a rather pure version of the Social Gospel idealism that Niebuhr wanted to make more realistic; and Carter has the most explicit interest in Niebuhr's Christian belief and in Niebuhr's being "quite intrigued" by the relationship of Christianity to politics.) Vice President Humphrey—as he then was— speaking at an anniversary dinner for a magazine Niebuhr founded, said of Niebuhr: "No American has made a greater contribution to political wisdom and moral responsibility." Humphrey said that Niebuhr taught Humphrey's generation, as they came out of the Great Depression, "how to combine *decisive action* with a *sensitive knowledge of the complexity of life*, including politics. We knew there were urgent demands of social justice that required direct action and idealism. At the same time, we had to learn that politics was complicated and many sided and that life wasn't simple. Dr. Niebuhr was the man—more than any other—who fit these two things together, and who showed how they are both connected with our religious faith."

As Humphrey's affectionate tribute implied, some links between Niebuhr and practical political man are elementary—so elementary that the sophisticated radar of modern political analysis may not pick them up. And the political writers who manage that radar may find these links uncongenial.

One tie between Niebuhr and a Jimmy Carter is simply that both men see a serious connection between religion and politics.

There can be such a connection, despite all the foolishness, error, and fanaticism with which it is ordinarily surrounded: despite all the nonsense that H. L. Mencken had such a good time deriding. Niebuhr himself repeatedly criticized, several cuts more profoundly than Mencken, those egregious errors of banality, utopianism, fanaticism, provincial prejudices baptized as the will of God, worthy causes overheated, unworthy causes propagated. He was the most pungent of modern critics of the confusion and error religion can introduce into politics. Now some who are wary about Carter have used quotations from Niebuhr to chide Carter for "mixing," "meddling" (familiar terms!) "bringing religion into politics." An article in *The Wall Street Journal*, for just one example, quoted Niebuhr's sentence, "religion is more frequently a source of confusion than of light in politics." Of course it is! But banishing it—*trying* to banish it—won't succeed. Therefore attend to it, in order that the confusion be diminished and light increased.

One could also quote Niebuhr as saying that "religion cannot be regarded as good per se" because of all the negative forms and results of religion; that "all men are inclined to obscure the morally ambiguous element in their political cause by investing it with religious sanctity"; and that "religion is frequently (and some believe always) the force of disharmony in life. It accentuates conflict, generates fanaticism and aggravates the pride and arrogance of individual and groups." There are dozens of such quotations, because one of the fronts on which Niebuhr was always fighting was against the dangerous and foolish amalgamations of religion with politics.

Nevertheless it was not his conclusion that "religion and politics" should be "kept separate." As Niebuhr certainly did not repeat the conventional pieties of the pulpit about "doing God's will" in a particular political fight, so on the opposite side he certainly did not repeat the conventional pseudowisdom of the cracker barrel that "religion and politics should never mix." The point was not to deny the connection but rather to try to make the profound and dialectical and critical connection that may rescue and redeem it. Because religiously understood politics leads to a lot of fanaticism and nonsense, it is important to interpret it in such a way as to make it lead instead to wisdom, compassion, and sound statecraft. In order to do that there must be a constant wariness. There are always the dangers of fanaticism on the one hand; escapism, pie in the sky, on the other.

Reinhold Niebuhr had a brother, H. Richard Niebuhr, who was to Reinie as Mycroft Holmes was to Sherlock Holmes—the brother less well known but even more respected by some in an inner circle. H. Richard Niebuhr once said that the point of religion is not to overcome irreligion but to displace bad religion with good. So it is in religion and politics. Reinhold Niebuhr's career may be interpreted as an elaborate effort to construct self-correcting and beneficial links between the Christian religion and politics—and men in history. He did not want to separate Christianity from politics; on the contrary—he spent his whole life making a sophisticated form of the connection.

And Carter? Are we to assume that an intelligent man growing up in a small town in Deep South Georgia is unaware of the dreadful forms of religion in politics? A man who has seen Christian preachers urging people to join the White Citizen's Council? One who heard his fellow parishioners argue in a Christian church against even admitting black persons to worship with them? Who has seen Lester Maddox's prayer services in the Governor's mansion (prayer services that as Governor he ended)? His wife had to shame the Baptist preacher into holding the funeral service for the child of a "controversial figure" (as they say) at interracial Koinonia Farm. Are we to assume that someone who went through the bigotry in his own community against the Catholic John Kennedy in 1960 does not know the sting of the wrong relationship of religion to politics? (Miss Lillian, who managed the Kennedy headquarters in those days, and Carter's sons still tell about how tough it was to be pro-Kennedy in their part of Georgia.)

As Presidential candidate Carter again and again faced "right to life" demonstrators, chanting absolute, sometimes nasty, slogans and carrying signs like these:

A large picture of a fetus in the womb; under
it the question: who imposed their morality
on these little people?

Born again?
Millions of little babies won't be born once.

Moral imposition?
Death vs. inconvenience.
Mr. Carter, who are you kidding?

Mr. Carter you are two faced on abortion.
Why not let them live?

Mr. Carter knows a great deal about the simple-minded absolutes that religion can interject into politics. In 1976 the largely
Catholic movement on abortion sometimes resembled the largely
Protestant movement on prohibition in 1928 or even the opposition to Al Smith and John Kennedy in 1928 and 1960.

And—perhaps worse still—there was the elaborate, many-
layered, sometimes subtly, sometimes blatantly snobbish attitude of the literati and the "enlightened," looking way down
their noses from New York and Cambridge at this strange
evangelical Baptist from southern Georgia—the nonreligious folk
who think that they are free of bigotry by definition, because only
religious people are bigots, so that their own closed minds are
exempt from any such charge.

I believe we can say that Mr. Carter knows from many sides
and in many ways, including the harrowing experience within his
own home church in Plains, the deficiencies religious people may
exhibit when they try to cope with political life.

Now, as an intelligent, life-long, church-going, Bible-reading,
believing Christian man, would it not come as an illumination to
hear Niebuhr speak out loud and bold? To discover an author who
made the intricate connection between Christianity and politics?

Carter was a man raised in the pieties of Amazing Grace and
Bible stories and smalltown sermons, who was himself involved
in very real struggles of the business world and then the political
world, where the stakes were real. "I've had a chance, as Governor, to deal with a multiplicity of problems from different kinds

of people—those who are mentally afflicted; those who are very
rich and want favors; those who are corporate giants and who
want to preserve a special privilege; those who are consumers and
are hungry for a chance at the marketplace." Might it not be for
such a man a—revelation, say—to discover Niebuhr? Here was a
writer who at his—Carter's—own intellectual level put together
the belief that Carter had dutifully stuck to from his youth with a
political wisdom that matched the world he was dealing with.
That happened for many people in their reading of Niebuhr. Why
should one not assume that that is what happened in the case of
the man who is now President?

I once asked Andrew Young about Carter and Niebuhr. Unlike
others who are wary about making any connection Young saw it
clearly.

He had told me on another occasion about an evening in which
Martin Luther King, Jr., gave a long spontaneous exposition of
Reinhold Niebuhr that left him—Young—stunned and moved in
admiration. Young himself, though an excellent interpreter of
the meaning of the Civil Rights Movement—I might say hereti-
cally a better interpreter to some audiences than King himself—
is not particularly articulate about Niebuhr. It seems a long time
since he read those books. Nevertheless they planted their seeds.
Bill Gunter said: "We [Gunter, Young, Carter] feel ourselves to
be on the same wave length."

And Young, feeling himself on the same wavelength, said this
about Carter: "He combines the simpler background of the
Southern Baptist upbringing with the solid intellectual approach
to Christianity that a Reinhold Niebuhr provided." Young said
that Niebuhr "gave an intellectual justification" to positions that
were forming in Carter "against the background of his Southern
Baptist piety."

The Plains Baptist Sunday School, whatever its merits, cannot
have provided much of an intellectual structure, or much of a
basis for linking that Christian religion to politics. On the contrary—the bias would have been against making any such link.
That absolutely predictable phrase of American culture that in-
volves the verb "to meddle" when religion and politics are mentioned together would be particularly ready at hand in a Southern
Baptist setting. (Of course religion and politics are mixed all the
time, by Southern Baptists and everyone else; what has always

been meant by denying that is that one disapproves of the particular mixture that somebody else is making.) For a man of Carter's ability and intellectual interests and yet basic conventionality, Niebuhr presumably helped to provide illumination and justification for serious politics. I make that presumption because I have seen it happen many times: a person of religious background whose political understanding receives an illuminating confirmation or a drastic upgrading by reading Niebuhr.

In Carter's religious and geographical setting it must have meant a lot simply to read an intelligent analysis of the connection between Christian belief and a politician's life. ("That's the most amazin' thing I ever read.")

I said there was a second rather elementary connection between Carter and Niebuhr. This has to do with the *content* of that Christian belief.

You can say like some hymn that it is always the same—tell me the old, old story—but a glance at a theological library or a look around churches in town will show you that it isn't. If Augustine, Niebuhr, and Moses are prisms, the Christian religion itself is the West's largest, most complicated, and intricate crystalline formation, casting out hundreds of lights in different directions. Just in the period when Niebuhr was writing there was a rainbow of theological revivals.

The old Protestant liberalism said Christianity is about "the teaching of Jesus." Some ferocious guttural European theologians responded with a whiplash insistence that Christianity is about *God* or about *Christ*. Bishops like to say that it is about the *Church*. The point is this: many religious flowers bloomed; Niebuhr and Carter picked the same one.

Niebuhr came in for some hard licks in the inner circle of theologians for not plucking the blooms some of his colleagues did. Where does he talk about the church? Not enough! said the churchly types. Why doesn't he write more centrally about *God*? (Snotty seminary students said he was not a *theo*logian but rather an *anthropo*logian—that means that he talked more about *man*—anthropos—than he did about *God*.) And he doesn't feature the "teachings of Jesus" as a ready daily guide for fixing up the troubles right here in River City by asking what would Jesus do, the way a series of American preachers and popular books—*enormously* popular books, like Charles M. Sheldon's *In His*

*Steps*—have done. Niebuhr's emphasis was none of these. His emphasis after all the paradoxes and ironical arrangements by which it was protected from being simple and sentimental was—love.

That is particularly evident in the book that Bill Gunter gave to Jimmy Carter: RNOP. In that book the foundation of thinking about politics is the "love ethic." This love ethic is impossible—but also possible. Also *relevant*. Davis and Good arranged in a numbered series the links between love—whole-hearted affirmation of the other person, which is impossible for human beings ever to do perfectly—and the link between that root of Christianity and "justice"—which is the way love moves over into the world of politics. The relationship is not a simple division of labor—love for individuals, justice when you're dealing with more than one person, with society. Instead there is a complicated pulling and checking so that love is always stirring justice to enlarge itself and deepen itself.

If one were forced to reduce Niebuhr's teaching to one word the way Orwell once said one could do with some of Shakespeare's plays (*Macbeth*: ambition; *Othello*: jealousy; *King Lear*: renunciation) the one word should not be, as is popularly supposed, "sin," but rather—these are the three candidates—"love" (his brother once in a fraternal technical argument accused him of turning around the Biblical proclamation "God is love" into "love is God"); "justice" (thus to reach beyond the sentimental-individual danger of "love" alone out to the realm of social life); or "humility" (a political thinker proposed that word once, as "what Niebuhr is all about"; it does catch his central thread—that "sin" has to do with, too—of the endless machinations of human pride, the subtle and manifold overestimating of the self, the never-ending need therefore for contrition and forgiveness). Niebuhr: love, justice, humility. The Sunday after Jimmy Carter was nominated at the convention in Madison Square Garden he taught the men's class at the Plains Baptist Church. His themes according to *The New York Times* headlines were: Love, Justice, Humility.

Even the quotation from Niebuhr that Carter uses may not be read as altogether the conservative version of realism: that sad duty is to *establish* (not just maintain) *justice* (not only order) and therefore—one may read it to say—to keep altering society. The duty of politics is to establish a social justice that is not here yet, and that is always in the process of arriving.

The two most notable specific reflections of Niebuhr in speeches by Carter bear out this interpretation.

One is his famous Law Day speech in 1974, a speech Carter was persuaded to give by Bill Gunter. On that occasion Carter's associating of Niebuhr with social justice came through with a force and passion that fully convinced those who were present— Hunter Thompson, who exploded in his own way in *Rolling Stone Magazine*, and also more sober witnesses.

The principal speaker, Senator Edward Kennedy, was sitting in the audience—no small point. Carter, as he explained, made new notes on the way to the occasion, and altered what he had planned to say.

He attacked the lawyers' failure to achieve justice in the criminal justice system. He linked Niebuhr to Bob Dylan's complaint about the situation of the exploited. He described himself as "a Sunday School teacher who knew the Christian ethic of love," knew it was a very high and perfect standard, and also knew the fallibility of man, and the contentions in society, "as described by Reinhold Niebuhr and many others," which don't permit us to achieve perfection. "We do strive for equality, but not with a fervent and daily commitment."

The flavor of the references to Niebuhr in Carter's Law Day speech was not cautionary and conservative but rather "prophetic," urging the achievement of a justice that has not yet been achieved.

That reference was linked, moreover, to a criticism of the callousness of those who are in the top places: "In general the powerful and influential in our society shape the laws and have great influence on the legislature or the Congress. This creates a reluctance to change, because the powerful and the influential have carved out for themselves or have inherited a privileged position in society, of wealth or social prominence or higher education or opportunity for the future." That paragraph seems to me to reflect a man, extemporizing, who wanted to say something forceful about social justice, and in doing so referred to Reinhold Niebuhr.

Carter went on to say that the young who are not yet caught up

in the compromises of society may have an openness to change
that later is lost. "As their interrelationship with the present
circumstances grows, they also become committed to approach-
ing change very very slowly and very very cautiously, and there's
a commitment to the *status quo*."

Anyone who reads the transcript of Carter's Law Day speech—
a moving and forceful, even though somewhat disorganized outburst—cannot but conclude that here is a man speaking from his
heart in the interest of a humane system of justice. He lays it on
his audience pretty hard as to their own failures—the failures of
the "privileged classes" as Niebuhr called them. And he indicts
himself along with them.

The other major seepage of Niebuhr into a Carter address—
this one is not explicit, but very plain—even more clearly con-
firms my present point. In his acceptance speech as the nominee
of the Democratic Party he delivered the sentence out of
Niebuhr that Congressman Bingham spotted. He said, "I have
spoken a lot of times this year about love. But love must be
aggressively translated into simple justice."

When he got back to Plains on the Sunday following his nomination, he asked the Men's Bible Class what he had said was "the
one more thing" that must come "out of love." The class did not
do very well. The eighty people, one-half regular Bible students
and one-half reporters and secret service men, provided only one
effort at an answer: "obedience." Mr. Carter gave the correct
answer softly: "simple justice."

Carter came in for some licks in the early stage of his arrival on the
scene in an article in *The Nation* by a theologically literate pastor
in Connecticut, Charles Henderson. Although basically rather
favorable, or at least open to Carter's candidacy, Mr. Henderson
criticized his too simple application of "love" to politics. When
you've got two or three or more neighbors you can't say just: "love
your neighbor." You have to decide among them, and you can't
run the board of zoning appeals or the finances of New York City
directly on the basis of love. Well, sure. I would say to Mr.
Henderson: I agree with what you say, but I wouldn't defend to
the death the appropriateness of your saying it. It's either rather a
technical argument among specialists—Carter isn't a seminary
graduate student—or it is a doubtful charge.

Is Carter in the end sentimental, unpolitical, unaware of the steps that politics goes through to translate love into justice? (I mean not in his words but in his deeds.) I think not. But in any case—I do not know whether he read Henderson's article or not—Carter dutifully then in his acceptance speech used the sentences quoted above to assert that love must be translated into justice, a Carterization of the central core of Niebuhr. It was followed by sentences critical of the way the "socially prominent" do not care enough for the people who are ill-treated in society.

The question about what religion means for justice in society was inescapably present in Jimmy Carter's life, as it was not for parishioners dozing in their pews up North.

There was the church, the Bible, the hymns, the universal embrace of the message. There were the blatant barriers of race: separated churches, stores, schools, drinking fountains, Jim Crow cars on the railroad to Americus; black folk in their "place"; epithets, lynchings. The white Protestants of the Deep South confronted in fact every day the most inescapable "social" injustice: race, the black/white division; lynching; a caste system.

Southern white liberals in the segregation days were a distinct species. Being "liberal" on race in that time and place blotted out most other social issues, and had a bite and reality it did not have in the North. Most of these people—a small minority in their time and place—were church people, and their rejection of the racial practices of their region was explicitly grounded in Christian belief. Though a small minority in their race and their region and their churches, they are still an important group of people: a Methodist lady (e.g., Lillian Smith) in almost every Southern town who took Christian teachings seriously on race; a minister or two braver than the others; a sober layman like Mr. Carter. In 1955 in the middle of the tense racial issue in Holmes County, Mississippi, I knocked on the Methodist minister's door in the little town of Tchula, and I remember yet the trembling honesty and scared voice with which the frail young minister's wife told me, as a Northern writer soon to escape this frightening country in his rented car, how, yes, she believed in integration; she and her husband had been to conferences at Emory in Atlanta and learned to know colored friends, learned about the Christian outlook on race.

A serious white churchgoer in the American South, however

individualistic and otherworldly his belief, could not altogether escape knowing about *institutional* evil, about *social* injustice of this world, because there it was every day in his town, his school, his church, his life.

Among the folk of an early generation who saw the injustice was Jim Jack Gordy, a populist in black-belt south Georgia (rare, for most of the populists were in north Georgia). He sang Methodist hymns at his kitchen table with his friend the black Bishop and held enlightened—or, let us say, "Christian"—views on race. His daughter Lillian Gordy, absorbing those views, holding to them despite the differing views of the man she married, Earl Carter of Plains, passed them on to her son. So her son had to know from his youth what this minority of Southern white Protestants knew: that those Christian beliefs and hymns and teachings had an inescapable social bite to them.

What Carter drew from Niebuhr is as much about love and justice as about a "sad duty" in a "sinful world."

# A PERSONAL
# CONCLUSION:
## The Capital and Carter

In the year and a half that followed my instructive visit to the balcony of the Second Christian Church in Indianapolis, I travelled not only to Plains, to Calhoun, Gainsville, Warm Springs, the Washington in Georgia and many times to Atlanta; not only to New York City and Chicago, and St. Petersburg; not only to South Bend and Indianapolis and other Indiana towns where the Carters were speaking, but also and above all to that other Washington that is the nation's capital.

It is a city for which I have a deep affection created by many visits, an interest in the city's one industry, an admiration for many of the city's insiders, and the advantage of never having lived in the city for very long.

I went to Harry Truman and Dwight Eisenhower's Washington mostly by train; John Kennedy and Lyndon Johnson's Washington by plane.

In 1967 I flew to Washington every week on Allegheny Airlines, a feat not to be taken lightly. The plane would come from Boston; during the World Series the pilot gave the scores of the Red Sox-Cardinals games.

I would come into the national airport sometimes from the West. The pilot might point out the Jefferson Memorial, the Lincoln Memorial, the Washington Monument. More recently pilots flying up the Potomac pointed out the Pentagon on the right and the Watergate complex on the left.

A city containing these last two eyesores cannot be treated sentimentally. The American government participates not only in the tragedy but also the evil of human history, in a way that the legend of our innocence did not allow for: Pentagon, Watergate, the CIA complex on the Virginia side of the river, the ugly J. Edgar Hoover building in downtown Washington.

There are perennial perils, as well as these particular recent ones in government. Washington has shown that often before. I once walked through the long hall leading to the office of the Secretary of the Interior looking for the picture of the Secretary 1921-23 (Albert Fall, one of the chief miscreants in the Teapot Dome scandal) and discovered it wasn't there. Much human greed, pride, selfishness, and especially love of power, struggle for power, exploitation of power has displayed itself in this capitol city.

Whoever deals with politics deals with the desire for power and therefore traffics with the devil. The skepticism about politics and government as having peculiar moral dangers is well grounded, but the disdain for those who enter that realm is not. Toward those who persist in this dangerous territory and serve honorably, the attitude should be the opposite of disdain.

It is part of Washington's meaning and appeal that despite the general and particular evils of collective life, of immoral society, of power, this democratic government has managed to do what the government of a great people must do in March of 1933, and in December of 1941, and in the fifteen weeks in the Spring of 1947 and in May of 1954 and (perhaps) in October of 1962 and in a different way from these others in November of 1963 (imagine passing the most powerful lever in this city of power from one hand to another under modern conditions as peacefully as that), and in the summer of the Ervin Committee, and in the four days of the House Judiciary Committee, and in August, 1974, and in the weavings and knittings of whole fabrics of legislation for Social Security and for housing and urban development and for health, education and welfare—all very defective fabrics, as we are continually reminded—but for all that, symbols of gropings for social justice.

The maligned bureaucrats who make their way by the new Metro or the buses or the bridges over the Potomac to the big ugly buildings that house the Federal bureaucracies include many people who have a genuine attachment to the field in which they work and to the good of the public. One of those ugly buildings is now named for a man who did love Washington, Hubert Humphrey.

More people than would admit it come to Washington with something of the old American moral impulse. The fault with that impulse as it has been shaped within our society, first, is its absolutism; and then the cynicism, or thoroughgoing relativism, it can turn into.

This simple scheme goes back in part to the Puritans and even more to the Evangelicals who followed the Puritans in the Baptist and Methodist churches down to Plains.

Recent generations since March of 1933 at least, have learned in Washington that the world is bigger and more complicated than the simple statement of their moral impulse implies. Some of them have therefore turned cynical. But not by any means all of them. Some stay without giving up the claim of justice, and seek to make it fit the real world of politics that Washington embodies. We now watch in Jimmy Carter's Presidency a rerun of this old and typical American story.

I went to Washington on January 19, 1977, and that night at 11:45—a bright, cold, moonlit , pretty night—we drove down Pennsylvania Avenue, past the bleachers and sawhorses being set up for the inauguration, in the reverse direction from that which the parade would take on the next day. Georgians in our car looked up at Blair House, where the Carters were staying temporarily, until they moved across the street.

"I wonder what Jimmy and Rosalynn are doing?"

"Oh, they've gone to bed."

At a party in the evening of inauguration day, with the presumed sleeper now President of the United States, Henry Brandon, the English journalist, said he did not like the inaugural address very well. It suggested an American drawing back from world-wide responsibilities.

"Would you have preferred something like Kennedy's inaugural?" I asked.

"Well . . . something in between."

For myself I did not miss the sweeping claims that we would bear any burden, pay any price—the overdone promises of a different age. At least in its comparative modesty about America's role I liked Carter's speech. The trumpet-sounding about our world role, begun in World War II and accentuated in the Cold War, was now out of tune with the many-sided complexity of world realities. Carter's Presidency offers the opportunity for a new formulation of our international role and of the "realistic" outlook that has recently accompanied it.

In domestic affairs reformulation is possible and appropriate, too. Is Mr. Carter the leader for that?

At that party at the end of inauguration day, I saw in the lobby of the Sulgrove Club on Massachusetts Avenue a large man who had been pointed out to me four months before in Warm Springs, then as Carter's choice for Governor, now as his designated OMB director, Bert Lance.

Although Mr. Lance is the son of a Methodist educator, I judged him, perhaps unfairly, by his manner, his bearing, his job, his house, his attitudes about budgets, and the huge luxury automobile he was driving, with license plates reading "BERT LANCE," not to be especially attuned—to refer back to Daddy King's morning sermon—to the sheep who need in particular to be fed. I did not then know about his banking practices.

He grinned happily to a black friend from Atlanta.

"Daddy King stole my text!" said Lance. "The *least* of these . . ." Mr. Lance, it seemed, had spoken at a memorial to Martin Luther King, Jr., in Atlanta shortly before that on that same text. The tall, white Georgian and the short, black Georgian grinned at each other in happiness about the triumph that the day represented, if not for the unfed sheep, at least for Georgians.

As to the sheep bein' fleeced: a White House staff person wrote that Carter was more than a Georgia Ben Franklin because he *does* have an understanding of social justice. I responded that I believed he did, but that it remained to be seen how that related to his fiscal conservatism. It remains to be seen how it relates to his resistance to the Washington political process, and the programs that are the heritage of liberalism.

I went to Washington again in March, after Carter had been President two months. A Carter friend who had been to a White House dinner reported that Rosalynn said, "The White House is *dirty.*" Each of the Georgia friends visiting the White House emphasized how much the Carters are still the *same*—a point the rest of us, it seemed to be assumed, would regard as significant: "Rosalynn is no different in the White House than in Plains,

Georgia, or the Governor's mansion." "The family is sitting around up there eating sandwiches." "I wish this country could see Rosalynn Carter walkin' in this house in her slacks."

A Georgian who stayed in the Lincoln bedroom, whom I had seen in Atlanta busily watching the television news every night, often with two sets, switching from channel to channel to see what Jimmy, Rosalynn, Miss Lillian, or Chip might be doing, made this memorable comment: "The nice thing about being in the White House is that you don't have to watch the news."

In July I talked to David Broder, Washington's "most respected political reporter," in Massachusetts. He said Carter would be a "transitional President."

I went again in October to a swearing in, where Mondale was being funny, Rosalynn was sitting soberly on the platform, and Joan Mondale was smiling beside her. Much of the Washington political community had by then returned to the negative view of Carter. It was now being said that he was inept and the Georgians around him were not up to the job. It was the second time there had been a swing of the pendulum of Washington opinion. In the early primary days, Carter was new and alone and different, an "outsider" loaded to the brim with the rectitude of the pious hinterland. The other candidates were familiar, ordinary, numerous and similar—old faces, born once, not interesting. But as the others dropped out he became fair game, the only media game in town; and the need for an ever newer newness turned on him.

In the first days of his Presidency the process began again. He was now at that still higher level of public attention where world leaders sit. He was no longer in a contest, in which balance and fairness were required; he was the fresh, interesting center of attention. He was surrounded by a cast of characters, and proved to be a fountain of symbolic newsworthy acts. But later he became familiar and this trendiness reversed itself again. His warts appeared.

"Washington" as a symbol, criticized by outsider Carter, returned the favor by developing fairly soon after an initial fascination some persisting negative lines about Carter, to the point by late 1977 of dismissing him as a one-term President.

But the two need each other—that is to say, the nation and its capital city need what is symbolized by the intense man from the provinces, and such a man needs what is symbolized by Washington.

In the long awkward age of this autobiographical Southern Yankee President he regularly referred to his own past: "My roommate and I would take all our slender earnings and spend it on classical records," he said at the Horowitz concert in the White House. A Chopin Polonaise brought him close to tears: "Maybe it was because of my experiences visiting Poland recently, but I just suddenly got emotional. I just couldn't help it. I was reaching for my handkerchief." Above all he lived still in the triumphs of his campaign days. He began his 1978 State of the Union message, having by then been President a full year, by saying: "Two years ago today we had the first caucus in Iowa, and one year ago tomorrow, I walked from here to the White House to take up the duties of President of the United States."

In the midst of one of those great presidential club sandwiches of unresolved problems—in the coal fields, the Middle East, the inflationary economy, the cities, the Senate debate over the Panama Canal, the SAL Talks— he returned to New Hampshire.

> It's good to be back in New Hampshire, back in Nashua. The first time I came here as a candidate, the crowd who met me was not quite so large as this. We had a political rally in a small front living room, and there were a lot of empty seats that faced me that evening. But as I campaigned for months here in your state I not only made many dedicated friends who later gave me a victory in your crucial primary, I not only learned a lot about New Hampshire, your special attitudes and your special hopes and dreams, but it gave me in microcosm a good preview of what I was to face in the 29 other primaries that I entered in 1976.

He'd been the nation's Chief Executive and "leader of the free world" for thirteen months, but he could still congratulate himself on the romance of his victory against odds in a Baptist missionary's person-to-person campaigning style:

> Here is focused in a unprecedented unequaled way, a sense of person-to-person campaigning. Your demands on candidates even for President are quite severe, because you want to know in detail stands on issues, personal characteristics, and the

dedication that that candidate has to win an ultimate victory in spite of tremendous, adverse odds.

Victories as *President* were not yet forthcoming.

In the old American story a lonely achiever and outsider, with a simple moral earnestness and a limited political and social understanding, moves out into a larger world that is not simple, not perhaps as earnest, and much more "realistic," perhaps excessively. The American "good' man has something he can contribute to that world, which regularly needs to recover its moral bearings. At the same time he has something to learn from Washington. For all its faults, it represents something "good," too: democracy making its endless adjustments of life to life, its continuous stream of proximate solutions to insoluble problems. The capital and Carter pulling on each other represent once again what Niebuhr called, in a phrase that Jimmy Carter marked, "the self-correcting powers of democracy."